ETHICS IN
QUALITATIVE
RESEARCH

ETHICS IN
QUALITATIVE
RESEARCH

ETHICS IN QUALITATIVE RESEARCH

edited by
Melanie Mauthner, Maxine Birch,
Julie Jessop & Tina Miller

SAGE Publications
London · Thousand Oaks · New Delhi

Introduction © Maxine Birch, Tina Miller, Melanie
Mauthner and Julie Jessop 2002
Chapter 1 © Rosalind Edwards and Melanie Mauthner
2002
Chapter 2 © Val Gillies and Pam Alldred 2002
Chapter 3 © Tina Miller and Linda Bell 2002
Chapter 4 © Linda Bell and Linda Nutt 2002
Chapter 5 © Maxine Birch and Tina Miller 2002
Chapter 6 © Jean Duncombe and Julie Jessop 2002
Chapter 7 © Andrea Doucet and Natasha Mauthner 2002
Chapter 8 © Pam Alldred and Val Gillies 2002

First published 2002

SAGE Publications Ltd
6 Bonhill Street
London EC2A 4PU

SAGE Publications Inc
2455 Teller Road
Thousand Oaks, California 91320

SAGE Publications India Pvt Ltd
32, M-Block Market
Greater Kailash – I
New Delhi 110 048

British Library Cataloguing in Publication data

A catalogue record for this book is
available from the British Library.

ISBN 0 7619 7308 7
ISBN 0 7619 7309 5 (pbk)

Library of Congress Control Number: 2002103173

Typeset by Photoprint, Torquay
Printed in India at Gopsons Papers Ltd, Noida

CONTENTS

CONTENTS

CONTRIBUTORS' BIOGRAPHIES

Editors

Melanie Mauthner is Lecturer in Social Policy at the Open University. She is developing multi-media teaching and learning resources for two courses: DD305 Personal Lives and Social Policy, and UI30 Get Connected: Studying with a Computer. She researches family and friendship cultures and her current work explores children's relationships with their siblings, funded by the Joseph Rowntree Foundation. She is co-editing *Gender and Education: Critical Perspectives* with Suki Ali and Shereen Benjamin, and Macmillan (2002) is publishing her sociological study of sisters entitled *Sistering: Narratives of Subjectivity and Change*.

Maxine Birch works as Staff Tutor and Research Fellow in the School of Health and Social Welfare at the Open University. Her present research project explores young people's narratives and how non-smoking and smoking lifestyles are commenced and maintained. Her PhD research was on group psychotherapeutic practices in alternative health and the reconstruction of self-identity stories. She has explored this psychotherapeutic medium and its connection with self-identity stories in relation to expressions of spirituality published in *Post-modernity, Sociology and Religion* (K. Flannagan and P. Jupp, Macmillan 1999). She has also written about the autobiographical approach in the research process in *Feminist Dilemmas in Qualitative Research* (J. Ribbens, and R. Edwards, Sage 1997). Her article in the *International Journal of Social Research* (2000) explores the qualitative interview relationship and processes when researching private and personal experiences.

Julie Jessop has recently completed her PhD at the Centre for Family Research, University of Cambridge looking at psychosocial aspects of post-divorce parenting. She has previously worked on research projects in the field of divorce and of children's definitions of family. She is currently working on a project looking at interventions and support services for children, which is funded by the Joseph Rowntree Foundation and based at the Centre for Family Research.

Tina Miller is a Senior Lecturer in Sociology and Assistant Director of the Centre for Family and Household Research at Oxford Brookes University. Her research and teaching interests include mothering and caring responsibilities, health and illness experiences, narrative and qualitative research methods. Her recent publications include 'Shifting layers of professional, lay and personal narratives' in the *Feminist Dilemmas in Qualitative Research* collection, 'Losing the plot: narrative construction and longitudinal childbirth research' (*Qualitative Health Research*, 2000), 'Inviting intimacy: the interview as therapeutic opportunity' (with Maxine Birch, *The International Journal of Social Research Methodology: Theory and Practice*, 2000). Her doctoral work explored women's journeys into first-time motherhood and was entitled 'An exploration of first-time motherhood: narratives of transition'.

Authors

Pam Alldred is researching education policy under New Labour, and sex education in particular, in the Education Department at Keele University. She has written about: the politics of representing children's voices in *Feminist Dilemmas in Qualitative Research*, the value of discourse analysis for research with children (in Hogan and Greene, 2002), and children's views of home–school relations (with Rosalind Edwards at South Bank University). She was part of the book collectives (E. Burman et al.) that produced *Challenging Women: Psychology's Exclusions, Feminist Possibilities* (Open University Press, 1996) and *Psychology, Discourse, Practice: From Regulation to Resistance* (Taylor & Francis, 1996). Her PhD was on policy and popular debates about lone mothers, absent fathers and lesbian mothers in the UK in the 1990s, and her lecturing interests include identity, research methods and the anti-capitalist movement.

Linda Bell is Principal Lecturer in the School of Health and Social Sciences, Middlesex University. She teaches research methods to student practitioners in social work and health and also works within the Masters in Social Research Methods programme. Her recent research has included work on communication training in health and social care, patients' views of complementary therapies, hospice services, and gender issues. Between 1991 and 1995 she was based at King's College, University of London where she researched inter-professional and organisational aspects of social work education and women's experiences with a therapy centre concerned with male violence. She completed her PhD entitled *My child, your child; mothering in a Hertfordshire town in the 1980s* in 1994. Her publications include journal articles and book chapters on mothering and evaluative research in health and social care.

Andrea Doucet is Associate Professor in the department of Sociology and Anthropology at Carleton University, Ottawa, Canada where her teaching and writing combine feminist theories and epistemologies and qualitative methodologies. Her current research is on economic restructuring in Canada, fatherhood and masculinities. Her work has appeared in numerous books as well as in *Women's Studies International Forum*, the *Journal of Family Issues*, *Community, Work & Family* and *Canadian Woman Studies*.

Jean Duncombe, formerly Senior Research Officer at Essex University is now Senior Lecturer in Social Studies at University College Chichester. Her interests include the sociology of the emotions (love and intimacy); family; childhood; and qualitative research. Her work on the gendered division of emotional labour has been published widely in academic journals and in *The Sociology of the Family: A Reader* (Blackwell, 1999).

Rosalind Edwards is Professor in Social Policy and Director of the Families and Social Capital ESRC Research Group at South Bank University, London. Her research focuses on family policies and a variety of aspects of family life, including mothers and education; lone and partnered mothers, employment and childcare; step-families; and children's understandings of aspects of family life. Her recent publications include: *Lone Mothers, Paid Work and Gendered Moral Rationalities* (with S. Duncan, Macmillan, 1999), *Risk and Citizenship: Key Issues in Welfare* (ed. with J. Glover, Routledge, 2001), *Children, Home and School: Autonomy, Resistance or Connection?* (ed., RoutledgeFalmer, 2002), *Analysing Families: Morality and Rationality in Policy and Practice* (ed. with A. Carling and S. Duncan, RoutledgeFalmer, 2002) and *Making Families: Moral Tales of Contemporary Parenting and Step-parenting* (with J. Ribbens McCarthy and V. Gillies, Sociologypress, 2002). She co-edits (with J. Brannen) *The International Journal of Social Research Methodology: Theory and Practice*.

Val Gillies is a Research Fellow in the Social Sciences Research Centre at South Bank University. She is currently researching and publishing in the area of families and social capital, having previously worked on projects focusing on step-parenting and the family lives of young people. She has recently completed a PhD thesis on marginalized mothers.

Natasha Mauthner is Deputy Director of the Arkleton Centre for Rural Development Research at the University of Aberdeen. Her research interests include work and family life, health and mental health issues, and qualitative research theory and practice. She is currently researching the impact of economic restructuring within the oil and gas industry on workers, families and children (ESRC and EU funded) and recently completed a study of the work, family and community life in rural areas (funded by the Joseph Rowntree Foundation). She has published numerous journal articles and book chapters (including a chapter in *Feminist Dilemmas in Qualitative Research*). Recent publications include *Work and Family Life in Rural Communities* (with L. McKee and M. Strell, York Publishing Services, 2001) and *The Darkest Days of My Life: Stories of Postpartum Depression* (Harvard University Press, 2002).

Linda Nutt is an independent child care consultant. She completed her doctoral research when employed by the National Foster Care Association (now the Fostering Network). Whilst there is an established body of research on children who are fostered, there is little work on the views of foster carers. Her research 'Foster carers' perspectives: the dilemmas of loving the bureaucratised child' therefore makes an original contribution to the field.

INTRODUCTION

Maxine Birch, Tina Miller, Melanie Mauthner
and Julie Jessop

This book examines the ethical dilemmas encountered in doing qualitative research. We are all confronted by ethical/moral questions as the boundaries in society shift and we are drawn into debates on the 'rights' and 'wrongs' of potential actions. The book integrates the theoretical and practical aspects of ethical dilemmas in research studies. The term ethics has traditionally been associated with disciplines such as philosophy and theology within which principles and abstract rules have been debated and developed in relation to particular moral philosophical positions. However shifts in late modern society, for example in the areas of biomedicine and technology, have led to ethical debates increasingly becoming part of everyday life. There is now a multiplicity of ethics and a recognition of different moral codes. Rather than appeal to philosophical principles and rules, we are more likely to respond in pragmatic ways, although this pragmatism may well be embedded in particular philosophical positions. Our ethical stance will also reflect our own moral, social, political and cultural location in the social world. In this edited collection we address the perplexing area of ethics in qualitative research from our positions as feminist researchers.

The turn to qualitative research as a means of exploring subjective experiences, meanings and voices has led to scrutiny of the research process, but less attention has been paid to ethics in the doing of qualitative research. Ethics in this context has largely been associated with following ethical guidelines and/or gaining ethics approval from professional or academic bodies before commencing data collection. Approval has been premised on notions of protection, confidentiality and anonymity. Ethics guidelines, and the committees established to administer applications, encompass different philosophical positions and principles, and pragmatic approaches. Yet ethical considerations encountered in research are much more wide-ranging than this: they are empirical and theoretical and *permeate* the qualitative research process. The complexities of researching private lives and placing accounts in the public arena raise multiple ethical issues for the researcher that cannot be solved solely by the application of abstract rules, principles or guidelines. Rather there are inherent tensions in qualitative research that is characterized by fluidity and inductive uncertainty, and ethical guidelines that are static and increasingly formalized. In this book we address the gaps between the practice of doing research and the ethical principles, both formal and informal, that guide it. How are theory and intention 'lived' in the research context?

This book arises from the research experiences of members of the Women's Workshop on Qualitative/Household Research who have previously written and published together (Edwards and Ribbens, 1995; Ribbens and Edwards, 1998). Building on our earlier edited collection, *Feminist Dilemmas in Qualitative Research: Public Knowledge and Private Lives*, which explored the interplay between theory and practice in the context of generating public knowledge about private lives, we now turn our attention to the theory and practice of ethical dilemmas encountered in qualitative research. As a group of women working as researchers and lecturers in higher education we meet regularly to share, critically appraise and support our research in progress, which explores subjectivity and personal experiences in relation to private lives, households, families and children. Although we work collaboratively as a group, we come from different disciplinary and social backgrounds, and have different ways of thinking ethically. While all the writers are members of the Women's Workshop, some members did not contribute a chapter to this book. As the academic practice of named authorship obscures the contributions which other members of the group made to our discussions and our thinking, we want to gratefully acknowledge their input here. Our discussions in the Workshop and in this volume explore ways of investigating and making sense of 'lived experiences' and the meanings of these experiences for both those being researched and the researcher.

Our own research experiences reflect the wider shifts in qualitative research from exploring accounts of personal experiences and subjectivity to the analysis of discourses, biographies, narratives, voices and stories (Chamberlayne et al., 2000; Denzin and Lincoln, 1998a+b; Josselson and Lieblich, 1993; Olesen, 1998; Plummer, 1995; Roberts, 2002). These 'personal experience methods' continue to influence our work, especially feminists' contributions to developing them (Denzin and Lincoln, 1998a; Josselson, 1996). Feminists have made a range of contributions – from drawing attention to the significance of research relationships and the need for reflexivity[1] to the crucial recognition of diversity and difference.[2] Ongoing debates concerning feminist critiques of the subject, feminist epistemologies and methods in relation to post-structuralist and postmodern positions also continue to inform and guide our practice.[3] However, while feminist debates have challenged traditional research standpoints and provided valuable tools with which to approach and analyse private and personal stories, we argue that feminist contributions have also produced an inherent ethical stance that we examine further here.

Being a feminist researcher

In our earlier work together we described ourselves as 'feminist researchers' (Edwards and Ribbens, 1998: 2; Ribbens and Edwards, 1995). This reflects our concern with conducting research about neglected aspects of women's lives, grounded in their own experiences and from a particular theoretical and methodological perspective that we call 'feminist' despite the breadth of the term (Maynard and Purvis, 1994; Ramazanoglu and Holland, 2002; Stanley, 1990). In *Feminist Dilemmas in Qualitative Research* (1998), we argued that the topics and dilemmas that we identified arose from the edge of mainstream, public academic debates and may be considered to belong to more hidden and private aspects of women's experiences (Ribbens and Edwards, 1998). We continue to share this interest in the interplay between public, social knowledge and private and personal lived experiences, and this concern shapes our discussions of ethical problems. Finding that we shared similar ethical dilemmas in our research experiences has led us to investigate this area further.

The chapters that make up this edited collection draw on both methodological and theoretical ethical concerns encountered by Workshop members in conducting qualitative research. Workshop meetings have enabled us to reflect on our actions and discuss practical ways forward. Yet ethical concerns are perplexing and require 'contextualised methods of reasoning' (Holm, 1997) not abstract rules. The meetings have provided a supportive forum for us to question standard practice or admit uncertainties and doubts. We continue to work in the gap between public and private tensions of women's experiences and practices of creating academic knowledge. Our aim here, therefore, is to suggest ethical ways of thinking rather than to provide answers or rules to be adhered to. As noted in the discussion of our previous edited collection, our meetings have 'emerged as a space in which to express doubt and admit the possibility of unanswerable questions, rather than falling prey to the certainty of academic rhetoric' (Edwards and Ribbens, 1998: 6).

As feminist researchers we appreciate the increased awareness of the private and personal in mainstream academic debates about qualitative research, and have found our research styles 'in tune' with developments in this area. Moreover, we have found that our positions as women academics on research advisory panels, supervising research students, submitting research proposals and working within research teams, involved the discussion of ethics from a limited perspective. Ethical components of these debates remain concerned with the tenets of coercion, risk and harm focused on protecting those being researched, the researcher, and the institution. This approach is based on a model of ethics, where ethical considerations are 'measured' against criteria designed to assess elements of risk and harm. Codes of professional behaviour are devised to set standards to cover this critical demand to protect all those involved in research. Consequently tensions may arise as a particular research centre and/or department may have differing priorities and demands, which conflict with the need to ensure that ethical codes of behaviour in research are followed. Therefore most ethical judgements applied to qualitative research designs are negotiated within an organisation's own internal regulatory body.

Further tensions may also arise where researchers also work as professional practitioners in education, health or welfare, for example. These practitioner-researchers will need to decide how to balance professional/occupational responsibilities with research ethics guidelines. Ethics applied to research can be seen as a method of self-regulation, whereby different disciplines and organisations attempt to demonstrate a professional approach to research. Several chapters address each of these areas.

This book questions the emergence of a professional ethical researcher as an 'ideal type' and explores whether the feminist contribution to this 'ideal type' leads to a perception of ethics as a promise to be a 'good human being' demonstrated through being a committed and responsible researcher. We are concerned that if the label 'feminist perspective' has become synonymous with ethical ways of working, then it can be misleading and offer more than it can deliver (Mauthner, 2000). Our research experiences demonstrate that ethical concerns arise at all stages of the research process and appear in many forms; our responses to them may not, on reflection, have always been ethical.

As a group of feminist researchers concerned with practising ethical ways of thinking in our research endeavours, we acknowledge the diversity of feminisms, which make it difficult to talk about feminism as a unitary shared set of ideas (Bulbeck, 1998; Hill Collins, 1990; hooks, 1989; Mirza, 1997; Spivak, 1992). From such wide and diverse areas of knowledge we focus here specifically on ethics in qualitative research concerned with personal experience methods. The methodological and theoretical ethical concerns we identify in this edited collection are examined from our substantive research experiences of being 'in the field', and against the backdrop of academic feminist research debates. The tick box approach to ethical standards, outlined in general research texts (Robson, 1993; Sarantakos, 1998), as a means of ensuring informed consent, confidentiality, anonymity, reliability and validity, represent ethics as an abstracted consideration. Whilst we do not argue that certain universal criteria to guide behaviour are irrelevant, or that general codes can be helpful, the constant neglect of detailed ethical discussions in all stages of research projects renders the enterprise open to being unethical.

A feminist perspective

The arguments we present here affirm the description of a feminist perspective as we understand and employ it within our research practices. As Bell has noted, 'feminism has been an articulation, set of demands, forces and strategies, the success of which I for one have inherited and benefited from' (1999: 1). It is the articulation, demands and strategies as applied to qualitative research that we explore here. We do not wish to induce any notion of exclusion by affirming this use of the word 'feminism' and wholeheartedly agree that a white, Western, social science perspective of feminism is a 'tiny fragment of the world and its knowledge' (Bulbeck, 1998). Nevertheless a feminist perspective provides a key starting point for us and enables us to re-examine and challenge the assumptions that underpin feminist research practices. For example, when combined with personal experience methods, a model of 'consequentialist-feminist ethics' is described as automatically committed to developing trusting and long-term research relationships. As Denzin and Lincoln assert: 'the research texts that are produced out of such material implicate the investigator in a feminist, caring, committed ethic with those who have been studied' (1998a: 39). However, ethical concerns can be perceived differently according to the ethical models employed, and researchers need to examine which mode of ethical reasoning informs their actions and why. This book therefore highlights two elements: first, how such feminist debates have influenced our perceptions of working as ethical researchers and secondly, how this perspective can be located in different ways of thinking ethically.

Ethical debates are increasingly wide-ranging and cover all areas of social life (Benhabib, 1992; Erben, 2000; Griffiths, 1995; Meyers, 1997). There are two dominant frameworks in relation to thinking about ethics applied to research (May, 1998). These emanate from the two distinct traditions in moral philosophy; deontological ethics and consequentialist ethics. The first of these ethical models, the deontological position is identified with Kantian philosophy and stems from the notion that certain absolute rules exist that must be upheld regardless of the consequences (Berglund, 1998; Holm, 1997). In contrast, the consequentialist position is based on a philosophy of the greatest good to the greatest number where the focus is on the consequences of an action (Holm, 1997). This model of ethical reasoning is identified with the philosopher, J.S. Mill and the tradition of utilitarianism. Whilst both these traditions are discernible in various guises in research ethics, in the practical 'doing' of research, more pragmatic approaches often shape the research enterprise.

Both models, importantly, focus attention on the conduct of the individual researcher and regulatory bodies through consideration of rights, duties, actions and consequences. However an over dependence upon these two Western dominant philosophical traditions may mask the complexities of ethical considerations that can be encountered in qualitative research. Researchers need to invoke contextualized reasoning and not just appeal to abstract rules and principles. This could be achieved through a more reflexive model of ethics where the self is placed within the ethical negotiations. Such a position is identified with Hegelian philosophy. Here the negotiation of ethics moves beyond a model of reasoning and rationality and enables the acknowledgment of feelings and emotions. The reflexive self becomes a key constituent in enabling ethical reflection through evaluation and reconsideration in the research process (Fraser, 2000; Hansenn, 2000). Thus ethics become part of our relationships, our interactions and our shared values portrayed in the sense of belonging to a community (Benhabib, 1992). It is apparent then that ethics in qualitative research require a combination of theoretical models to enable us to make sense of ethical decision-making and a reflexive self to develop and guide ethical thinking. In this book, the empirical and theoretical examples of grappling with ethical dilemmas in our work illustrate how, in practice as researchers, we are probably influenced by elements from both the deontological and consequentialist positions. Principles guide our perceptions of how to conduct ethical research and yet ultimately, specific circumstances and contexts inform our decisions.

The writing process

In this edited collection, each chapter provides a detailed analysis of the ethical concerns raised by the authors. We chose to write each chapter with a co-author to promote collaboration and cohesion in the practice of sharing and developing our ideas and experiences. During this period of working on the book we have held a series of book meetings where our discussions have stimulated and provided much food for thought. We have valued these precious spaces for 'talk', away from the pressurised working environments of higher education, which all of us find ourselves within. The introduction to the book presented here is the result of one of our group discussions and reflects our evolving arguments. Nevertheless it ultimately consists of our views as editors. Although we choose to present our text within the established academic framework of named authors and editors, deemed necessary for our professional credibility, we have been tempted to challenge academic writing conventions and be more imaginative and radical in our collective writing. Resisting this temptation and notwithstanding the conventional textual representation you find here, we hope that our use of personal pronouns and personal research experiences succeed in making this an accessible research text. By presenting our personal, private research stories we seek to counteract the production of academic texts, which transform everyday understandings into complex interpretations. We feel that the issues we raise here need to be produced in the customary academic format in order to reach a majority academic audience.

In the following chapters each pair of authors introduce the different ethical issues they identified and continue to identify while actively involved in qualitative research. As a result of this approach many aspects of the research process are explored. These include ethical issues related to: access and informed consent, negotiating participation in the research relationship, developing rapport, eliciting particular types of research accounts and the tensions inherent in being a professional researcher and being a 'caring' professional. The intentions of feminist research, and the analysis of data, are also explored in relation to our aspirations to be ethical researchers and developing ethical research practices. In this way we seek to explore and build upon the feminist contributions to ethical research practices.

Outline

The key themes of the book concern responsibility and accountability in applied feminist research practice based on personal experience methods. The contributors approach these themes from several angles: some challenge the practical reality and desirability of achieving such elevated ethical standards, others question whether being a feminist researcher requires such a caring responsible identity, while others propose some practical frameworks for doing things differently. The book is divided into eight chapters. The first two chapters set the context for the discussion in the rest of the book by indicating the relevance of theoretical debates about ethics for research purposes and by highlighting the ethics of intention in how we conceive of the goals of research. Rosalind Edwards and Melanie Mauthner draw out practical guidelines to guide ethical decision-making rooted in a feminist ethics of care, and Val Gillies and Pam Alldred dissect how feminist researchers formulate the intentions they have for their research as a political intervention.

Rosalind Edwards and Melanie Mauthner discuss the practical and theoretical context for a focus on ethics in conducting feminist research. They consider the growing interest in ethical issues among health, medical and social research as well as legal frameworks and implications from distinct epistemological perspectives. They review current ethical concerns and assess prevalent models. They then consider political approaches to theories of ethics and morality, and feminist theorizing of an ethic of care, and their respective value bases. Finally, they bring a feminist ethics of care to bear on the research process and explicitly elaborate some practical guidelines.

Val Gillies and Pam Alldred engage with debates among post-structuralist feminists who have problematized the notion of 'truth' as a justificatory foundation underpinning statements, claims or actions. They argue that this epistemological shift necessitates a new scrutiny of the intentions underlying feminist research. From this alternative perspective, the goal of feminist research is likely to be transformed from an attempt to better understand or represent women's experience, to, for instance, a more pragmatic, political aim of challenging oppression and improving women's lives. Focusing in particular on feminist efforts to represent women's voices, initiate personal change and to undermine oppressive knowledge structures, they identify potential ethical dilemmas contained within each approach.

Next, several authors examine in detail the ethical implications of using personal experience methods in the field and how viable or desirable a feminist ethic of working towards a responsible committed research relationship is. Tina Miller and Linda Bell focus on issues of access, gate-keeping and consent. Linda Bell and Linda Nutt examine ethical dilemmas faced by health and welfare professionals conducting research. Maxine Birch and Tina Miller unravel the different meanings of 'participation' in the research process. Jean Duncombe and Julie Jessop revisit the links between rapport and friendship in interview settings.

Tina Miller and Linda Bell argue that issues around access and gate-keeping, and notions of what constitutes 'informed' consent have clear ethical implications for feminist research. They explore the interplay between access, coercion and motive/motivation in three

research projects that encompass issues of gender, power and ethnicity. They examine the role of the gate-keeper in relation to access
being granted to those who may be in less powerful positions. They
suggest that consent should be ongoing and renegotiated throughout
the research process and that researchers need to continually reflect on
what it is that research participants have consented to.

Linda Bell and Linda Nutt explore how professional and occupational responsibilities translate into empirical research dilemmas.
They focus on the ethical difficulties that accompany divided loyalties
towards research and employment, specifically in the health and
social care fields. They draw on two examples from different parts of
the social work 'practitioner spectrum' to explore issues of 'confidentiality' and 'negotiation'. One example involves research ethics
and student practitioners and the other, an experienced social worker's doctoral research on foster care. They argue that the range of
responsibilities, which practitioner-researchers have to negotiate, constitute, in themselves, an 'ethics of caring'; and that decisions about
emphasizing or playing down the role of practitioner whilst conducting research may therefore be an important part of such
negotiations.

Maxine Birch and Tina Miller elaborate on the notion of participation in the research process. They note the shift in terminology from
research subject to research participant that is reflected in academic
professional codes of conduct, and question how far participation is
practical or even desirable throughout the research process. They
draw on their own research experiences to show the difficulties
encountered in maintaining participation during the various phases of
their research projects. Maxine and Tina argue that carrying out
ethically responsible research requires the researcher to negotiate participation at the outset of a project and be sensitive to the dimensions
of participation that have been agreed, which may be partial and may
shift.

Jean Duncombe and Julie Jessop pick up on the themes of consent
and negotiation. They evaluate the idea of 'rapport' that supposedly
promotes empathy, genuineness, authenticity and disclosure in 'the
good interview', particularly where women talk to women. However,
interviewing is becoming a 'job' they maintain, where interviewers are
trained, using skills from counselling, to 'do rapport' consciously in
order to encourage the disclosure of intimate information and feelings. In effect, as the emotions and emotion work of 'doing rapport'
become professionalized and commercialized, they argue, the 'skills'
of negotiating rapport become a substitute for the awkward ethical
problems of negotiating consent.

In the final two chapters, other authors discuss some of the wider
ethical implications of conducting qualitative research. Andrea Doucet

and Natasha Mauthner draw out epistemological issues in carrying out ethical analysis of qualitative data. Pam Alldred and Val Gillies reflect on the ethics of producing modernist subjects by reinforcing normative expectations of the individual in research through standard and good practice in qualitative research.

Inspired by the Canadian philosopher Loraine Code's writings on ethics and feminist approaches to epistemologies and methodologies Andrea Doucet and Natasha Mauthner describe a research practice aimed at 'knowing well' and 'knowing responsibly'. Drawing on Code's idea that one way of grounding a theoretical discussion on the inseparability of epistemology and ethics into actual research practice is to seek ways of conducting and then presenting 'responsible knowledge of human experience' (Code, 1993: 39), they ask what it means to 'know responsibly' or to 'know well'. First, they highlight the importance of maintaining relationships with research subjects during data analysis processes, particularly those who may not 'fit' our theoretical, epistemological and political frameworks. They also highlight inherent tensions in this process partly because research respondents are not homogenous groups and thus it is impossible to maintain relationships with *all* respondents and their voiced perspectives, and partly because research involves multiple sets of relationships and commitments to varied persons, communities and interests. Secondly, they argue for accountability in research through transparency about our epistemological, theoretical and political assumptions, particularly to the readers, users as well as varied communities within which our work is located (interpretive, epistemological and academic). Through a case study of American geneticist Barbara McClintock (1902–1987) and their own research, they reflect on the dilemmas inherent in attempting to enact ethical research practice that is both responsible and accountable.

Pam Alldred and Val Gillies consider understandings of 'the subject' as a site of ethical practice in interviewing and data analysis. They argue that researchers construct interviewees as modernist subjects through both the interview interaction and in research accounts because conventional ways of negotiating, conducting and transcribing interviews rest on this understanding of 'the individual'. Unsurprisingly, interviewees, as well as researchers, re/produce themselves through the dominant individualist subjecthood, and ethical practice rests on this. This means that we reinforce the Western model of the subject, with its exclusions and oppressive view of its Others, even as we strive to do 'ethical research'. They discuss two sites of ethical concerns for research: ethical practice in relation to the individuals who participate (the focus of conventional 'research ethics'), and in relation to broader cultural politics and the relations of knowledge we re/produce. The latter may impact on participants indirectly. These two sites may provide contradictory ethical pulls within a given piece of research. Affirming normative understandings of subjectivity may be 'ethical' in the interaction, but undesirable politically. Furthermore, it may benefit a particular social group's representation and so be ethical in terms of cultural politics, but leave assumed the centrality and normality of the modernist subject. This raises questions about whether our desire for radical social change is inevitably compromised in interview-based research: owing to its reliance on the modernist subject on the one hand (in the requirements of ethical practice on the immediate level, and in the strategic requirements of cultural politics), and for its thoroughly modernist foundations in truth and rationality, on the other.

The ethical issues discussed in this book, whilst informed by a broadly feminist perspective, are obviously applicable to other aspects of social science research. Although they represent the particular ethical dilemmas that we encountered as researchers working mainly within family and household studies, they are relevant for any research which aims to increase knowledge through the use of personal experience methods. Whilst our endeavour has not been to provide a comprehensive account of ethical dilemmas which may arise, we believe that drawing attention to areas which are not always seen as problematic will open up and expand much needed ethical debates. As society becomes more complex, and researchers are urged to become more reflexive, ethical dilemmas are set to increase. There is therefore a growing need to formulate guidelines for research, which take a much broader ethical stance; it is hoped that this book will be a step towards that goal.

Notes

[1] Cotterill, 1992; DeVault, 1990; Edwards, 1993; Finch, 1984; Lather, 1991; Oakley, 1981; Reissman, 1987; Ribbens, 1989; Skeggs, 1995; Stanley, 1992; Stanley & Wise, 1983, 1993.

[2] Bulbeck, 1998; Hill Collins, 1990; hooks, 1989; Kitzinger & Gilligan, 1994; Mirza, 1997; Spivak, 1992.

[3] Butler, 1992; Code, 1993; Harding, 1987; Maynard & Purvis, 1994; Roberts, 1981; Smith, 1987; Stanley, 1990.

References

Bell, V. (1999) *Feminist Imagination*. London: Sage.
Benhabib, S. (1992) *Situating the Self*. Cambridge: Polity Press.
Berglund, C.A. (1998) *Ethics for Health Care*. Oxford: Oxford University Press.

Bulbeck, C. (1998) *Re-orienting Western Feminisms: Women's Diversity in a Postcolonial World.* Cambridge: Cambridge University Press.

Butler, J. (1992) 'Contingent foundations: feminism and the question of post-modernism', in J. Butler and J. Scott (eds), *Feminists Theorise the Political.* London: Routledge.

Chamberlayne, P., Bornat, J. and Wengraf, T. (2000) *The Turn to Biographical Methods in Social Science.* London: Routledge.

Code, L. (1993) 'Taking subjectivity into account', in L. Alcoff and E. Potter (eds), *Feminist Epistemologies.* New York and London: Routledge.

Cotterill, P. (1992) 'Interviewing women: issues of friendship, vulnerability and power', *Women's Studies International Forum,* 15(5/6): 593–606.

Denzin, N.K. and Lincoln, Y.S. (1998a) *Collecting and Interpreting Qualitative Materials.* Thousand Oaks: Sage.

Denzin, N.K. and Lincoln, Y.S. (1998b) *The Landscape of Qualitative Research: Theories and Issues.* Thousand Oaks: Sage.

DeVault, M. (1990) 'Talking and listening from women's standpoint: feminist strategies for interviewing and analysis', *Social Problems,* 37: 96–116.

Edwards, R. (1993) 'An education in interviewing: placing the researcher and the research', in C.M. Renzetti and R.M. Lee (eds), *Researching Sensitive Topics.* London: Sage.

Edwards, R. and Ribbens, J. (1995) 'Women in families and households: qualitative research', *Women's Studies International Forum,* 18(3): 247–386.

Edwards, R. and Ribbens, J. (1998) 'Living on the edges: public knowledge, private lives, personal experience', in J. Ribbens and R. Edwards (eds), *Feminist Dilemmas in Qualitative Research, public knowledge and private lives.* London: Sage.

Erben, M. (2000) 'Ethics, Education, Narrative Communication and Biography', *Educational Studies,* 26(3): 379–390.

Finch, J. (1984) ' "It's great to have someone to talk to": the ethics and politics of interviewing women', in C. Bell and H. Roberts (eds), *Social Researching: Politics, Problems, Practice.* London: Routledge and Kegan Paul.

Fraser, N. (2000) 'Recognition without ethics', in M. Gaber, B. Hanssen and R.L. Walkowitz (eds) *The Turn to Ethics.* London: Routledge.

Griffiths, M. (1995) *Feminisms and the Self: The Web of Identity.* London: Routledge.

Hanssen, B. (2000) 'Ethics of the other', in M. Gaber, B. Hanssen and R.L. Walkowitz (eds) *The Turn to Ethics.* London: Routledge.

Harding, S. (1987) 'Is there a feminist method?', in S. Harding (ed.), *Feminism and Methodology.* Bloomington, IN: Indiana University Press.

Hill Collins, P. (1990) *Black Feminist Thought: Knowledge, Consciousness and the Politics of Empowerment.* London: Routledge.

Holm, S. (1997) *Ethical Problems in Clinical Practice.* Manchester: Manchester University Press.

hooks, b. (1989) *Talking Back: Thinking Feminist, Thinking Black.* Boston: South End Press.

Josselson, R. (1996) Introduction in R. Josselson (ed.), *Ethics and Process in the Narrative Study of Lives.* California: Sage.

Josselson, R. and Lieblich, A. (eds) (1993) *The Narrative Study of Lives,* Vol. 1. Newbury Park: Sage.

Kitzinger, C. with Gilligan, C. (1994) 'The spoken word: listening to a different voice', *Feminism and Psychology,* 4(3): 399–403.

Lather, P. (1991) *Getting Smart: Feminist Research and Pedagogy with/in the Postmodern*. New York: Routledge.

Mauthner, M. (2000) 'Snippets and silences: ethics and reflexivity in narratives of sistering', *International Journal Social Research Methodology*, 3(4): 287–306.

May, T. (1997) *Social Research: Issues, Methods and Process*. Buckingham: Open University Press

Maynard, M. and Purvis, J. (eds) (1994) *Researching Women's Lives from a Feminist Perspective*. London: Taylor and Francis.

Meyers, Tietjens, D. (ed.) (1997) *Feminists Rethink the Self*. London: HarperCollins.

Mirza, S.H. (ed.) (1997) *Black British Feminism: A Reader*. London: Routledge.

Oakley, A. (1981) 'Interviewing women: a contradiction in terms', in H. Roberts (ed.), *Doing Feminist Research*. London: Routledge and Kegan Paul.

Olesen, V. (1998) 'Feminisms and models of qualitative research', in N.K. Denzin and Y.S. Lincoln (eds), *Handbook of Qualitative Research*. London: Sage.

Plummer, K. (1995) *Telling Sexual Stories: Power, Change and Social Worlds*. London: Routledge.

Ramazanoglu, C. and Holland, J. (2002) *Feminist Methodology: Challenges and Choices*. London: Sage.

Reissman, C.K. (1987) 'When gender is not enough: women interviewing women', *Gender and Society*, 1(2): 172–207.

Ribbens, J. (1989) 'Interviewing: an "unnatural situation"?', *Women's Studies International Forum*, 12(6): 579–92.

Ribbens, J. and Edwards, R. (eds) (1998) *Feminist Dilemmas in Qualitative Research, public knowledge and private lives*. London: Sage.

Roberts, B. (2002) *Biographical Research*. Buckingham: Open University Press.

Roberts, H. (1981) *Doing Feminist Research*. London: Routledge and Kegan Paul.

Robson, C. (1993) *Real World Research*. Oxford: Blackwell.

Sarantakos, S. (1998) *Social Research*. Basingstoke: Macmillan.

Skeggs, B. (1995) 'Theorising, ethics and representation in feminist ethnography', in B. Skeggs (ed.), *Feminist Cultural Theory: Process and Production*. Manchester: Manchester University Press.

Smith, D. (1987) *The Everyday World as Problematic: A Feminist Sociology*. Milton Keynes: Open University Press.

Spivak, G. Chakravorty (1992) 'The Politics of Translation', in Michele Barrett and Anne Phillips *Destabilising Theory: Contemporary Feminist Debates*. Cambridge: Polity Press.

Stanley, L. (ed.) (1990) *Feminist Praxis. Research, Theory and Epistemology in Feminist Sociology*. London: Routledge.

Stanley, L. (1992) 2 *The Auto/biographical I: The Theory and Practice of Feminist Auto/biography*. Manchester: Manchester University Press.

Stanley, L. and Wise, S. (1983) *Breaking Out: Feminist Consciousness and Feminist Research*. London: Routledge and Kegan Paul.

Stanley, L. and Wise, S. (1993) *Breaking Out Again: Feminist Ontology and Epistemology*. London: Routledge and Kegan Paul.

CHAPTER I

ETHICS AND FEMINIST RESEARCH: THEORY AND PRACTICE

Rosalind Edwards and Melanie Mauthner

Introduction

Ethics concerns the morality of human conduct. In relation to social research, it refers to the moral deliberation, choice and accountability on the part of researchers throughout the research process. General concern about ethics in social research has grown apace. In the UK, for example, in the late 1980s and early 1990s, a number of professional associations developed and/or revised ethical declarations for their members. The guidelines available from these bodies include: the Association of Social Anthropologists of the Commonwealth's Ethical Guidelines for Good Practice, the British Educational Research Association's Ethical Guidelines, the British Sociological Association's Statement of Ethical Practice, the British Psychological Society's Revised Ethical Principles for Conducting Research on Human Participants, and the Social Research Association's Ethical Guidelines. Indeed, it would be interesting to trace the genealogy of these statements as they all seem to acknowledge drawing on each other's declarations. Research funders may also produce ethical statements, such as the Economic and Social Research Council (see www.esrc.ac.uk/esrccontent/researchfunding/sec22.asp), which is the UK's leading research and training agency. The Association of Research Centres in the Social Sciences is, at the time of writing, reviewing ethical guidelines from an institutional perspective. Moreover, it also seems that academic institutions themselves, individually, are setting up ethics committees to which researchers (and in some cases students) should submit their projects for approval, and research ethics committees have been a feature for social (not just medical) researchers working with and through statutory health organisations for some time now (see www.corec.org.uk). In addition, ethical guidelines have been published addressing particular social groups on whom researchers may focus, such as Priscilla Alderson's (1995) for social research on and with children.

Researchers themselves have written extensively on ethics in social research. While feminist researchers certainly have not been the only authors to undertake reflexive accounts of the politics of empirical research practice, it is fair to say that such reflections have done and do form a substantial feature of feminist publications on the research process. Indeed, some have characterized feminist ethics as a 'booming industry' (Jaggar, 1991). These pieces, however, are not usually explicit investigations of ethics per se. In discursive terms, they are posed in terms of politics rather than ethics. Nonetheless, they represent an empirical engagement with the practice of ethics. As such, they pose the researcher as a central active ingredient of the research process rather than the technical operator that can be inferred by professional ethical codes.

Mary Maynard (1994) has characterized feminist work in this area, in the early stages of second wave scholarship, as concerned with a critique of dominant 'value-free' modes of doing social research, the rejection of exploitative power hierarchies between researcher and researched, and the espousal of intimate research relationships, especially woman-to-woman, as a distinctly feminist mode of enquiry (see also Jean Duncombe and Julie Jessop, this volume). In particular, detailed attention was given to the empirical process of collecting data for analysis.

In this chapter we are concerned with ethical perspectives on qualitative social research, from a feminist perspective in particular. We start from a position that an explicit theoretical grounding in a feminist ethics of care would enhance many feminist and other discussions of the research process where this is concerned with ethical dilemmas. Such work, however, rarely draws on these theories, although authors may often implicitly work within or towards just such an ethics. In turn, though, few feminist analyses and elaborations of an ethics of care at the epistemological level (a vibrant feature of feminist political philosophy) pay attention to the empirical process of conducting social research. We feel, however, that feminist discussions of the research process and of the ethics of care have a lot of concerns in common.

Our focus is on philosophical theories of ethics and the difficulties we face as researchers in applying these models in our practice when we conduct research projects. There are clear tensions between the range of models of ethics that we can draw on to negotiate our way through the competing demands of research, both practical and theoretical. We are often left in isolation to ponder and plot our decisions about how best to draw on these perspectives. This chapter connects theoretical ethical models with the complex dilemmas we encounter in the 'doing' of research. We begin our exploration of such issues by laying out explanations for the rise of concern about the practice of ethics in social research. We then pinpoint ethical concerns in social research, which subsequent chapters explore in more depth. We review specific ethical models including deontology, consequential-ism, virtue ethics of skills, rights/justice ethics and the ethics of care. After considering some of the care-based ethical debates we suggest some practical guidelines for researchers to consider rooted in a feminist ethics of care.

Why the rise in concern with ethics in social research?

Martyn Hammersley has argued that what he calls 'ethicism' is one of the four main tendencies operating in contemporary qualitative social research. The others are empiricism, instrumentalism and post-modernism. Although not explicitly referring to feminist researchers, he perhaps has them, amongst others, in mind when he points to:

> . . . a tendency to see research almost entirely in ethical terms, as if its aim were to achieve ethical goals or to exemplify ethical ideals . . . Whereas previously ethical considerations were believed to set boundaries to what researchers could do in pursuit of knowledge, now ethical considerations are treated by some as constituting the very rationale of research. For example, its task becomes the promotion of social justice. (Hammersley, 1999: 18)

Hammersley sees this posing of research as ethics as leading to the neglect of research technique – the better or worse ways of carrying out the processes of research in terms of the quality of research knowledge that they generate. He also sees the dominance of ethicism as attributable to the effects of the tendencies of instrumentalism – the idea that the task of research is to relate to policymaking and practice (on which see also Homan, 1991; Simons, 1995) – and of postmodern-ism, especially the 'turn' to 'irony' and scepticism. For Hammersley, they both lead to the down-playing or questioning of the possibility and desirability of knowledge, and he argues that a concern with ethics has expanded to fill this space.[1] We feel, however, that there may well be other factors at work in the rise in concern with research ethics. In its institutionalized form we see this as, at least in part, related to a concern with litigation.

An overt and similar preoccupation in professional ethical state-ments or guidelines, given the way they draw on each other, is with the contract between research funder or sponsor and the researcher (see also CVCP, 1992). There are two main linked issues here. First, there is a concern that researchers should retain their academic free-dom. They should not accept contractual conditions that conflict with ethical practice, such as confidentiality of data and protection of participants' interests, and should consider carefully any attempt to place restrictions on their publication and promotion of their findings. Indeed, there has been recent concern about the way that Government departments can place restrictions on research that they fund, requiring researchers to submit draft reports, publications and so on, so that the department in question can vet these (for examples, see *Times Higher* 31.3.00, 31.3.01).

Secondly, and conversely, we can also detect a concern that researchers need to protect themselves from any legal consequences that might arise if they unwittingly contractually agree to research funders' restrictions and then break that agreement. It is here that we also see the possibility of litigation concerns on the part of the academic institutions that employ researchers: this is why these institutions have a vested interest in these posed ethical issues, for they are implicated in the contractual obligations. Institutional preoccupations with ethics can sometimes appear to be more premised on avoiding potentially costly litigation than with ethical practice itself. Moreover, the pressures of time, bureaucratic administration and funding, our training as social scientists and the prevailing ethos of professional detachment can all mitigate against our giving ethical dilemmas the focused attention that they require in the research process.

There are no laws (at least in the UK) requiring researchers to submit their proposals and modes of practice to ethics committees, and professional association guidelines hold no legal status. Like journalists, however, researchers do not enjoy the protection of the law if they seek to keep their data confidential when its disclosure is subpoena'd (see discussion in Feenan, 2002). Furthermore, as Linda Bell and Linda Nutt discuss in Chapter 4, where researchers work within, or are associated with, a welfare professional context where disclosure of certain types of data is mandatory, such as social work and an interviewee revealing child abuse, they may be required to reveal their source.

Institutional concerns about legal redress being pursued by research participants are equally an issue, especially in the UK with an untested (in this area at least) Copyright, Designs and Patents Act 1988 (see www.qualidata.essex.ac.uk/). This legislation concerns breaching interviewees' copyright in their spoken words in publication of data collected from them. Professional association ethical statements also place an emphasis, in an absolutist way, on researchers' responsibilities for ensuring informed consent to participation in research, protecting research participants from potential harm (and sometimes also wider society), and ensuring their privacy by maintaining confidentiality and anonymity. The University Ethics Committee Code of Practice at one of our institutions, which is not dissimilar to codes being adopted at other universities that we know, thus requires researchers to obtain written ethical approval from any collaborating organisations involved in the research. It also requires researchers to ask research participants to sign a consent form basically stating that they have had the nature and purpose of the research explained to them and that they fully and freely consent to participate in the study. Such an approach implies an either/or position: either consent is informed, participants are protected, and so on, or they are not, as Tina Miller and Linda Bell, and Maxine Birch and Tina Miller write about in this volume. It also implies that all the ethical issues involved in a research project can be determined at the start of the project being carried out, that any potential harm may be offset by research participants' stated willingness, and that an ethics committee sanctioned project is by definition an ethical one. The aim appears to be to avoid ethical dilemmas through asserting formalistic principles, rather than providing guidance on how to deal with them. Indeed, while some pose codes of ethical practice as alerting social researchers to ethical issues (for example, Punch, 1986), others argue that they may have the effect of forestalling rather than initiating researchers' reflexive and continuing engagement with ethical research practice (for example, Mason, 1996).

We are not suggesting, however, that such institutionalized concerns with litigation are necessarily what motivates social researchers in their considerations about, and reflections on, ethics, both here in this book and elsewhere. Nor would we agree with Hammersley that their/our focus on ethics is driven by instrumentalism or by postmodernism in the terms in which he poses the latter, as ironic scepticism. Rather, we would see it as rooted in a genuine and legitimate concern with issues of power. We acknowledge that research is a political, rather than neutral, process – as Val Gillies and Pam Alldred describe in Chapter 2 – in a world that is characterized by awareness of difference and a questioning of the motives and rights of 'experts' to define the social world and to proscribe templates for what constitutes the 'correct' course of action (see Edwards and Glover, 2001).

Ethical concerns in social research

As we noted earlier, there is an extensive literature on ethics in social research. The Social Research Association Ethical Guidelines, for example, contains over 90 key references (www.the-sra.org.uk/). These cover a range of aspects of ethical practice. There are numerous other examples of publications concerned with ethics in social research as well, including a strand of feminist pieces. Few of the SRA-cited publications seem to be written from a feminist perspective, even though a number of influential feminist pieces concerned with aspects of ethical research have been published (early examples include Finch, 1984; Oakley, 1981). Indeed, discussions of the research process related to ethical issues have become a feature of feminist research, especially qualitative empirical work.

Ethical decisions arise throughout the entire research process, from conceptualization and design, data gathering and analysis, and report, and literature on the topic reflects this. Regarding access, the issue of informed consent has been subject to fierce debate among qualitative social researchers generally: in particular the ethics of carrying out covert research (see reviews in Hornsby-Smith, 1993; Lee, 1993; May, 1993; Wise, 1987) and the nature and time frame of consent (David et al., 2001; Denzin, 1997; Morrow and Richards, 1996). The time frame involved in assessing the benefits or harm of social research has also been an issue in discussion (for example, Wise, 1987). There have also been debates amongst feminists concerning the ethical merits and consequences of qualitative versus quantitative methods (see review in Maynard, 1994), and the ethical problems involved in secondary qualitative data analysis have been raised (Mauthner et al., 1998).

The epistemologies of the theoretical perspective informing research have also been discussed as generating ethical questions, allied to debates around research as involved empowerment or distanced knowledge production (see Andrea Doucet and Natasha Mauthner, Chapter 7). Mary Maynard (1994) poses the issue of the ethics of epistemology as the current focus of much debate within feminism, and feminists have also engaged in debate with other perspectives on this topic (see, for example, contributions to *Sociology*, 1992, 26: 2). Other examples of feminist work in this vein include Sue Wise's (1987) argument that ethical issues are inherent in the researcher's definition of social reality; that is the epistemologies of the theoretical perspective framing research questions, analysis of data, and writing up of findings. She argues that the 'cognitive authority' of the researcher's view in producing knowledge, and assessments as to whether or not that knowledge is empowering, are knotty ethical issues. She poses a series of questions, including: who decides, and how, what counts as knowledge? What if one research group's empowerment is another's disempowerment? Hilary Rose (1994) has unpacked the way the scientific knowledge system is entwined with other power systems, and shaped by a masculinist instrumental rationality that denies emotion. In contrast, Rose (1994: 33) puts forward a feminist epistemology that 'thinks from caring' and that is 'centred on the domains of interconnectedness and caring rationality'

Underlying these sorts of discussions and debates over ethical concerns in the research literature are various models of how to understand and resolve ethical issues.

Ethical models

Professional association ethical guidelines and textbook discussions of
social research ethics usually pose the sorts of ethical issues outlined
above as being formed around conflicting sets of rights claims and
competing responsibilities. Steiner Kvale (1996) outlines three ethical
models that provide the broader frameworks within which researchers reflect on these issues (see also Kent, 2000 for a similar categoriza-
tion). These are derived from mainstream political philosophy and
draw out their implications for conducting social research.

In the *'duty ethics of principles'* or deontological model, research is
driven by universal principles such as honesty, justice and respect.
Actions are governed by principles that should not be broken, and
judged by intent rather than consequences. As Kvale (1996: 121) points
out, however, 'carried to its extreme, the intentional position can
become a moral absolutism with intentions of living up to absolute
principles of right action, regardless of the human consequences of an
act'.

The *'utilitarian ethics of consequences'* model prioritizes the 'good-
ness' of outcomes of research such as increased knowledge. Thus the
rightness or wrongness of actions are judged by their consequences
rather than their intent. This model is underlain by a universalist cost-
benefit result pragmatism. In extremis, though, as Kvale notes, such a
position can mean that 'the ends come to justify the means' (1996:
122).

In contrast to the two universalist models above, a *'virtue ethics of
skills'* model questions the possibility of laying down abstract principles. Rather, it stresses a contextual or situational ethical position,
with an emphasis on the researchers' moral values and ethical skills in
reflexively negotiating ethical dilemmas: 'Ethical behaviour is seen
less as the application of general principles and rules, than as the
researcher internalising moral values' (ibid: 122). Researchers' ethical
intuitions, feelings and reflective skills are emphasized, including
their sensibilities in undertaking dialogue and negotiation with the
various parties involved in the research.

Feminist writers on ethics, however, have put forward another
basis for reflecting on ethical issues (although not specifically in
relation to research), with an emphasis on care and responsibility
rather than outcomes, justice or rights. In other words, this is a model

that is focused on particular feminist-informed social *values*. Elisabeth Porter (1999) argues that there are three inter-related features of feminist thinking on ethics: personal experience, context and nurturant relationships. Daily life dilemmas are shaped by social divisions of gender, class and ethnicity: experiences of these dilemmas generate different ethical perspectives. These perspectives are not only obtained in particular contexts, but those contexts also alter and inform the ethical dilemmas that we face as researchers and the range and appropriate choices in resolving them. These dilemmas are not abstract but rooted in specific relationships that involve emotions, and which require nurturance and care for their ethical conduct.

While some, such as Elisabeth Porter, see a clear distinction between the virtue ethics of skills and the value-based feminist model, our own stance is that there are some overlaps as well as distinctions between the two. Both stress context and situation rather than abstract principles, and dialogue and negotiation rather than rules and autonomy. A virtue skills model, however, can imply that the skills that researchers acquire through practice in making ethical decisions are impartial and neutral 'good' (virtue) research standards, even with awareness of particular context. In contrast, a value-based model explicitly advocates a 'partial' stance based on analysis of power relations between those involved in the research and society more broadly, and admits emotion into the ethical process. Here, partiality refers to the importance of acknowledging power relations and taking up a position:

> Ethics encourages partiality, the specific response to distinctiveness . . . partiality does not preclude impartiality . . . partiality varies according to the [relationships] involved . . . responding to this particularity is fundamental to ethics. (Porter, 1999: 30)

A contingent virtue and/or value, rather than universalist approach has become predominantly advocated in texts discussing ethics in social research (examples include Davidson and Layder, 1994; Fielding, 1993; Hornsby-Smith, 1993; Punch, 1986). Professional association guidelines, however, often weave a difficult balance between various models. So, for example, the British Sociological Association's Statement of Ethical Practice both 'points to a set of obligations to which members should normally adhere as principles for guiding their conduct' and 'recognises that often it will be necessary to make . . . choices on the basis of principles and values, and the (often conflicting) interests of those involved'. While difficult balancing acts will always remain, it may be that the awkward tensions in the aims of professional association ethical statements would be eased if they were explicitly informed and guided by a theoretical and feminist approach to ethical dilemmas, as we elaborate later.

Tensions between different ethical models or situational shades of grey, however, do not often seem to be apparent on the part of ethics committees who vet research proposals. Moreover, some researchers seem to want them to apply abstract universalistic principles. Ann Oakley (1992), for example, in discussing her experiences with hospital and health authority ethics committees, points to evidence concerning inconsistencies in their judgements. Such criticism may well be fairly made, but it also implies that there are universal principles and abstract criteria that can be applied regardless of situational context. This is a puzzling stance for researchers like Oakley, whose research practice has been informed by feminism. Indeed, much feminist work addressing aspects of ethical research practice that we discuss below draws on complex situationally informed debates.

There are, nonetheless, contrasts and tensions between positions within any virtue or value based ethical approach – although what they have in common is an ethical approach that calls for attention to specificity and context. These range from complete postmodern relativism through to post-traditional positions (such as feminist, communitarian, new critical theory) that have a particular set of ethical values underlying their situated approach. Even with feminist or feminist-inspired value approaches to ethics there are significant debates around issues of care and power, focused around relationships with 'the Other', as we address below.

There are also debates about the extent to which justice-based ethical models and an ethics of care are in conflict, inter-related or can be reframed (see Porter, 1999; Ruddick, 1996; Sevenhuijsen, 1998). Eva Feder Kittay (2001) summarizes the main elements of an ethics of care in contrast with an ethics of justice, which we have adapted from a medical/health environment to a research context (see table below).

Kittay's discussion, however, poses the two ethics as if they were in opposition to one another. Sarah Ruddick (1996) has taken a similar position, arguing that ethics of care and justice cannot be subsumed under each other and that they cannot be integrated, because in her view justice depends on a notion of the individual as a detached rather than relational being. Nevertheless, Ruddick also argues that justice as well as care applies to the moral domain. Others regard justice and care as complementary, and argue that they need to be integrated in thinking about moral issues (see review in Porter, 1999). This proposition retains the integrity of each ethical framework, as laid out in the table below, but sees them each as providing enabling conditions of moral adequacy for the other ethic.

In contrast, Selma Sevenhuijsen (1998) has gone further to argue for a reformulation of the concept of justice so that it is no longer

Care	Justice
Self as self-in-relation	Autonomous self
Characteristic of informal contexts	Characteristic of formal contexts
Emphasis on contextual reasoning	Emphasis on principles
• Situations as defining moral problems and resolutions	• Hierarchy of values
• Use of narrative	• Calculation of moral rights and wrongs
Emphasis on responsibilities to others and ourselves	Emphasis on rights and equality
Acceptance of inevitable dependencies	Emphasis and valuing of independence
Moral importance of personal connections	Impartiality valued
Values and attempts to maintain connections among individuals	Protects against or adjudicates conflict between individuals
Temptations:	Temptations:
• Sacrifice or loss of self	• Failure to be merciful
• Failure to recognize autonomy of other	• Over-reliance on impersonal institutions
• Over-identification with other	• Overly rule-bound
Harm when connections are broken	Harm when there is a clash between individuals

opposed to or separate from, and thus does not require reconciling with, an ethic of care. Feminist criticisms of justice from care perspectives, she says, have been directed towards a specific variety: that of liberal, rational, distributive models of justice. In her view, discussion about the compatibility of care and justice can usefully be freed from these parameters. There is a need to have concepts of justice that are not framed exclusively in distributive, sameness or universal terms, but which take into account situations and consequences. Thus Sevenhuijsen fundamentally reframes justice to see it as a process rather than rules: a process involving an ethics of care in a situated way based on values of reconciliation, reciprocity, diversity and responsibility, and with an awareness of power. Justice thus does not stand alone but is simultaneously incorporated into, and informed by, care. It is within this understanding of justice as part of care that we proceed to examine care-based ethical debates and then generate our own guidelines for ethical research practice.

Care-based ethical debates

Kittay (2001) refers to care and caring as a labour, an attitude and a 'virtue' (or value in our terms). The central catalyst to writings on a feminist ethics of care was the work of Carol Gilligan (Porter, 1999). She first used the concept in her work on gender differences in moral reasoning between boys and girls (Gilligan, 1983), in which she argued that girls and women deliberate in a 'different [ethical] voice' to boys/men because they find themselves dealing with dilemmas over their own desires and the needs of others, and the responsibilities that they feel for those within their web of connections in ways that are gendered. Other feminist work addressing a feminist ethics of care includes Nel Noddings' (1984) discussion of the central places of responsibility and relationships as an empathetic way of responding to others in an ethical manner; and Joan Tronto's (1993) analysis of the way that the practical, relational, caring work primarily undertaken by women is excluded from mainstream moral and political philosophy and theorizing because it is regarded as instinctual practice rather than willed action based on rules.

The work of these and other feminist theorizers in the field, however, has rarely been applied to a consideration of ethics in social research. Norman Denzin (1997) provides a notable exception here. He has put forward a strong argument for feminist theorizing to inform ethical research, expressly in relation to ethnography and specifically addressing the writing of it. As part of his critique of traditional voyeuristic and utilitarian knowledge-making protocol, Denzin takes issue with those who, like Martyn Hammersley, want a focus on 'better' techniques, and who pose the 'turn' to postmodernism as if it is a choice or an option. Rather, for Denzin, we inhabit and *live* in just such a cultural moment, and one in which morality and ethics are central issues:

> The ethnographic culture has changed because the world that ethnography confronts has changed. Disjuncture and difference define this global, postmodern cultural economy we all live in . . . Global and local legal processes have problematicized and erased the personal and institutional distance between the ethnographer and those he or she writes about . . . We do not own the field notes we make about those we study. We do not have an undisputed warrant to study anyone or anything . . . The writer can no longer presume to be able to present an objective, noncontested account of the other's experiences . . . ethnography is a moral, allegorical, and therapeutic project. Ethnography is more than the record of human experience. The ethnographer writes tiny moral tales. (Denzin, 1997: xii–xiv)

Denzin castigates modernist ethical models as resting 'on a cognitive model that privileges rational solutions to ethical dilemmas (the rationalist fallacy), and it presumes that humanity is a single subject (the distributive fallacy) . . . This rights-, justice-, and acts-based system ignores the relational dialogical nature of human interaction' (Denzin, 1997: 271, 273). The universalist ethical models of duty and of utilitarianism are rejected and replaced by a personally involved care-based ethical system, based on a body of work Denzin refers to as the 'feminist, communitarian ethical model'. He sees this work as defined by its contention that:

> . . . community is ontologically and morally prior to persons, and that dialogical communication is the basis of the moral community . . . A personally involved, politically committed ethnographer is presumed and not the morally neutral observer of positivism . . . In this framework every moral act is a contingent accomplishment measured against the ideals of a feminist, interactive, and moral universalism. (Denzin, 1997: 274)

Denzin explicitly draws on the work of feminist political theorists and philosophers such as Patricia Hill Collins (1991) and Syela Benhabib (1992). From a Black feminist position, Hill Collins critiques the traditional, positivist, masculinist and Euro-centric knowledge-making enterprise. She offers four criteria for interpreting truth and knowledge claims of social science: the first focuses on the primacy of concrete lived experience; the second on the use of dialogue in assessing knowledge claims; the third on the ethic of caring; and the fourth on the ethic of personal accountability. Hill Collins' ethical system for knowledge validation is concerned with ethics of care and accountability that are rooted in values of personal expressiveness, emotions and empathy. These are made accountable through an interactive 'call-and-response' dialogue. In such a mode, there is no need to 'decentre' others in order to centre our own 'expert' voice and arguments adversarially. Rather, the centre of discussion is constantly and appropriately pivoted, so that participants can all exchange wisdoms, and acknowledge that experience and knowledge are partial at the same time as they are valid. Benhabib reworks Habermas' ideas around discourse ethics (including through her notion of 'open-ended moral conversations' which Maxine Birch and Tina Miller refer to in Chapter 5), to reject traditional liberal, abstract, autonomous and rights-based justice reasoning as the basis for moral deliberation. She argues that ethics is about concrete rather than generalized situations, in which relations of care belong at the centre rather than the margins. What is moral and ethical is arrived at through an active and situationally contingent exchange of experiences, perspectives and ideas across differences (particularly around gender, but also in terms of other social divisions). She puts forward 'moral respect' as 'symmetrical reciprocity', comprising a relation of symmetry between self and other that involves looking at issues from the point of view of others or putting ourselves in the place of others.

As Denzin (1997) conceives it, the personally involved care-based ethical system for social research that he derives from feminist communitarianism, privileges emotionality in the ethical decision-making process. It presumes a dialogic rather than autonomous view of self, and asks the researcher 'to step into the shoes of the persons being studied' (Denzin, 1997: 273) and build connected and transformative, participatory and empowering relationships with those studied. Researchers need to be what is often termed 'with and for the Other'. Ethnographic writing should be 'a vehicle for readers to discover moral truths about themselves' (Denzin, 1997: 284) and should be judged for its ability to 'provoke transformations and changes in the public and private spheres of everyday life' (Denzin, 1997: 275).

This view necessarily is a simplification of the complex and valuable arguments that Denzin makes, as well as those of the 'feminist communitarian' thinkers upon whom he draws. Parts of them, however, may be subject to the sorts of questions Sue Wise (1987) directed at previous feminist work (see earlier). What if one research group's empowerment is another's disempowerment, especially where both are considered oppressed groups? What happens if, as Donna Luff (1999) experienced in her study of women in the moral lobby, we find ourselves researching individuals or groups whom we dislike and/or consider socially damaging even if oppressed? And what if what is beneficial at one moment turns out to be the opposite in the long-run? Indeed, Denzin seems to imply that research following the feminist communitarian ethical model will not face these sorts of ethical questions:

> This framework presumes a researcher who builds collaborative, reciprocal, trusting, and friendly relations with those studied. This individual would not work in a situation in which the need for compensation from injury could be created. (Denzin, 1997: 275)

Other feminist theorists have criticised the approaches on which Denzin's work is based. Iris Young (1997), for example, challenges feminist and other ethical frameworks that imply a relation of symmetry between self and other, which involve looking at issues from the point of view of others or putting ourselves in the place of others (including Benhabib's notion of symmetrical reciprocity). The 'stepping into each other's shoes' that Denzin recommends assumes an easy reversibility of positions that is neither possible nor desirable according to Young. This is because individuals have particular histories and occupy social positions that make their relations asymmetrical. Young points out the difficulties of imagining another's point of view or seeing the world from their standpoint when we lack their personal and group history. Instead, Young argues for 'asymmetrical reciprocity' which means accepting that there are aspects of another person's position that we do not understand, yet are open to asking about and listening to. Asymmetrical reciprocity involves dialogue that enables each subject to understand each other across differences without reversing perspectives or identifying with each other. In other words, rather than ignoring or blurring power positions, ethical practice needs to pay attention to them. (See also Maxine Birch and Tina Miller, Chapter 5, for a further critique of attempting open-ended moral conversations.)

Selma Sevenhuijsen's (1998) work on an ethics of care also raises shortcomings in Denzin's particular feminist-derived position on ethics in social research. Like him, she also regards postmodernism as a social condition based on diversity, ambiguity and ambivalence, which brings moral and ethical issues to the fore. Like Young, however, she does not accept 'being with and for the Other' as a sufficient basis for formulating ethics. For her, though, this is because this stance does not capture the concrete relations of dependency and connection that are central to an ethics of care.

> First of all, the ethics of care involves different moral concepts: responsibilities and relationships rather than rules and rights. Secondly, it is bound to concrete situations rather than being formal and abstract. And thirdly, the ethics of care can be described as a moral activity, the 'activity of caring', rather than as a set of principles which can simply be followed. The central question in the ethics of care, how to deal with dependency and responsibility, differs radically from that of rights ethics: what are the highest normative principles and rights in situations of moral conflict? (Sevenhuijsen, 1998: 107)

So, while Denzin calls for a care-based ethical system to shape the research process, he slips away from fully recognizing its implications back towards the autonomous separateness he rejects.

Furthermore, while Denzin seems similar to Sevenhuijsen in seeing emotionality and empathy as central to ethical judgement, unlike her he does not also stress the need for caring and 'care'ful judgement to be based on practical knowledge and attention to detail in the context of time and place. Within Sevenhuijsen's version of an ethics of care, ethics thus needs to be interpreted and judged in specific contexts of action – it is fundamentally contingent practice-based.

Feminist ethics of care and practical guidelines

Feminist political theorists who advocate an ethic of care perspective on issues argue that a feminist approach to ethics should not seek to formulate moral principles that stand above power and context. Ethics is about *how* to deal with conflict, disagreement and ambivalence rather than attempting to eliminate it. A feminist ethics of care can help researchers think about how they do this by 'illuminating more fully the sources of moral dilemmas and formulating meaningful epistemological strategies in order to deal with these dilemmas, even if only on a temporary basis' (Sevenhuijsen, 1998: 16). The importance and centrality of attention to specificity and context means that ethics cannot be expected to be a source of absolute norms. It has to connect to concrete practices and dilemmas, as the chapters in the rest of this book illustrate. It is attention to these issues that can provide the guidelines for ethical action.

•Thus we conclude with a – contingent – attempt to generate some guidelines for ethical research practice arising out of a feminist ethics of care, indicating where they are elaborated empirically in following chapters by our co-contributors. Importantly, it should be noted that when we refer to 'the people involved' below, we include the researcher as well as participants, funders, gate-keepers and others. We suggest that these guidelines framed as questions can be useful for researchers to consider in deliberating dilemmas, choosing from alternative courses of action, and being accountable for the course of action that they ultimately decide to pursue.

• *Who are the people involved in and affected by the ethical dilemma raised in the research?*

Maxine Birch and Tina Miller address these issues in their chapter on participation in the research process (Chapter 5).

• *What is the context for the dilemma in terms of the specific topic of the research and the issues it raises personally and socially for those involved?*

Andrea Doucet and Natasha Mauthner consider this in their chapter on how we come to produce ethical knowledge (Chapter 7).

• *What are the specific social and personal locations of the people involved in relation to each other?*

Linda Bell and Linda Nutt explore these elements in their discussion of professional and research loyalties (Chapter 4), as do Andrea Doucet and Natasha Mauthner in the context of analysing data (Chapter 7).

• *What are the needs of those involved and how are they inter-related?*

Jean Duncombe and Julie Jessop delve into this issue in their examination of emotions and 'rapport' in interviews (Chapter 6).

- *Who am I identifying with, who am I posing as other, and why?*

Linda Bell and Linda Nutt tackle this question in their chapter on divided loyalties to professional considerations and research etiquette (Chapter 4). Pam Alldred and Val Gillies' chapter on the implicit notion of the modernist subject that researchers work with in interview-based research also touches on some of these issues (Chapter 8).

- *What is the balance of personal and social power between those involved?*

Val Gillies and Pam Alldred address this question explicitly in their chapter about research as a political tool (Chapter 2), as do Linda Bell and Linda Nutt in their focus on conflicting expectations when researchers are also working professionals in other spheres – health, welfare and social work in particular (Chapter 4).

- *How will those involved understand our actions and are these in balance with our judgement about our own practice?*

Both Val Gillies and Pam Alldred (Chapter 2), and Jean Duncombe and Julie Jessop (Chapter 6) write about these issues in their chapters in relation to the intentions researchers espouse for their research on the one hand, and regarding the intimacy between researcher and respondent that can resemble friendship on the other.

- *How can we best communicate the ethical dilemmas to those involved, give them room to raise their views, and negotiate with and between them?*

Both Tina Miller and Linda Bell (Chapter 3), and Maxine Birch and Tina Miller (Chapter 5) consider these issues in the context of seeking access to participants and gaining their consent to taking part in research projects.

- *How will our actions affect relationships between the people involved?*

Both Linda Bell and Linda Nutt (Chapter 4), and Jean Duncombe and Julie Jessop (Chapter 6) address this question in their respective chapters: in relation to professional and research motivations, and to forms of friendship that are created in the research process.

We hope that other researchers will find these guidelines useful for consideration in deliberating ethical dilemmas in their research practice. We are not claiming that this list of guidelines for working with a feminist ethics of care in social research constitutes a definitive model. Rather, we see it as work in progress. We offer it here in the spirit of working towards a means of implementing a feminist ethics of care as a guide for how ethical dilemmas in empirical research may be practically resolved.

Note

[1] It is something of an irony (although not in the Hammersleyite postmodern sense) that his late colleague, Peter Foster, who shared many of his views, could be regarded as feeding into Hammersley's charge of ethicism. Foster (1999) argued that the pursuit of truthful objective knowledge through the application of systematic research triangulation should in fact be a key guiding principle elaborated in professional association *ethical* guidelines, and which pursuit Foster also saw as a casualty of postmodern relativism.

References

Alderson, P. (1995) *Listening to Children: Ethics and Social Research*. Barkingside: Barnardos.

Benhabib, S. (1992) *Situating the Self: Gender, Community and Postmodernism in Contemporary Ethics*. New York: Routledge.

Committee of Vice Chancellors and Principals (CVCP) (1992) *Sponsored University Research: Recommendations and Guidance on Contract Issues*. London: CVCP.

David, M., Edwards, R. and Alldred, P. (2001) 'Children and school-based research: "informed consent" or "educated consent"?', *British Educational Research Journal*, 27(3): 347–365.

Davidson, J. O'Connell and Layder, D. (1994) *Methods, Sex and Madness*. London: Routledge.

Denzin, N. (1997) *Interpretive Ethnography: Ethnographic Practices for the 21st Century*. London: Sage.

Edwards, R. and Glover, J. (2001) 'Risk, citizenship and welfare: an introduction', in R. Edwards and J. Glover (eds), *Risk and Citizenship: Key Issues in Welfare*. London: Routledge.

Feenan, D. (2002) 'Researching paramilitary violence in Northern Ireland', *International Journal of Social Research Methodology: Theory and Practice*, 5: 2: 147–63.

Fielding, N. (1993) 'Qualitative interviewing', in N. Gilbert (ed.), *Researching Social Life*. London: Sage.

Finch, J. (1984) ' "It's great to have someone to talk to": ethics and politics of interviewing women', in C. Bell and H. Roberts (eds), *Social Researching: Politics, Problems, Practice*. London: Routledge.

Foster, P. (1999) 'Some critical comments on the BERA Ethical Guidelines', *Research Intelligence*, No. 67. pp. 24–28.

Gilligan, C. (1983) *In A Different Voice: Psychological Theory and Women's Development*. Cambridge, MA: Harvard University Press.

Hammersley, M. (1999) 'Some reflections on the current state of qualitative research', *Research Intelligence*, No. 70. pp. 16–18.

Hill Collins, P. (1991) *Black Feminist Thought*. London: Routledge.

Homan, R. (1991) *The Ethics of Social Research*. Harlow: Longman.

Hornsby-Smith, M. (1993) 'Gaining access', in N. Gilbert (ed.), *Researching Social Life*. London: Sage.

Jaggar, A. (1991) 'Feminist ethics: projects, problems, prospects', in C. Card (ed.), *Feminist Ethics*. Lawrence: University Press of Kansas.

Kent, G. (2000) 'Ethical principles', in D. Burton (ed.), *Research Training for Social Scientists: A Handbook for Postgraduate Researchers*. London: Sage.

Kittay, E.F. (2001) 'Ethics of Care Workshop: Tools and Methods in Bioethics', *EURESCO Biomedicine Within the Limits of Human Existence Conference*, Davos, Switzerland, 8–13 September.

Kvale, S. (1996) *InterViews: An Introduction to Qualitative Research Interviewing*. London: Sage.

Lee, R.M. (1993) *Doing Research on Sensitive Topics*. London: Sage.

Luff, D. (1999) 'Dialogue across the divides: "moments of rapport" and power in feminist research with anti-feminist women', *Sociology*, 33(4): 687–703.

Mason, J. (1996) *Qualitative Researching*. London: Sage.

Mauthner, N., Parry, O. and Backett-Milburn, K. (1998) 'The data are out there, or are they? Implications for archiving and revisiting qualitative data', *Sociology*, 32(4): 733–745.

May, T. (1993) *Social Research: Issues, Methods and Process*. Buckingham: Open University Press.

Maynard, M. (1994) 'Methods, practice and epistemology: the debate about feminism and research', in M. Maynard and J. Purvis (eds), *Researching Women's Lives From a Feminist Perspective*. London: Taylor & Francis.

Morrow, V. and Richards, M. (1996) 'The ethics of social research with children: an overview', *Children & Society*, 10: 90–105.

Noddings, N. (1984) *Caring: A Feminine Approach to Ethics and Moral Education*. Berkeley: University of California Press.

Oakley, A. (1981) 'Interviewing women: a contradiction in terms', in H. Roberts (ed.), *Doing Feminist Research*. London: Routledge and Kegan Paul.

Oakley, A. (1992) *Social Support and Motherhood*. Oxford: Blackwell.

Porter, E. (1999) *Feminist Perspectives on Ethics*. Harlow: Pearson Education.

Punch, M. (1986) *Politics and Ethics of Fieldwork*. London: Sage.

Rose, H. (1994) *Love, Power and Knowledge: Towards a Feminist Transformation of the Sciences*. Cambridge: Polity Press.

Ruddick, S. (1996) *Maternal Thinking: Towards a Politics of Peace*. Boston: Beacon Press.

Sevenhuijsen, S. (1998) *Citizenship and the Ethics of Care: Feminist Considerations on Justice, Morality and Politics*. London: Routledge.

Simons, H. (1995) 'The politics and ethics of educational research in England: contemporary issues', *British Journal of Educational Research*, 21(4): 435–449.

Tronto, J. (1993) *Moral Boundaries: A Political Argument for an Ethic of Care*. London: Routledge.

Wise, S. (1987) 'A framework for discussing ethical issues in feminist research: a review of the literature', in V. Griffiths, M. Humm, R. O'Rourke, J. Batsleer, F. Poland and S. Wise, *Writing Feminist Biography 2: Using Life Histories*. Studies in Sexual Politics No. 19, University of Manchester.

Young, I.M. (1997) *Intersecting Voices: Dilemmas of Gender, Political Philosophy and Policy*. Princeton: Princeton University Press.

CHAPTER 2

THE ETHICS OF INTENTION: RESEARCH AS A POLITICAL TOOL

Val Gillies and Pam Alldred

Introduction

Many feminists have criticized the traditional approach of Western scientific research, questioning in particular the premise that facts can be gathered objectively. This chapter argues that the epistemological shift from a reliance on the positivist paradigm of scientific truth necessitates a new scrutiny of the intentions underlying feminist research. Whilst feminists take up a range of positions in relation to the implications of the critique of positivism for their research – which means that our aims can range from the production of more inclusive or less biased research to the rejection of this type of knowledge claim altogether – the questions raised about the politics or ethics of research can usefully inform feminist research of whatever hue. Once our faith in objective positivism is shaken, the goals of feminist research tend to be transformed from attempting to better understand or represent women's experiences, to the explicitly political aim of challenging gender oppression and improving women's lives. Research therefore becomes an explicitly political tool to be used strategically to make political interventions. But how do we address issues of intention for research when feminist aims themselves have also been subject to the same questioning as has 'Truth'?

Within a modernist research paradigm, ethics have been seen as abstract, transferable principles. Moreover, they are concerned with the research process itself: the rights and wrongs of how knowledge (as objective fact) is collected. Research ethics have therefore focused on how well participants are treated, but has not been extended to encompass broader questions about the ethics of knowledge itself, for instance, the political role played by research findings or by the relations set up by the knowledge claims (Burman, 1992). We argue for the need to broaden our conception of ethics to include the political objectives or intentions for research, as well as such questions about the ethics of knowledge relations. That is, who claims to know, and how, and the power relationship produced by this. Once research is acknowledged to be a political activity (e.g. Mayall, 1999), questions of ethics cannot be separated from political aims and intentions. Judgements of ethical practice therefore become situation specific, with criteria tied to politically informed intentions, which is why ethics can no longer be abstracted into codes of practice (as Rosalind Edwards and Melanie Mauthner argue in Chapter 1). This redefining of ethics to encompass knowledge relations as well as the relations set up within the practices of research, collapses established boundaries between political activism and ethical feminist research.

The political and personal perspectives of researchers inform the intentions we have for the research. They are also the means by which we evaluate the impact and the indirect implications of our research. Although all feminist research may be regarded as 'transformative' (Harding, 1987), precise political aims are rarely discussed or critically evaluated. While most feminist researchers rely on some basic abstractions and universal categories for good reasons, few of us explicate our motivation beyond the aim of generating 'feminist knowledge' or 'doing feminist research'. Taken-for-granted notions of what is progressive in research can therefore be left unquestioned, with good intention seemingly adequate justification. This might be partly because of the difficulty of warranting 'feminist' interventions as the terms of feminist politics have been queried, but perhaps it is also partly a legacy of the depoliticization of research in positivist empiricism. It forecloses the space we wish to open up for discussion of our, and others', intentions for research. Questioning the intentions that lie behind someone's research must not be interpreted as questioning their feminist commitment, but rather as trying to help clarify political aims and means. In some situations, such as when negotiating hostile audiences, we might not fully expose our political intentions in order to keep our place on the platform, as chapters in *Feminist Dilemmas* argued (Alldred, 1998; Standing, 1998). Strategic silences, such as when we present our research 'findings' without our account of the political role we hope they will play, may be seen as politically and ethically legitimate, but in contexts of feminist debate and reflexivity we argue for making explicit the links between research, politics and ethics.

This chapter focuses on three main areas of feminist research, which might be positioned differently along the epistemological continuum in terms of the political aims and intentions they embody. First we examine feminist efforts to represent women in order that their voices and experiences are heard. Secondly we focus on feminist attempts to initiate personal change through action research. Thirdly, we look at feminist post-structuralist aims to deconstruct and thereby undermine oppressive knowledge structures. We aim to highlight the assumptions that underpin each approach, and the potential ethical dilemmas raised by them. We begin by exploring how knowledge has been conceptualized in recent Western feminist thought because these epistemological debates are crucial to the (re)definition of ethics. We argue that if knowledge is understood as essentially political, then ethical principles must also be understood in terms of political practice.

Epistemological debates

Having identified positivism as oppressive and as failing in its own terms to be truly objective, some feminists have attempted to produce knowledge that is closer to the 'truth' about women. For some, the identification of bias and androcentricism in traditional scientific research pointed to male scientists' failure to live up to the principles of good science. An approach that Sandra Harding (1990) termed 'feminist empiricism' suggested increasing the numbers of female scientists to help eliminate distortion, ignorance and prejudice, and thereby reform the otherwise inadequate practices of positivist research. As many feminists, including Harding herself, pointed out, this aim left untouched the gendered assumptions that underlie the very project of science itself, and merely incorporated women scientists within a male defined framework. As an alternative to this positivist approach, Harding called for a scientific epistemology to encompass a 'feminist standpoint', suggesting that research grounded in women's experiences could produce a more complete picture and less distorted knowledge claims.

Feminist research has provided a critique not only of the findings of positivist research, but also of the aims, assumptions and methods that underpin the empiricist approach to knowing. Feminists have questioned the notions of neutrality and objectivity, arguing that reason cannot be separated from emotion or subjective interest. The universal validity of knowledge produced by a male-dominated elite was also challenged, revealing the way this ignored or marginalized women's perspectives and experiences (Harding, 1991). By highlighting the way claims of objectivism naturalize particular embedded perspectives, issues of gender and power were implicated in the process of creating 'scientific knowledge' and therefore also its 'findings'. Critics thereby exposed the essentially political nature of claims to truth, and feminists in particular showed how women's subjectivities come to be defined through masculinist knowledge structures.

According to Harding (1990), epistemologies are 'justificatory strategies', necessary both to defend the value of feminist 'knowledge' and to guide theory, practice and politics. In this sense, justificatory strategies are regarded as tools to develop and validate alternative truth claims made by feminists, enabling and justifying feminist action to effect change. However, for many other feminists, any claim to objective truth raises a number of problematic issues about knowledge and power (Burman, 1996; Hollway, 1989; Weedon, 1987). Although Harding's endorsement of the feminist standpoint approach as a 'successor science' has been influential, it has also been widely criticized for its reification of a single, universal feminist standpoint, which allows the continued marginalization of, for example, black, lesbian, working-class or post-colonial women's perspectives (Burman, 1996; hooks, 1990; Stanley and Wise, 1993).

A rigid reliance on supposedly universal categories, such as women, excludes and manipulates by policing legitimate 'insides' and constructing ineligible 'outsides'. As Diane Elam argues 'a feminism that believes it knows what a woman is and what she can do both forecloses the limitless possibilities of women and misrepresents the various forms that social injustice can take' (Elam, 1994: 32). Yet without access to basic generalizations, feminism struggles to preserve its moral and political role in challenging the oppression(s) of women. Many feminists are wary of attempts to effect social change by unqualified universal appeals to 'women' and 'women's interests' (Riley, 1988; Spelman, 1988), but some have gone further and, drawing on postmodernist work, reject altogether universalizing classifications such as gender or identity (Butler, 1990, 1993; Fraser and Nicholson, 1990). Many feminists saw how postmodernist and post-structuralist[1] critiques resonated with long-standing feminist critiques of *'whose truth'* counts. They question the essentialising implications of some feminist theory and are suspicious of any reliance on a unitary system of justification (Elam, 1994; McNay, 1992). Instead they highlight the pluralistic, complex social identities that individuals draw on, and recast 'knowledge' as a situation-dependent resource. The resulting focus on difference and multiplicity has led many to consider the implications of the postmodern approach for feminist research and politics. Whilst methodologies which emphasize the contingent and situated nature of knowledge and subjectivity have been broadly taken up amongst feminist researchers, the accompanying challenges to assertions of feminist knowledge or perspectives have provoked intense debate. Concerns have been voiced over the value or dangers that such an approach generates for feminist politics, and the ethical dilemmas it raises in terms of research (Jackson, 1992; Soper, 1991).

In particular, there is a concern that a focus on the heterogeneity of women's experience dissolves many of the assumed commonalities that feminism was built on. Without a central, definable notion of the female subject, established theoretical and political distinctions seem to become redundant. As Janet Ransom points out 'what threatens to disappear is the hook on which to hang our feminism' (Ransom, 1993: 166). There is also concern that the rejection of theoretical abstractions or generalizations, in favour of an exclusive focus on plurality and cultural diversity, obscures the existence of broad and systematic structures of inequality and oppression. The understandable concern is that with no recourse to legitimation through claims of justice or truth, feminism becomes merely one of many equally valid perspectives.

While most feminists recognise the risk that gender generalizations may be made at the expense of individual, contextual experience, many also oppose an exclusive focus on difference. Although the debates about 'difference' amongst Western feminists during the 1980s and early 1990s have been crucial in identifying the exclusionary potential of universalizing any single feminist perspective, important subsequent arguments have highlighted the risks that a sole focus on 'difference' can present to feminist political analyses. As critiques of multiculturalism have revealed, 'respect for difference' sometimes conceals a vacuum in the critique of injustice and of the existing power-relations. Postmodern critiques of the concepts of truth and justice have therefore been accused of paralysing practical efforts towards social progress, by levelling the ground on which moral judgements are made. At the extreme or theoretically pure end of postmodernist approaches is a relativism which is regarded by many as delegitimising feminist (or any other political) action. Relinquishing the warrant of truth may be seen as kicking the platform that feminists and others have recently had (some) access to, out from under our feet (Burman, 1990). Furthermore, such an epistemologically orientated focus, can reduce feminist struggle to a mere theoretical exercise which can conceal and leave unchallenged the embedded structures of privilege. The promotion of epistemological theory over political prac- tice and physical experience has been criticized on theoretical as well as ethical grounds. Susan Bordo (1990) has argued that a postmodern approach exchanges a positivist preoccupation with objectivity and neutrality ('a view from nowhere') for an equally problematic fantasy of protean dislocation characterized by constantly shifting viewpoints ('a dream of everywhere'). Bordo also draws attention to the inescap- able physical and material locatedness that works to shape and limit human thought and action:

> we are standing in concrete bodies, in a particular time and place in the 'middle' of things, always. The most sophisticated theory cannot alter this limitation on our knowledge, while too-rigid adherence to theory can make us too inflexible, too attached to a set of ideas, to freshly assess what is going on around us. (1998: 96)

Confronted with the problematic consequences and ethical dilemmas associated with modernist and postmodernist epistemologies, some feminists have argued for a progressive synthesis of the two approaches. For instance, Nancy Fraser and Linda Nicholson have suggested that each perspective illuminates significant shortcomings of the other, claiming that a 'postmodernist reflection on feminist theory reveals disabling vestiges of essentialism, while a feminist reflection on postmodernism reveals androcentricism and political naivete' (Fraser and Nicholson, 1990: 20). Some feminists informed by post-structuralism or postmodernism have sought to move beyond the essentialising tendencies of some approaches to feminist epistemology, but claim to avoid relativising by demonstrating how individual women's lives are shaped by multiple influences and experiences that interweave to produce intricate power relations. Fraser and Nicholson view gendered experience as fragmented, diverse and situated, but attempt to link such analyses to wider social theory to construct a practical politics of emancipation. Similarly, Erica Burman claims that local analyses in which the researcher does not claim to have privileged access to the truth or to be presenting the only possible interpretation of events can still guard against relativism by attending to both the micro- and the macro-politics of the situation (Burman, 1992, 1993). Nevertheless, some feel there are intractable contradictions between postmodernism and feminism (McNay, 1992), and have expressed unease at the incorporation of such a radically undermining critique of traditional emancipatory objectives. These theoretical and epistemological debates have important implications for feminist research and ethics in terms of political practice.

Feminist intentions: why research is political

By questioning the way that we justify our political statements about women's lives, a whole league of questions are raised about the nature of current feminist research. The ethical dilemmas posed include, for example, how do we know such a thing to be true, and that a particular response will be in (even specific) women's interests? Most feminist researchers tread an uneasy path between retaining certain abstractions and general categories (such as gender or ethnicity), while also recognizing diversity and critiquing essentialism. We suggest that a consequence of this struggle to reconcile aspects of foundationalism with post-structuralist critiques should be a magnified spotlight on intention and political praxis. Feminist researchers need recourse to concepts of justice and morality in order to make claims about (how we see) the world, and as Fraser and Nicholson argue, we need access to 'the large scale theoretical tools needed to address large political problems' (1990: 34). But to ensure sensitivity to the heterogeneity of experience and power, there is a responsibility to place ourselves in the picture that we are 'describing', thereby revealing the partiality of our own perspective. This involves locating research in terms of its objectives and outcomes, by fully articulating the motivating political intentions.

Within modernist accounts, the intent is to find 'truth', and while a political intent may be recognized, it is believed that knowledge itself will prove emancipatory. It is this very aspect of modernism, the myth of progress towards 'enlightenment' which produces the corollary presumption that Western (modernist) knowledge practices represent the furthering of 'civilization'. It was the West's presumed purchase on superior knowledge which has underpinned and justified the colonization of 'less civilized nations' and the neo-imperial relations still maintained. Critiques of such modernist tropes first made postmodernist, postcolonial and post-structuralist approaches of interest to feminists. First wave Western feminism emerged as a modernist movement believing emancipation would follow from the discovery of 'truth', whereas contemporary feminists have differing views about the role 'truth' might play in achieving emancipatory aims. For some feminist researchers abandoning theoretical purity has lead to a more practical focus on challenging inequality and improving women's lives. According to Liz Stanley (1990), feminists should be transcending the theory/research divide, and recognizing the symbiotic relationship between manual and intellectual activities. This is one approach to re-valuing knowledge for its pragmatic use to feminists, rather than valuing its status as truth in the conventional modernist paradigm. From this perspective, it is not simply knowledge of women's lives, but knowledge that *works for* women that counts. In which case it is necessary to discuss what knowledge is for, in terms of what we want it to do or achieve with it.

Although we may make certain compromises in the light of funders' or other practical concerns, as researchers we are broadly guided in our choices by what we believe is 'for the best'. But despite good intentions, feminists cannot transcend the personal accountability and partial nature of knowledge production. As such, both our intentions for our research and the political assumptions underpinning these, need to be personally recognized and publicly acknowledged. This is not to suggest that we are incapable of promoting causes outside of our own experience or personal involvement, but it is to re-assert that such interventions are conducted from our own particular frames of reference. While particular concepts of morality and justice are vital, they are actively constructed, deconstructed or maintained through particular political struggles and perspectives. As Susan Bordo points out 'we always "see" from points of view that are invested with our social, political, and personal interests, inescapably "centric" in one way or another, even in the desire to do justice to heterogeneity' (Bordo, 1990: 140).

Knowledge and empowerment: three key strands in feminist research

While the will to make a difference is understood as a basic feminist principle, it is generally recognized that there are multiple, contested 'feminist' readings of what needs to change. It is this disconnection from abstract notions of 'truth' for a broad acceptance of multiple 'feminisms' that brings the ethics of intention more sharply into view. We will now examine three distinct strands within feminist research in order to draw out the implicit political/ethical issues associated with each approach.

Representing women

A fundamental objective of much feminist research is to represent the views and experiences of women, in order to challenge their marginalized status. This was a key strategy for second wave Western feminists. Many regarded themselves as conduits, channelling perspectives and voices which would otherwise remain silent, muted or invisible. Asserting that knowledge always embodies a perspective means that the researcher's own role in constructing 'knowledge' about other women needs to be recognized as an active and particular one, as opposed to being a neutral, 'objective' research instrument. Recognition of the researcher's role in constructing 'knowledge' about women has generated numerous debates about the ethics and politics of 'representing the other' (see for instance, Wilkinson and Kitzinger, 1996). In this section we consider the dilemmas which characterize these debates before moving on to emphasize the central significance the ethics of intention assumes in relation to feminist attempts to represent women other than ourselves.

A central issue for feminist research is whether individuals can, or should attempt to represent groups that they do not belong to, especially groups with less power and influence, as many of the chapters in *Feminist Dilemmas* discussed (e.g. Alldred, 1998; Ribbens and Edwards, 1998; Standing, 1998). Although feminist researchers often

emphasize the commonalities between themselves and the participants of their research as a validation of their right to represent other
women, structural and individual differences sometimes conflict with
similarities (e.g. Maxine Birch and Tina Miller in Chapter 5). As bell
hooks has argued, efforts by dominant groups to represent those who
are oppressed can amount to a form of colonization, reinterpreting
and thereby erasing the 'voice' of the speaking subject (hooks, 1990).
Similarly, Daphne Patai (1991) argues forcefully that the intractability
of the power relation between Western academic feminists and 'Third
World' women means that research by the former on the latter is never
ethically justifiable. Like hooks and Patai, many feminists are uneasy
about over-attribution to the concept of gender as a universal experience across 'race', class and other social distinctions.

Even when specific experiences or identities are shared by the
researcher and researched, affinity in itself cannot be regarded as an
authoritative basis for representative research. Paradoxically, when an
emphasis is placed on sameness, power differences are highlighted in
terms of whose version of the account is eventually told, even if the
research is presented as a co-construction. Fore-grounding commonality at the expense of difference risks generating a falsely homogen-
ised view of particular experiences, and may result in an over
representation of issues that resonate with white, middle-class
researchers. Thus, although sharing an experience or standpoint may
generate empathy and a desire to speak on behalf of others, it can
compromise critical reflexivity by encouraging a reliance on unchallenged assumptions and inferences (Hurd and McIntyre, 1996; Reay,
1996). In particular, political intentions might remain unexplicated
behind assumed shared political perspectives. As critiques of identity
politics have shown (Butler, 1990), even if we do share identities, we
cannot assume that common identities produce common political
perspectives.

In response to these ethical/political concerns, some feminists have
argued against speaking for others, suggesting that a researcher's
warrant extends only to representations of themselves and their
immediate communities. Inevitably, this proposal has generated much
debate and dispute, not least over what constitutes a common identity.
Many writers point to the highly specific experience of being an
academic feminist (Kitzinger and Wilkinson, 1996), while others stress
the multifaceted nature of an individual's identity and subjective
positioning in order to highlight the unfeasible basis of this idea
(Bhavnani and Phoenix, 1994; Stanley and Wise, 1993). Taken to its
logical conclusion, the call to 'only speak for ourselves' would preclude all discussion other than solipsistic reflections on personal
experience, given that no two individuals will share exactly the same
standpoints. Clearly, we would not want to draw this conclusion

because it forecloses possible political alliances including acts of sol-
idarity which fully recognize difference and the power relations that
the act is embedded in.

While valid ethical concerns have been expressed about the practice of speaking for others, equally valid questions have been raised
about the morality of not speaking for them. As Rosalind Edwards
states:

> Can, or should, white middle-class women academics, such as myself,
> research and represent in writing the voices of black, mainly working-class
> women? For me, the question has always been another way around: can I
> possibly be justified in leaving them out? (Edwards, 1996: 83)

The argument that researchers should avoid representing individuals or groups who inhabit less powerful social positions is a difficult
one to sustain morally, never mind epistemologically. Feminist
researchers cannot begin to challenge women's oppression without
addressing wider social hierarchies and divisions, and this requires
that women use any power and influence that they have on behalf of
others. Not to speak about, or for 'others' encourages silences and
gaps, which marginalize and exclude, while cementing the privilege
of those with the more powerful voices. As Christine Griffin points
out, when we speak for others we cannot become them, we can only
tell our story about their lives (Griffin, 1996). What we can do,
however, is make explicit our intentions for telling our story of their
lives, and our intentions for the processes of participation, interpretation and writing/representation.

One way that feminists have responded to the issue of representing
others has been for researchers to 'put themselves in the picture', so
that the research account is not a disembodied 'view from nowhere'
(Fraser and Nicholson, 1990) or reveal the contingent nature of their
analysis (Burman, 1992). This then raises questions about how such
'stories of life-stories' (research accounts) can be judged as more or
less appropriate. If notions of authenticity and 'truth' are problematized, we are left to evaluate the legitimacy of particular representations, not in terms of accuracy, but according to what we reveal about
the basis of our interpretation or on the grounds of an account's
effects. In some situations, members of an oppressed group may be
better placed to represent other members of the same group because
they are likely to have a situated (personally invested) understanding
of what needs to change. For example, black feminists pushed the
issue of 'race' onto feminist agendas, highlighting previously neglected issues of white power and privilege. However, this does not
proscribe 'less'/differently oppressed others from speaking against
injustice. Nor does it excuse those who do not.

The choice feminist researchers face between remaining 'respect-fully silent' for fear of appropriating the experiences of 'others', and speaking out on their behalf, must be seen as an instrumental, political choice, rather than an abstract, theoretical ethical dilemma. It requires reflection on a number of questions concerning the research, the researcher and the researched. First, the overall intention of specific representational research needs to be acknowledged and clarified in terms of what might be achieved by speaking for or about 'others'. Secondly, the researcher's position in relation to those whom she is representing needs to be thoroughly explored, in terms of her own social, political, and personal interests, and the assumptions she brings to her understanding of those she is researching. As Caroline Ramazanoglu and Janet Holland argue 'In connecting theory, experi-ence and judgement, the knowing feminist should be accountable for the sense she makes of her own and other people's accounts, and how her judgements are made' (1999: 386). Thirdly, there needs to be careful consideration of the likely impact of the 'knowledge' pro-duced, to ensure that it could not work against the interests of those it seeks to represent, or against another group. This includes trying to imagine the different political contexts into which the research account might play, and the deployment of the material in ways that are contradictory to the researcher's politics or intentions. As Chris-tine Griffin notes 'Researchers are always speaking for others. This is not something to be denied or avoided: it is a (potential) power and a responsibility' (1996: 100).

Initiating personal change through action research

Another key strand of feminist research focused on initiating a more direct form of change through a politicization of those taking part in the research. Sharing a similar rationale to the 'consciousness raising' associated with the late 1960s and 1970s women's liberation move-ment in the West, 'action research' aims to generate insight, confidence and mutual support for research participants. Indeed, action research today has a precedent in Paulo Friere's (1972) concept of 'conscientiza-tion' – a process by which people 'deep[en] awareness of [their own] sociocultural identity and their capacity to transform their lives' (Taylor, 1994: 109). 'Empowering' the women who take part is a primary aim of this kind of research, with fully participatory research involving participants in all stages of the research process, including the identification of the initial question or problem to be studied. The focus of the research intervention is on those who experience the research personally, rather than on how the research represents par-ticipants or their social group generally in the broad political arena.

The notion of empowering women through the research process is appealing to many feminists. However, the associated ethical dimensions are complex. By definition, action research is intervening in people's lives and so entails a use, and potential abuse of power. Maye Taylor argues that because of this the 'ethical guidelines for research have to be stringently applied' and there must be 'respect for the whole life of the person, not just as a research subject' (1994: 112). However participant-led the research may be, the researcher plays a crucial role in initiating, facilitating and constructing meanings – a point that is often played down in the emphasis on democratic rapport and participant empowerment. Simplistic ideas of participation and empowerment can obscure other aspects of the researcher's power and responsibility: 'It is we who have the time, resources and skills to conduct methodological work, to make sense of experience and locate individuals in historical and social contexts' (Kelly et al., 1994: 37; Birch and Miller, see Chapter 5). While participants may engage with the research and exercise a high degree of autonomy in organising and reflecting on the topic, the researcher herself remains central to the process. Valuable as they were at the time, second wave feminist attempts to develop egalitarian research relationships (as well as therapeutic and pedagogic ones), have been criticized (along with the whole framework of liberal humanist political narratives) by later feminist and post-structuralist work for being naively optimistic and theoretically weak regarding its analysis of power (Fraser, 1989; Probyn, 1993; Ticeneto Clough, 1992). In particular, the democratized research ideal is shown to rest on the fantasy that power can be shared and the differing positions occupied by researcher and researched neutralized (Burman, 1992; Marks, 1996). Not only does this fail to recognize the power the researcher may retain in the research interaction despite attempts to allow participants to set the agenda (Burman, 1992), the pre-occupation with relations in the interview itself distracts from the relations of power set up within the academy (Probyn, 1993). Applying the same reflexivity to the institutionalized power relations of researcher–researched highlights the dynamic of representation where one party has little or no say and the other has full authorial power: the researcher is not merely author, but interpreter, editor and political editor/ambassador (Burman, 1992).

At a fundamental level, a feminist researcher brings to the research her judgement or assumption that there is a need for social change – a principle that lies at the root of feminism. In models of participatory research in which the end goal is not fixed at the outset, specific notions of what, where and how this change should be affected are supposed to emerge during the course of the project. But the researcher and perhaps each of the participants will have particular understandings and interpretations of the process of change being studied in action research, and may attach different values to the dynamics identified. The enabling of participants to reflect differently on their experiences is an intention that directly connects to a political agenda. Affecting participants' understandings is clearly a political impact, and while participants in action research may themselves identify problems, research questions and be encouraged to develop their own solutions, the parameters of 'enlightenment' are likely to be drawn by the researcher and funder. For example, in the context of action research, few feminist researchers would be prepared to 'facilitate' the interpretation of racist or homophobic discourse as empowering to participants. If a women's group identified asylum seekers as the source of their housing problem and decided to picket a local hostel, would the researcher be justified in challenging this construction? Again this question could be reversed: would the researcher be justified in not challenging this construction?

This illustrates the political nature of the researcher's role and the need for reflexive thinking about research ethics to be extended to what are sometimes set aside as 'political issues'. The example above shows how an ethical researcher necessarily makes political decisions, and the political role of a researcher is more complex than simply to accept and represent participants' perspectives. Even those working within an empirical realist perspective would probably share the view that they are responsible for considering the impact of the views that by publishing they are re-presenting or 'giving voice' to. For some of us, this would limit even the 'voice-as-empowerment' approach to research, so that where 'giving voice' to individual participants conflicted with our broader political judgements, the latter would be more decisive. However, the dilemma presented might be far more complex than this. If ethical research means taking responsibility for the political consequences of the accounts we produce, it entails trying to imagine unintended consequences, how the crudest versions of our accounts might function, how the findings might function when stripped of our qualifiers. It is hard to see how far one ought to take this responsibility, but by tying our research to an explicitly political agenda we might block extreme readings of our accounts and retain some control over the political uses to which the 'knowledge' we produce might be put. The political judgements that inform such decisions about representation contribute to the reflexivity 'in the academy' that Probyn (1993) urges, and analysis of the personal interpretive resources drawn on would enter into reflexive discussions about the micro-politics of research that Burman (1992) highlights. Both strands inform the politics/ethics of research and produce the relations of power between researcher and researched.

Although the emphasis may be on participants' own negotiation of change, action research projects are inevitably structured around particular definitions of empowerment and politicization. Without an exposition of these politically informed intentions, the value of such projects is difficult to measure either empirically or ethically. Furthermore, vague notions of empowerment can obscure the limitations of research as well as any potentially negative consequences. Where the aim is to raise consciousness, many feminists have agonized over whether politicizing participants is necessarily helpful, when it makes apparent the limitations on their autonomy or resources without actually challenging these limitations themselves (see Birch, 1998, chapter in *Feminist Dilemmas*). Similarly, Kelly et al. (1994) highlight the more 'grandiose' claims made for the emancipatory impact of some projects, and reassert the constraints of feminist research, drawing our attention to the level at which change is prompted:

> Participating in a research project is unlikely, in the vast majority of cases, to transform the conditions of women's lives. We cannot for example, provide access to alternative housing options, childcare places or a reasonable income. Nor are the women's services to which we may refer women, especially in the resource-starved voluntary sector, always able to meet their needs. (Kelly et al., 1994: 37)

If these limitations are not acknowledged and understood, there is a risk that participants may feel further disempowered by the research because of their perceived inability to live up to raised expectations to effect meaningful change in their lives. More significantly, participants living with oppression are likely to have constructed vital defence mechanisms and coping strategies to enable them to survive.

Approaching a research project with the aim of encouraging participants to 'enlighten' themselves, may at times be simplistic and patronizing, particularly given the amount of feminist research that is conducted by middle-class academics on or 'for' working-class women. Despite the critique of the notion of false consciousness, middle-class intellectuals might still implicitly construct working class or other disadvantaged people as victims of distorted perceptions unable to recognize and address their oppression. As Valerie Walkerdine asks:

> The idea of a true as opposed to a false consciousness simply assumes a seeing or a not seeing [yet] what if a working-class person sees and yet has myriad conscious and unconscious ways of dealing with or defending against the pains and contradictions produced out of her/his social and historical location? (Walkerdine, 1996: 149)

Awareness and sensitivity to an individual's social, cultural and historical location is crucial in facilitating any meaningful, constructive reflection on experiences. Certain interpretations or strategies regarded as counterproductive by the researcher may make perfect sense from the participant's point of view. If these constructions are challenged or disrupted during the course of the research, it is important that realistic, practical alternatives are actually available. Otherwise, well-intentioned action research which aims to raise women's consciousness of the injustices of their situation could leave individual women feeling more vulnerable.

Deconstructing and undermining 'knowledge' structures

In another distinct approach to research, feminists have sought to challenge and destabilize the knowledge structures through which power is exercised and oppression maintained. Feminists informed by post-structuralism have drawn attention to the productive function of language, highlighting the relationship between knowledge and power and effectively problematizing gendered truth claims. The resulting social critiques can be seen as offering a focus for resistance, demonstrating how language or 'discourse' may constrain women, and shape their experiences and subjectivities (Hollway, 1989; Radtke and Stam, 1994; Wilkinson and Kitzinger, 1995). A major aim of this work is to identify and undermine dominant, coercive networks of 'knowledge', thereby opening up discursive space for manoeuvre and resistance (Burman, 1990; Burman et al., 1996; Probyn, 1993).

However, the principle of deconstruction concerns many feminists who are critical of the relativistic tendencies of some analyses. Theorists engaged in deconstruction may produce analyses that lack an ethical and political context, leaving them open to charges of nihilism (Seidman, 1995). Debates concerning the ethics of post-structuralist feminism often centre on the consequences of deconstructing the category of women and of undermining the guarantors of truth. While some feminist theorists, such as Elam (1994), stress the potential benefits of re-negotiating feminism's gains to generate a more radical, non essentialist, non identity-based approach to politics, others, such as Jackson (1992), emphasize the responsibilities of feminists to preserve and build on what has already been achieved through a collective notion of womanhood. Concern about abstract theory also focuses on the extent to which postmodern deconstruction promotes academic hegemony at the expense of practical, realisable politics. Those engaged in feminist theory and research are orientated towards a political aim of critiquing and changing the social world, yet in order to pursue this goal personal investments must be made in the academic mode of production (Stanley, 1990). As Beverley Skeggs (1995) also notes, feminists in academia are locked into a paradox, in which ensuring the survival of feminist departments within universities may clash with basic feminist principles.

Most academic feminist research is conducted to obtain a research degree or publications, and while a basic intention of the work may be to understand and transform, there is also the more immediate incentive of furthering individual careers. These two functions of feminist research, abstract social change and more instrumental personal gain, can conflict, particularly when feminist work is located in an exclusively academic context, as several of the chapters in *Feminist Dilemmas in Qualitative Research* (Ribbens and Edwards, 1998) explored. While the discourse of women's studies created feminist spaces and jobs within universities, the pressure now to 'sell' material under the title of 'gender' raises dilemmas about incorporation, regulation and de-radicalization for feminist research.

Deconstructive research, informed by postmodernist approaches, may seek to expose assumptions that may be damaging to women, but without careful consideration of the impact of such deconstruction, the act of exposure itself may become the primary goal, and the particular impacts it has in specific local contexts not fully considered. Applying the critique of knowledge to one's own practice involves reflecting fully on the research intervention to question what social relations and 'facts' it corroborates and bolsters, and what meanings it blocks, undermines implicitly or questions directly. The production of theory, explanation and criticism can work to sustain, reify and legitimize some forms of social action, while excluding, deterring or problematizing others. By seeking to identify the politics of 'knowledge', post-structuralist informed feminists themselves produce political 'knowledge', which reflects their own grounded, partial interpretations of the world. Encouraging and enabling resistance to oppressive discourses and practices through a destabilization of the 'truths' which underpin them, necessarily requires a consciously motivated, political stance. Feminists use deconstruction as a device to make way for more empowering constructions, but the struggle to produce 'better' 'knowledge' will always be fought in the context of complex, shifting political debates, and local effects as well as potentially historically shifting conditions.

Reflexivity: thinking forwards as well as back

The conclusion that the research we produce and the values we promote are inevitably grounded in partial, invested viewpoints does not detract from the crucial role that feminism, and other social criticism must play in defining or struggling towards a better world. It does, however, undermine any notion that feminism necessarily represents the universal interests of women. The recognition that women are oppressed in contradictory ways highlights the importance for feminists of thoroughly deconstructing any assumed commonalities with other women before reconstructing a contingent basis for progressive research, theory and or practice. This process involves an open evaluation of the specific political intentions underpinning feminist-inspired work, and an observant consideration of the ethical dimensions in terms of who may be marginalized or excluded as a result. In other words, this involves a shift of emphasis from the justification of feminist claims on the grounds of moral absolutes, to a more specific, situated warranting of particular representations or actions.

The practice of reflexivity is generally regarded as an acknowledgement of the researcher's constitutive role, but emphasis feminists have traditionally placed on the research process itself, can, in some cases, actively draw attention away from the wider political context it is situated in. Focusing on methods and the interaction between researcher and researched has become so important within feminist research that, at times, it seems to substitute for feminist practice, as if the research was the political action in itself. Miriam Glucksmann (1994), amongst others, has pointed to the angst-ridden efforts of feminists to foster egalitarian relationships with the women they are researching, and she suggests that reflexivity and reciprocity is potentially confused with actual feminist politics:

> Nobody imagines that we could transform the various relations between women: we do not and could not overcome the structured inequalities between women *within the research process*. Yet the creation of a transparent and equal relation between researcher and researched where each is equally involved and each gets something from the process does sometimes appear to become the objective of the research . . . We find a quasi solution for frustration in the current political climate by focusing down onto the research process, perhaps the one situation in which we can have an active role, and over which we do have some control. (Glucksmann, 1994: 151) [italics added]

While conducting research constitutes a political activity, in that knowledge produced is knowledge subsequently lived, there are limits to what can be achieved through the process of feminist research. Paying careful attention to the 'internal' dynamics of a particular project reveals the messy, complex and subjective nature of research, but does not generate 'knowledge' that is somehow more authentic, or necessarily more progressive. Neither does it alter the very real, and sometimes institutionalized differences that exist between researchers and those being researched. This form of reflexivity is limited, providing a localized, bounded account of a researcher's subjectivity and research subjects' active participation. 'Silences' remain despite efforts to acknowledge the contradictions, complexities and dilemmas of doing research (Kelly et al., 1994).

Within feminist research the principles of self-reflection and transparency that have been developed and applied to the research dynamic are rarely extended to include the overarching political intentions or commitments inspiring specific projects. We argue that without the guarantees of 'a feminist politics' or 'feminist perspectives' to fall back upon, we are obliged to reflexively explore the ethics of our intentions for research, a process that could be described as forward reflexivity. Voicing the hopes that lie behind research interventions is novel in mainstream methodology discussions because it contrasts starkly with the positivist assumption that the social relations being researched are left unaltered by the research process, and that findings merely represent or reflect the world neutrally. However, a careful consideration of the possible impacts of a research project both on immediate and broader relations highlights many of the pitfalls and ethical dilemmas raised by feminist research. Without linking specific research to a wider commitment to social change, that is, discussing our intentions for research in the light of our political hopes, we miss the opportunity to develop more effective, ethically responsible, research interventions. In addition, when we produce information that is disconnected from our political aims, we might be risking our findings being invoked to back analyses we would not support politically. Exposing the political project we as researchers are engaged in clarifies our objectives, attempts to account for personal understandings and assumptions, and ultimately provides the only justification we can for our judgements about the representations or interventions we make.

Note

[1] In particular, we are identifying the theoretical strands that postmodernism and poststructuralism share in terms of their critiques of modernity and 'truth'.

References

Alldred, P. (1998) 'Ethnography and discourse analysis: dilemmas in representing the voices of children', in J. Ribbens and R. Edwards (eds), *Feminist Dilemmas in Qualitative Research: Public Knowledge and Private Lives*. London: Sage.

Bhavnani, K-K. and Phoenix, A. (1994) *Shifting Identities, Shifting Racisms: A 'Feminism and Psychology' Reader.* London: Sage.

Birch, M. (1998) 'Re/constructing research narratives: self and sociological identity in alternative settings', in J. Ribbens and R. Edwards (eds), *Feminist Dilemmas in Qualitative Research.* London: Sage.

Bordo, S. (1990) 'Feminist, postmodernism, and gender-scepticism', in L.J. Nicholson (ed.), *Feminism/Postmodernism.* New York: Routledge.

Bordo, S. (1998) 'Bringing body to theory', in D. Welton (ed.), *Body and Flesh: A Philosophical Reader.* Oxford: Blackwells.

Burman, E. (1990) 'Differing with deconstruction: a feminist critique', in I. Parker and J. Shotter (eds), *Deconstructing Social Psychology.* London: Routledge.

Burman, E. (1992) 'Feminism and discourse in developmental psychology: power, subjectivity and interpretation', in *Feminism & Psychology,* 2 (1): 45–60.

Burman, E. (1993) 'Beyond discursive relativism: power and subjectivity in developmental psychology', in H. Tam, L. Mos, W. Thorngate and B. Kaplan (eds), *Recent Trends in Theoretical Psychology* (Vol. 111). New York: Springer Verlag, pp. 208–20.

Burman, E. (1996) 'Introduction', in E. Burman, P. Alldred, C. Bewley, B. Goldberg, C. Heenan, D. Marks, J. Marshall, K. Taylor, R. Ullah and S. Warner, *Challenging Women: Psychology's Exclusions, Feminist Possibilities.* Buckingham: Open University Press.

Burman, E., Alldred, P., Bewley, C., Goldberg, B., Heenan, C., Marks, D., Marshall, J., Taylor, K., Ullah, R. and Warner, S. (1996) *Challenging Women: Psychology's Exclusions, Feminist Possibilities.* Buckingham: Open University Press.

Butler, J. (1990) *Gender Trouble: Feminism and the Subversion of Identity.* New York: Routledge.

Butler, J. (1993) *Bodies that Matter.* New York: Routledge.

Edwards, R. (1996) 'White woman researcher – black women subjects', in S. Wilkinson and C. Kitzinger (eds), *Representing the Other.* London: Sage.

Elam, D. (1994) *Feminism and Deconstruction: Ms en Abyme.* London: Routledge.

Fraser, N. (1989) *Unruly Practices: Power, Discourse and Gender in Contemporary Social Theory.* Cambridge: Polity Press.

Fraser, N. and Nicholson, L. (1990) 'Social Criticism without Philosophy', in L. Nicholson (ed.), *Feminism/Postmodernism.* New York: Routledge.

Friere, P. (1972) *Cultural Action for Freedom.* Harmondsworth: Penguin.

Glucksmann, M. (1994) 'The work of knowledge and the knowledge of women's work', in M. Maynard and J. Purvis (eds), *Researching Women's Lives from a Feminist Perspective.* London: Taylor and Francis.

Griffin, C. (1996) ' "See whose face it wears": difference, otherness and power', in S. Wilkinson and C. Kitzinger (eds), *Representing the Other.* London: Sage.

Harding, S. (1987) *Feminism and Methodology.* Milton Keynes: Open University Press.

Harding, S. (1990) 'Feminism, science, and the anti-enlightenment critiques', in L. Nicholson (ed.), *Feminism/Postmodernism.* New York: Routledge.

Harding, S. (1991) *Whose Science? Whose Knowledge? Thinking from Women's Lives.* Milton Keynes: Open University Press.

Hollway, W. (1989) *Subjectivity and Method in Psychology: Gender, Meaning and Science.* London: Sage.

hooks, b. (1990) *Yearning: Race, Gender and Cultural Politics.* Boston: South End Press.

Hurd, T.L. and McIntyre, A. (1996) 'The seduction of sameness: similarity and representing the other', in S. Wilkinson and C. Kitzinger (eds), *Representing the Other.* London: Sage.

Jackson, S. (1992) 'The amazing deconstructing woman', *Trouble and Strife*, 25: 25–31.

Kelly, L., Burton, S. and Reagan, L. (1994) 'Researching women's lives or studying women's oppression? Reflections on what constitutes feminist research', in M. Maynard and J. Purvis (eds), *Researching Women's Lives from a Feminist Perspective.* London: Taylor and Francis.

Kitzinger, C. and Wilkinson, S. (1996) 'Theorizing representing the other', in S. Wilkinson and C. Kitzinger (eds), *Representing the Other.* London: Sage.

Marks, D. (1996) 'Constructing a narrative: moral discourse and young people's experience of exclusion', in E. Burman, G. Aitken, P. Alldred, R. Allwood, T. Billington, B. Goldberg, A.J. Gordo-Lopez, C. Heenan, D. Marks and S. Warner, *Psychology, Discourse, Practice: From Regulation to Resistance.* London: Taylor and Francis.

Mayall, B. (1999) 'Children and childhood', in S. Hood, B. Mayall and S. Oliver (eds), *Critical Issues in Social Research: Power and Prejudice.* Buckingham: Open University Press.

McNay, L. (1992) *Foucault and Feminism: Power, Gender and the Self.* Cambridge: Polity Press.

Patai, D. (1991) 'US academics and third world women: Is ethical research possible?', in S. Berger Gluck and D. Patai (eds), *Women's Words: The Feminist Practice of Oral History.* London: Routledge.

Probyn, E. (1993) *Sexing The Self: Gendered Positions in Cultural Studies.* London: Routledge.

Radtke, H.L. and Stam, H.J. (eds) (1994) *Power/Gender: Social Relations in Theory and Practice.* London: Sage.

Ramazanoglu, C. and Holland, J. (1999) 'Tripping over experience: some problems in feminist epistemology', *Discourse: Studies in the Cultural Politics of Education*, 20(3): 381–392.

Ransom, J. (1993) 'Identity, difference and power', in C. Ramazanoglu (ed.), *Up Against Foucault, Explorations of Some Tensions Between Foucault and Feminism.* London: Routledge.

Reay, D. (1996) 'Insider perspectives or stealing the words out of women's mouths', *Feminist Review*, 53, Summer: 57–73.

Ribbens, J. and Edwards, R. (eds) (1998) *Feminist Dilemmas in Qualitative Research: Public Knowledge and Private Lives.* London: Sage.

Riley, D. (1988) *'Am I That Name?' Feminism and the Category of 'Women' In History.* London: Macmillan.

Seidman, S. (1995) 'Deconstructing queer theory', in L. Nicholson and S. Seidman (eds), *Social Postmodernism: Beyond Identity Politics.* Cambridge: Cambridge University Press.

Skeggs, B. (1995) 'Women's studies in Britain in the 1990's', *Women's Studies International Forum*, 18(4): 4775–88.

Soper, K. (1991) 'Postmodernism and its discontents', *Feminist Review*, 39: 97–108.

Spelman, E.V. (1988) *Inessentially Speaking: Problems of Exclusion in Feminist Thought.* London: Women's Press.

Standing, K. (1998) 'Writing the voices of the less powerful: research on lone mothers', in J. Ribbens and R. Edwards (eds), *Feminist Dilemmas in Qualitative Research: Public Knowledge and Private Lives.* London: Sage.

Stanley, L. (1990) 'An editorial introduction', in L. Stanley (ed.), *Feminist Praxis.* London: Routledge.

Stanley, L. and Wise, S. (1993) *Breaking Out Again: Feminist Ontology and Epistemology.* London: Routledge.

Taylor, M. (1994) 'Action research', in P. Banister, E. Burman, I. Parker, M. Taylor and C. Tindall, *Qualitative Methods in Psychology: A Research Guide.* Buckingham: Open University Press.

Ticeneto Clough, P. (1992) *The End(s) of Ethnography: From Realism to Social Criticism.* London: Sage.

Walkerdine, V. (1996) 'Psychological and social aspects of survival', in S. Wilkinson (ed.), *Feminist Social Psychologies: International Perspectives.* Buckingham: Open University Press.

Weedon, C. (1987) *Feminist Practice and Poststructuralist Theory.* Oxford: Blackwell.

Wilkinson, S. and Kitzinger, C. (eds) (1995) *Feminism and Discourse: Psychological Perspectives.* London: Sage.

Wilkinson, S. and Kitzinger, C. (eds) (1996) *Representing the Other.* London: Sage.

CHAPTER 3

CONSENTING TO WHAT? ISSUES OF ACCESS, GATE-KEEPING AND 'INFORMED' CONSENT

Tina Miller and Linda Bell

Introduction

This chapter examines ethical issues that arise in the course of accessing potential participants. Gaining 'informed' consent is problematic if it is not clear what the participant is consenting to and where 'participation' begins and ends. We argue that 'consent' should be ongoing and renegotiated between researcher and researched throughout the research process. We also argue that satisfactorily completing an ethics form at the beginning of a study and/or obtaining ethics approval does not mean that ethical issues can be forgotten, rather ethical considerations should form an ongoing part of the research. In this chapter we explore the ongoing ethical dilemmas around gate-keeping, access, *re*-access and consent through examples from three projects, two employing single interviews and another with a longitudinal component. A further key concern involves the ways in which the researcher and any 'gate-keepers' (Miller, 1995, 1998) influence who eventually become research participants.

The first of these research projects involved a woman researcher (Linda) accessing and interviewing partners of 'violent men'. These men were attending a therapy centre that was being evaluated by Linda's male colleagues. The issues involved in this project will be discussed later. The second study involved accessing and interviewing Bangladeshi women living in a town in southern England, about antenatal practices. The final project was a longitudinal study exploring women's experiences of first-time transition to motherhood. The ethical issues that we address in this chapter are enmeshed, in the context of these particular projects, with the important issues of gender and ethnicity.

The shift towards a focus on subjective experience and the meanings individuals give to their actions has led to a concern with the research process itself and the ways in which qualitative data are gathered. Feminist researchers have influenced debates around the research process, reflecting upon their own roles in the co-production of research data and questioning the power relationships that are produced and underpin data gathering (Edwards and Ribbens, 1998; Oakley, 1981; Ribbens and Edwards, 1995; Stanley and Wise, 1990, 1993). In turn this has led to a questioning of the ongoing ethical dimensions of the research process (Wise, 1987). In Britain there is no law requiring the submission of research proposals to ethical committees. However professional and academic research guidelines and committee structures have been available to researchers for many years and are widely used to guide the early stages of the research process (BSA, 1993). Yet, whilst initial guidance is welcomed it is argued that this can obscure the need to continually reflect on the ethical implications of researching people's lives. Ethics committee requirements that the research relationship must be formalized through written consent at the outset also has implications for those trying to research hidden groups or those who are difficult to access (Renzetti and Lee, 1993). Individuals who identify themselves as socially excluded or belonging to a marginalized group, are unlikely to formally consent in writing to participation in a study.

As feminist researchers we identify knowledge production as being grounded in individual and collective experiences and this means that the course of a project may only be guessed at initially. While informing participants about the research aims at the outset of a project is vital, final research findings may not resonate with those aims. The precise nature of 'consent' for the participants might only become clear eventually, at the end of a study, when the researchers' impact on shaping the study is visible. This raises questions about what is it that the participant is consenting to. Just 'participation', in the sense of being interviewed? (For a further discussion of dimensions of participation see Maxine Birch and Tina Miller in Chapter 5). However, if we are to enable/empower participants to share in this construction of more than the interview data, suggesting an 'egalitarian' or participatory focus to the research, might we tacitly expect interviewees also to be interested in reading their own interview transcripts, or to contribute in other ways to the analysis or to the final written product? Is this 'egalitarian' focus somehow ethically 'more acceptable' although, at the same time, it requires a greater contribution from participants than they may have thought they were consenting to? (These issues are developed further in Chapter 5).

Accessing potential participants not only requires providing information about the research, but also that individuals are in a position to

exercise choice around whether or not to give their consent to participate. Yet much qualitative research relies upon gate-keepers as a route
of initial access to participants. The notion of 'gate-keeper' has frequently been used in sociological and anthropological research[1] (Burgess, 1982; Liebow, 1967; Whyte, 1955), referring to those who are in a
position to 'permit' access to others for the purpose of interviewing.
This is important from an ethical perspective because it suggests the
potential exercising of power by some individuals over others. Some
research projects may consider a representative of a particular group
as a gate-keeper (with all the methodological implications this may
imply – see Wallman, 1984 on 'resource keepers' in households). In the
research examples below we discuss how gate-keepers' power was
exerted in differing ways in relation to those individuals we wished to
access for interview purposes. Controls the gate-keepers exercised
varied, for example from the cultural and hierarchical (Bangladeshi
women study) to the therapeutic and paternalistic ('male therapy
centre' study). We argue that issues around access and gate-keeping
and notions of what constitutes 'informed' consent have clear ethical
implications for feminist research.

In the following sections we use examples from three research
projects to explore the ethical dilemmas that can surface in gaining
access and *re*-access to research participants. Interplay between
notions of access, 'coercion' and motive and/or motivation provides a
recurrent theme across these discussions in which issues of gender,
power and ethnicity are implicit. Our concerns lead us to reflect upon
the ethical dilemmas raised by notions of 'informed' consent and the
sometimes tenuous link between research aims and research outcomes. Finally, we consider practical ways in which feminist ethical
guidelines can be used to alert researchers to the ongoing ethical
considerations that can arise in qualitative research.

Ethical dilemmas encountered in gaining access to research participants

Decisions taken around access are closely bound up with questions of
ethics. Similarly, the differences between gaining access and consent
are not always clear. Access to research participants is both a crucial
aspect of the research process and one that is often dealt with as
relatively unproblematic in mainstream research methods textbooks
(see Robson, 1993[2]). The potential dilemmas encountered around
access can become subsumed within discussions about 'sampling' and
'populations' (see Mason, 1996). As noted above, other issues, for
example around 'gate-keepers', may also be significant. An overriding

concern within professional research guidelines is often that 'coercion' has not been exerted and participation in any research project is 'voluntary' (see also Linda Bell and Linda Nutt in Chapter 4).

Implicit within such guidelines is the assumption that providing consent is 'voluntary', 'coercion' is deemed not to have occurred. Yet such an assumption ignores the potentially complex power dynamics that can operate around access and consent especially where issues of gender and/or ethnicity are manifest. Nor do such guidelines take account of ethnographic research. So, in the process of moving from the written research proposal to operationalizing the research plan – which may or may not have been submitted to an ethics committee – the researcher can experience problems around access and encounter ethical dilemmas. Having decided *who* is to be accessed the problem of *how* arises. Even supposing that this is straightforward, the researcher must continually reflect on the ways in which decisions around *routes* of access can affect the data collected.

Access to potential research participants can be achieved through employing a range of strategies. Participants can be recruited via highly structured and selective strategies, for example quota sampling, or through much less formal channels such as snowballing using the researcher's own social networks. Whichever approach is adopted, the *motives* around why some people become participants and others resist should concern the researcher and be documented in a research diary. Clearly some potential participants may find resistance more difficult. The control of gate-keepers has been noted in previous research (Miller, 1998) but not specifically in relation to their power to sanction access to less powerful individuals and groups such as Bangladeshi women for example. So, whilst feminist researchers have recognized and increasingly documented the need to reflect on the relationship between the ways in which participants are accessed and the data collected (Edwards and Ribbens, 1998; Mauthner, 2000), the ways in which decisions taken around access can be closely bound up with questions of ethics are less well explored. Our initial concern is with the ways in which judgements are made about who might be 'suitable' interviewees and the lengths that might be gone to in order to access those identified as such. Moreover, does the researcher feel that s/he can be more tacitly 'coercive' of potential participants, as in the case of the 'male therapy centre' research, if s/he perceives that the research is underpinned by a good ethical motive? Or if interviewees view their participation as minimal, a single interview for example rather than a longer-term commitment as in a longitudinal study? We explore these questions in the following sections through a focus on different research projects we have been involved in individually.

Accessing women respondents for single interviews via male gate-keepers

The first of these studies, the 'male therapy centre' project was com-
missioned to evaluate the work of a therapy centre concerned with
male violence. This example illustrates protracted, and ethically
fraught dimensions of accessing hard to reach participants perceived
(though not necessarily self-defined) as potentially vulnerable.[3] The
role of gate-keepers in this project is particularly relevant to feminist
research ethics, since two 'layers' of male gate-keepers controlled
access, in different ways, to women whose partners used the therapy
centre. Interviews with these particular women emerged as a key
feature of the overall evaluative study. Potentially, gate-keeping issues
had serious implications for being able to work confidentially with
these women partners. The sensitive nature of the topic of investiga-
tion also meant that the research eventually had to be based on single
rather than repeat interviews with women. This avoided some other
ethical dilemmas noted initially but also precluded any attempts to
involve interviewees more closely in interpreting research findings
over a longer period. However the sensitive topic of male violence
also raises a question as to whether the female interviewees or the
funders of the research, in this case the therapy centre, were the main
beneficiaries of the project's findings, especially given the small number of women eventually accessed.

In this project Linda's male academic colleagues initially planned
to interview men using the therapy programme in order to examine
whether there were any changes over time to their perceptions or
violent behaviour as a result of the therapy. However, the (male)
researchers and therapists felt that this 'before' and 'after' data available from interviews with men would only give a partial indication of
'success' or 'failure' of the centre's programme. They decided that
what was called an 'independent check' was needed on the validity of
the men's accounts, so it was planned to ask women partners of men
attending the centre whether they 'really had improved' following
therapy. After the project had started, Linda was therefore asked if she
would join the research team and interview women partners on that
basis. She rejected this original plan since, as a feminist, she objected
to the idea that women were just there to confirm or deny someone
else's 'reality'. Her first reaction was that it was no use trying to 'link'
women in to the men's versions or accounts of their 'realities' in this
way, but that taking a feminist perspective meant that women should
be asked to give their own accounts of their experiences.

Beyond this initial objection, however, it soon became clear that
questions of accessing 'women partners' for interview were going to

be the key issue (see Hoff, 1990: 148, 249 on 'the problem of access'). Linda felt it was unlikely that women would be willing to come forward to be interviewed if contact with them stemmed from a men's centre. The therapists and male researchers had designed a project into which the women were then 'fitted' and for whom they acted as gate-keepers. A second 'layer' of gate-keeping involved the 'violent men' themselves and, as discussed below, it was not clear initially how to gain access specifically to women whose partners used the centre *without* involving their male partners in some way.[4]

Reactions from women's groups to Linda's developing work were sometimes negative (see also Hoff, 1990: 249–50 on feminist activist concerns). This underlined that a significant emerging feature of this research was that the centre could be having a profound impact on women, but was primarily set up to assist men. Due to the nature of the whole project, including evaluation of the therapy programme with individual men by male colleagues, Linda felt that ethically it was essential that these women partners' voices should be heard in relation to the centre and its programme.[5] Linda made a judgement that, due to the nature of the research, it was *these* women (whose partners were currently using the centre) that she should interview, despite the difficulties of access, rather than any other women who had been subjected to violence.

Linda and her colleagues realised that she would have to take *active* steps in order to reach these particular women. This suggests persuasion, even tacit coercion, would be needed in order to access and interview what she might consider 'a reasonable number of women partners'. Two further gendered aspects of the project emerged. The first was the tacit assumption on the part of Linda's colleagues that partners of men using the centre would actually be women. Linda acknowledged that this might not be the case, and offered to interview any partners, male or female. However, she also felt that due to the frequently gendered nature of violence, and especially if she were working with a small sample of interviewees, that accessing a small mixed group could seriously affect the nature of the research in terms of the 'representativeness' being sought by the therapists. At this stage Linda therefore began to think in terms of a sample of 'all women' or 'all gay men'.

At the outset Linda deliberately avoided contact with men using the centre. She took this decision to help ensure future confidentiality for any partners who might agree to be interviewed. Nevertheless Linda had not realized initially, that some of her potential 'sample' of women partners were well known to the centre therapists. Some partners had been in direct contact with the centre by phone or in person (as she was to discover during the research) and a majority of these partners were women. Colleagues suggested that Linda should simply ring up these partners and ask them to talk about their partner's violence towards them. However, Linda felt that this was again a potential breach of confidentiality and felt unease at the prospect of raising the issue of violence directly with these women. By this stage women's centres and other organisations had contacted Linda concerned in particular with the ethics of doing research with male abusers. Linda explained that she was doing research that was intended to give the partners of 'violent' men more of a 'voice' in relation to the male therapy centre. However their fears highlighted Linda's own intentions to behave in ways which would not be, inadvertently or otherwise, damaging to women partners.

This process of accessing and interviewing women partners illustrates a number of ethical issues, for example the difficulties of access via (male) gate-keepers. Furthermore Linda decided to 'distance' her interviewees from the therapy centre and male partners by using her own university connections to further ensure the confidentiality of women's participation and of their interview accounts. Linda and her colleagues agreed that she would 'reach' these women partners by letter in which the 'serious' nature of the research would be conveyed. By adopting an 'impersonal' stance and linking herself specifically to her University, Linda hoped that women might not feel 'intruded' upon personally, and would feel able to come forward to be interviewed.

Research Study

An independent research project run through the University of Y is investigating women's experiences of violence, particularly in a domestic setting. We are contacting you to ask whether you would be willing to take part in this research.

The research will involve talking to a woman researcher working at University of Y in confidence, and completing an anonymous questionnaire. We are keen to talk to as many women as possible, and to give them the opportunity to discuss their concerns with us. This project is part of a wider study being run in association with the Z Centre, but the woman researcher will have no contact with men using the Centre, and interviews will be arranged confidentially and in places agreed between her and women taking part in the study.

Information on services and projects that aim to help women experiencing violence will be available from the researcher.

If you would like any further information about the study, or wish to take part, please contact Linda Bell on the following numbers:

Please leave a telephone number and name for us to contact if you wish, but you do not need to leave your surname, or address.

Thank you

Linda Bell

After designing the letter Linda became dependent on the centre for distributing it. The only way seemed to be to give copies to men attending for therapy, asking them to pass it on to their partners. As noted earlier, these 'gate-keeping' activities yielded one interviewee whose partner was currently having therapy. Linda also asked the centre to make the letter available to any partners who contacted them. Through this latter route two more interviewees were recruited. Another woman who had heard about the research contacted Linda artd offered to be interviewed. However she rang back some days later to cancel the proposed meeting, as her partner had attacked her and broken her arm. It was never clear to Linda whether or not this was as a result of her attempt to participate in the research.

Each of the three women who gave full interviews perceived herself as a 'survivor' from the circumstances around the violence, and all had suggestions as to how women's perspectives could be taken on board more effectively by the centre in its work with 'violent' men. The interviewees all used their interviews to 'sound off' about the centre and the effects its work was having on them. For example, one interviewee complained her ex-partner 'hassled' her, using his attendance at the centre to suggest he was 'cured' of violent behaviour.[6] She contacted the centre, asking them to tell him to stop hassling her. One woman was hopeful that the therapy would be effective (she was still living with her partner), whilst the others had separated from their partners and were also more pessimistic that the man would stop being violent. Although Linda suggested repeat interviews and offered to keep in contact, no interviewees actually maintained contact with her. However, once the effects of the centre's work on these women had been revealed, re-interviewing them was felt to be unnecessary by all the researchers. Despite the limited sample, the interviews had thus served a useful purpose from a policy perspective. Specifically, a woman counsellor was recruited to work with centre partners and closer links were also developed with supportive women's centres.

A further dilemma remained. With only three interviewees Linda decided to try a different approach to boost the response. She had by now come into contact with a women's group who actively supported the work of the therapy centre and arranged with them to meet a potential interviewee on their premises (although she did not turn up in the event). The women's group suggested holding a meeting with their members and an 'open letter' was written inviting them to meet. Interestingly however, despite (or perhaps because of) its much more 'direct' approach, this letter was not effective and the proposed meeting had to be abandoned due to lack of response. The letter had a very different tone to the earlier one; Linda was much more up-front about her own intentions, saying for example – 'my way of doing this

research is to *listen to everything women want to tell me*, in confidence
. . .'. With such a sensitive topic, perhaps with hindsight this person-
alized the issue too much. Although no more interviews were
arranged, Linda developed a short questionnaire that was posted to
some members of this women's group, whose partners used the
therapy centre and this provided further background material for the
research.

By now Linda had also reported to colleagues that she herself was
feeling intimidated by demands to increase the sample. This made her
realise the *similarities* between herself and her interviewees, in their
experiences of power, control or even, coercion by men. Ethically,
Linda felt that despite the small number of women accessed, these
accounts did justify the time and effort spent on obtaining them. For
the women who came forward with a story to tell, the interviews
provided a sort of catharsis, which they acknowledged. For the therapy centre and male researchers, the research findings had revealed
women (including Linda herself) describing their perceived lack of
power and effective involvement with the centre. The political and
therapeutic implications of this were subsequently acknowledged by
the therapists and acted upon, particularly by recruiting a female
counsellor. The research process therefore raised ethical dilemmas
relating not only to issues of access and confidentiality, but also to
male power in relation to women.

Using gate-keepers in accessing those who may be less powerful

The need to *re*think routes and modes of access both at the outset *and*
once a study is underway is clearly necessary in research that explores
groups who may be difficult to access for a whole range of reasons.
The question of *who* is actually giving consent and to what must be
considered throughout. However, control over decision-making
around access is not always in the hands of the interviewer and even
when this appears to be so, can still be problematic when gate-keepers
are used. The role of the gate-keeper in accessing those who may be
less powerful and therefore less able to resist 'voluntary' participation
became a concern in Tina's research on Bangladeshi women (Miller,
1995). The small-scale pilot study was set up to explore Bangladeshi
women's experiences of maternity services in a town in southern
Britain. Tina had lived and worked in Bangladesh and was sensitive to
the religious beliefs and cultural traditions of the women she hoped to
interview. She also recognized that in order to access this largely

hidden group she would have to find a gate-keeper. This proved to be more difficult than anticipated.

Initially, Tina hoped to access potential participants through a health visitor contact. Although Tina realized that this might result in a 'biased' sample (i.e. women who were regular users of maternity services) she anticipated that snowballing could then be used to access other women. The health visitor who was approached felt unable to act as a potential gate-keeper as she was concerned about being perceived as coercive and mis-using her professional role. She suggested that Tina contact her colleague who was Bangladeshi and a community worker. When contact was finally made, Tina was surprised and dismayed to find that this colleague was not in fact Bangladeshi but Indian and therefore unable to act as a gate-keeper. Tina's dismay arose from the apparent cultural insensitivity demonstrated by the health visitor. However this contact was able to provide Tina with the name of a Bangladeshi woman who worked in the community assisting in language classes for members of the local Bangladeshi population. Contact was eventually made with J and she agreed to meet Tina and discuss her research. Fortunately she was interested in the research and agreed to let Tina 'join' a recently formed Bangladeshi women's group. Yet whilst the difficulty of accessing a gate-keeper was an initial and protracted problem it is the power that the gate-keeper was then able to assert in *volunteering* women that is of particular importance to this discussion.

The Bangladeshi women who came to the group – where amongst other activities, English language classes were offered – were both vulnerable and largely powerless. The context in which they experienced and exercised agency was regulated by religious and cultural practices that encompassed all aspects of their lives. When, at the next meeting, Tina was introduced to the women she realized that in effect *wholesale access* had been provided by the gate-keeper. These women would find it difficult not to agree to participate in the study as it was J who had 'let her in'. J was not only responsible for setting up the women's group but she also occupied a respected position in the local community; she was more powerful than the other women in terms of her perceived social class and status. However, although the women had been volunteered and access given to a hard-to-reach group, the interviews themselves provided an opportunity for the women to exercise some agency and to resist talking about certain aspects of their lives. But in situations where those in more powerful positions, for example line managers, are asked to act as gate-keepers to potential respondents, how feasible is it for them subsequently to resist taking part? Similarly when powerful gate-keepers are used notions around access, coercion and, more importantly, consent can become very difficult for the researcher – and researched – to disentangle. Who is actually giving consent and to what?

Access and longitudinal research

Further ethical dilemmas can arise for the researcher in longitudinal research. Here access clearly needs to be renegotiated prior to each interview (Miller, 1998). Ethical concerns can emerge when re-negotiation of access is clouded by advice from others and when participants may be feeling particularly vulnerable. The point made earlier about whether researchers should ever be more 'coercive' when they perceive their research to be underpinned by good ethical motives is revisited here. In her research on first-time transition to motherhood (Miller, 2000), Tina planned to interview the 17 women who had agreed to participate in her study, on three separate occasions – once at seven months antenatally, then at six to eight weeks postnatally and finally at eight to nine months postnatally. She had accessed all the women through snowballing and they were verbally willing at the outset to participate over the course of the study. The first round of interviewing took place at seven months antenatally with the women consenting to be contacted once their baby had been born so that a further interview could be arranged. All the women reiterated their 'consent' at this first interview although they had no way of knowing how they might be feeling in the early weeks following the birth of their baby and whether they would want to talk about their experiences.

For one participant the early postnatal period was much more difficult to cope with than she had anticipated and she initially 'chose' not to be interviewed when the first postnatal interview was due. It was this action that raised particular ethical concerns for Tina. These concerns arose because the participant had commented during telephone conversations with Tina that she had been diagnosed as having postnatal depression (a label she rejected) and that her husband and health visitor felt that she should not be interviewed. The lengthy telephone conversations with Tina suggested that she really did want someone to talk to and that she was clearly feeling lonely and isolated. Tina felt uneasy that her research should in some way be seen as a possible catalyst for reflection leading to unhappiness – or at least not helpful – by her health visitor and that this participant was, it seemed, being silenced by others. Tina was at the same time frustrated that this participant's experiences of early mothering might not be voiced thereby helping to perpetuate the myths that surround mothering being 'natural' and therefore easy. Was this a 'good enough' ethical motive for Tina to pursue this participant further, to be 'coercive'? In the extracts below taken from Tina's fieldwork diary she contemplates what course of action to take:

[24/1/96] Spoke to respondent 4 again (having phoned her last week). We spoke for 15–20 minutes – apparently both the respondent's husband and her health visitor don't think she should progress with the interviews – but I feel she wants to, if only to have someone to talk to. I said I did not want to put any pressure on her, especially as others thought she should not proceed. She was unhappy that the health visitor had asked her to fill out a depression scoring questionnaire – she had scored 16 points and then 17 on the next occasion and so had been 'labelled'/diagnosed as suffering from postnatal depression and prescribed anti-depressants. She was angry that she had been labelled in this way and treated with drugs (the implication was that she was not taking the drugs). She spoke of being lonely and 'stuck out here', isolated. After a long talk – with me telling her that not all women found becoming a mother easy – she arranged to meet me next Tuesday at her house for a [first] postnatal interview. I gave her my home number and said to phone me on Tuesday morning if she didn't feel up to being interviewed – although I sense that she will be relieved once she has been interviewed (fulfilled her 'obligations' to me?). I am also aware of my position/role as researcher and not professional counsellor, but as a mother I empathise and realise I may find it difficult to disentangle/keep my various 'roles' separate.

[30/1/96] I have just been telephoned by respondent 4 who sounded cheerful – hysterical almost – but said that she was phoning from her parents and therefore could not be interviewed today. She apologised but said she was cooking lunch for her dad. She said she would phone me (I suggested Thursday) at the office, or at home to arrange another time. I feel frustrated as I had my coat on ready to leave and had prepared to 'do' the interview after what had already been a frustratingly long build up. Will she contact me??

[15/2/96] Respondent 4 hasn't phoned, I wonder if I should send my interview prompt sheet in the form of a self-administered questionnaire? I will talk to (supervisor) about this (Ethics?!).

After discussions with my supervisor I decided to write to the participant and request that she contact me if she wanted to re-enter the study for the final interview. I was surprised, and pleased, when she did contact me once her child had reached nine months of age. My decision not to pressure her eventually yielded a positive result.

'Informed' consent – to what?

The research studies above relied upon obtaining verbal consent. The requirement that researchers increasingly obtain written consent from participants poses new ethical considerations. The differences between access and consent are not always clear. As we noted in our earlier discussion, gate-keepers may in effect (unknowingly) imply and authorize consent where they provide access to less powerful groups. Similarly, researchers may choose to take 'consent' as given once a potential participant agrees to be interviewed and to participate in the research. Whilst ethics committees increasingly require researchers to produce consent forms for them to vet and for research participants to sign, the formality of such procedures will certainly alienate some groups and individuals. This shift in academic social research mirrors concerns around coercion and safety that have existed for some time in health services research. It also resonates with growing concerns around risk and consumerism in research (Annandale, 1998). The practice of research is increasingly regarded as a risky enterprise in which the 'protection' of parties involved and issues of accountability come to the fore in written guidelines and contracts. Yet, in research focusing on less visible aspects of the social world, for example domestic violence, access to research participants may be tenuous, based on notions of trust in the individual researcher. Any formal requirement to obtain written consent could fundamentally challenge such relationships.

Even more problematic than written consent are notions that consent is 'informed'. Research handbooks and ethical guides emphasize that consent must be obtained prior to any research commencing. Yet, what is it that participants are consenting to when they agree to join a study? If the focus of the research is to explore a period of transition, how can the outcome of the research be known? Feminist principles of research – reciprocity and empowerment – may be embraced by the researcher at the outset of research, yet goals may shift, prompting a more instrumental approach, for example assembling a viable sample or meeting deadlines (see Duncombe and Jessop in Chapter 6). Whilst the dynamic nature of the research process is increasingly acknowledged in social research literature, the ethical dilemmas that this presents for feminist researchers and their research participants are less well explored (although see Luff, 1999 and Mauthner, 2000 for recent contributions to this area).

Obtaining 'informed consent' at the start of a project should not mean that it does not have to be thought about again. Researchers need to decide what they are inviting participants to consent to. Is consent just about participation in the research in terms of being interviewed or does it go further, involving reading and commenting on transcripts and the analysis of data? Even if the terms of participation are clearly agreed and consented to at the beginning of a study these can change. In her research on transition to motherhood (Miller, 2000) Tina offered to provide a summary of the research findings at the end of the study to the women who had participated. Yet by the end of the longitudinal research Tina recognized that her findings would not in some cases resonate with the participants own expectations. Whilst the women had all consented to participate by allowing themselves to be accessed, Tina admits to feeling some trepidation in returning to the participants at the end of the study with her findings. Tina's anxiety arose because she felt certain the women in the study had anticipated a different 'product', a more practical 'how to' guide to first-time mothering, when they agreed to join the research. Their overriding interest had been with how other women in the study had experienced and coped with becoming mothers. In contrast Tina's interpretation of the data led her to focus on the epistemological and ontological shifts discernible in the stories that were constructed at different times through the women's transition. Whilst participants were informed prior to the first interview that the research was about 'transition to motherhood' the findings could not be known before the research was carried out. Yet the women in the study had their own ideas about the research and its possible outcomes as noted in the extract below taken from one end-of-study questionnaire,

> I would hope being a participant in the research would help other women . . . Tina is making a great achievement for women. I hope in enlightening us all, that we are allowed to feel the way we do. Well done Tina and thank you!

Tina was aware, retrospectively, that although some of the women had experienced their participation in the research as 'therapeutic' (see Birch and Miller, 2000) the research could only ever make a small contribution (if any) to changing societal attitudes to motherhood. Tina's research would almost certainly not be 'enlightening' everyone, as one participant clearly hoped in the extract above. However it may also be the case that as feminist researchers we are overly sensitive to the potential (ethical?) impact of our research on those involved. This was demonstrated in one response Tina received when she wrote to confirm participants' addresses before returning their tape-recorded interviews to them at the end of the study. Abigail replied to the letter and, as well as confirming her address details, wrote '. . . it seems so long ago, that to be honest I'd forgotten about it'.

Some thoughts on practical guidelines around ethical issues in relation to access and consent

We have argued that decisions taken around access, re-access and gaining consent can be closely bound up with questions of ethics. Moreover, the differences between gaining access and consent are not always clear. From our examples, it is clear that researchers must continually reflect upon access routes in order to address complex issues around representation of individual voices; ethical concerns over 'consent' to participating in a research study; and activities of those acting as 'gate-keepers' who may perceive some potential interviewees as 'vulnerable', or otherwise be in a position of some power over them. Researchers should examine how far those 'volunteered' by such gate-keepers can resist participation, or alternatively whether some potential participants are being effectively excluded. Researchers should also examine the ways in which gender and ethnicity can affect who is accessed and by whom. Does apparent or tacit 'coercion' invalidate our notions of 'informed' consent? Furthermore, may there be a danger of excluding those groups who are difficult to access by using inflexible and formal methods of gaining consent (e.g. written consent)? Judging by our own experiences 'consent' needs to be ongoing and renegotiated between researcher and researched – not just at the time of access but possibly as transcripts are analysed and findings are published. Using a research diary to document access routes and decisions made throughout the research process is one practical way of developing an ethics checklist. This practice of regular reflection helps ensure that ethical and methodological considerations are continually reassessed.

Notes

[1] This notion of 'gate-keeper' is related to that of the 'key informant' (Tremblay, 1957; Whyte, 1955). Unlike key informants, however, we would also define a 'gate-keeper' as someone who gives access to other interviewees but who would not necessarily actually take part in a study by being interviewed themselves (which was the postion in the studies discussed in this chapter).

[2] Robson does acknowledge, however, that different research designs imply different problems: 'If you are clear about your [research] intentions, perhaps with a pretty tight, pre-structured, design then the task [getting access] is probably easier initially, in that you can give them a good indication of what they are letting themselves in for. With a looser, more emergent design, there may be more difficulties . . . as it is impossible to specify in advance exactly what you will do' (1993: 295).

[3] However genuine issues of 'partner safety' should not be underestimated here. See Bell (1998).

[4] As Dobash et al. note: 'Increasingly, evaluators [of programmes for violent men] have proposed the use of self-reports of victims. Unfortunately existing evaluations do not routinely include self-reports of women who have been victimised by the men receiving whatever form of intervention is being evaluated' (1999: 210).

[5] There were concerns about the 'representativeness' of women's accounts in relation to the centre, and Linda was specifically urged to interview as many women as possible.

[6] Recent research suggests male abusers may attempt to neutralize or eradicate women's experiences of abuse, including using their own participation in therapy to present themselves as non-violent (Anderson and Umberson, 2001; Cavanagh et al., 2001).

References

Anderson, K. and Umberson, D. (2001) 'Gendering violence: masculinity and power in men's accounts of domestic violence', *Gender and Society*, 15(3): 358–80.

Annandale, E. (1998) 'Working on the front line: risk culture and nursing in the new NHS', in M. Allott and M. Robb (eds), *Understanding Health and Social Care*. London: Sage.

Bell, C. (1998) 'Counselling intervention with men who batter: partner safety and the duty to warn', *Counselling*, August.

Birch, M. and Miller, T. (2000) 'Inviting intimacy: the interview as therapeutic opportunity', *International Journal of Social Research Methodology*, 3(3): 189–202.

British Sociological Association (BSA) (1993) *Statement of Ethical Practice*. Mountjoy Research Centre, Durham.

Burgess, R. (1982) 'Early field experiences', in R. Burgess (ed.), *Field Research: a Sourcebook and Field Manual*. London: Allen and Unwin.

Cavanagh, K., Dobash, R.E. and Dobash, R.P. (2001) ' "Remedial work": men's strategic responses to their violence against intimate female partners', *Sociology*, 35(3): 695–714.

Dobash, R. et al. (1999) 'A research evaluation of British programmes for violent men', *Journal of Social Policy*, 28(2): 205–33.

Edwards, R. and Ribbens, J. (eds) (1998) *Feminist Dilemmas in Qualitative Research*. London: Sage.

Hoff, L.A. (1990) *Battered Women as Survivors*. London: Routledge.

Liebow, E. (1967) *Tally's Corner: A Study of Negro Street Corner Men*. Boston: Little Brown.

Luff, D. (1999) 'Dialogue across the divides: "moments of rapport" and power in feminist research with anti-feminist women', *Sociology*, 33(4): 687–703.

Mason, J. (1996) *Qualitative Researching*. London: Sage.

Mauthner, M. (2000) 'Snippets and silences: ethics and reflexivity in narratives of sistering', *International Journal of Social Research Methodology*, 3(4): 287–306.

Miller, T. (1995) 'Shifting boundaries: exploring the influence of cultural traditions and religious beliefs of Bangladeshi women on antenatal interactions', *Women's Studies International Forum*, 18(3): 299–309.

Miller, T. (1998) 'Shifting layers of professional, lay and personal narratives: longitudinal childbirth research', in R. Edwards and J. Ribbens (eds), *Feminist Dilemmas in Qualitative Research*. London: Sage.

Miller, T. (2000) 'An Exploration of First-Time Motherhood: Narratives of Transition', PhD dissertation, University of Warwick.

Oakley, A. (1981) 'Interviewing women: a contradiction in terms', in H. Roberts (ed.), *Doing Feminist Research*. London: Routledge and Kegan Paul.

Renzetti, C.M. and Lee, R.M. (eds) (1993) *Researching Sensitive Topics*. London: Sage.

Ribbens, J. and Edwards, R. (1995) 'Introducing qualitative research on women in families and households', *Women's Studies International Forum*, 18(3): 247–58.

Robson, C. (1993) *Real World Research*. Oxford: Blackwell.

Stanley, L. and Wise, S. (1990) 'Method, methodology and epistemology in feminist research processes', in Stanley, L. (ed.), *Feminist Praxis: Research Theory and Epistemology in Feminist Sociology*. London: Routledge.

Stanley, L. and Wise, S. (1993) *Breaking Out Again. Feminist Ontology and Epistemology*. London: Routledge.

Tremblay, M.A. (1957) 'The key informant technique: a non-ethnographic application', *American Anthropologist*, 59(4): 688–701.

Wallman, S. (1984) *Eight London Households*. London: Tavistock.

Whyte, W. (1955) *Street Corner Society*. Chicago: Chicago University Press.

Wise, S. (1987) 'A framework for discussing ethical issues in feminist research: a review of the literature', in V. Griffiths et al. (eds), 'Writing Feminist Biography: Using Life histories', *Studies in Sexual Politics*. No. 19. University of Manchester.

CHAPTER 4

DIVIDED LOYALTIES, DIVIDED EXPECTATIONS: RESEARCH ETHICS, PROFESSIONAL AND OCCUPATIONAL RESPONSIBILITIES

Linda Bell and Linda Nutt

Introduction

This chapter examines how professional and occupational respons-ibilities 'translate' into actual research situations, and the ethical dilemmas which accompany 'divided loyalties' towards research and employment, in the fields of health and social care. We define 'practitioner-researchers' here as those who have responsibilities as health/social care practitioners (including trainee practitioners) and who are also conducting research (see Fuller and Petch, 1995; Robson, 1993: chapter 15). We explore two examples suggesting ethical dilem-mas and potentially divided loyalties. The first focuses on social research that overlaps with paid professional employment as a social worker involved in foster care in the voluntary sector. The second involves the construction of a set of ethical guidelines for university student-practitioners embarking on research projects related to pro-fessional education. We suggest that despite the efforts of a number of different professional bodies, to ethically regulate the activities of their practitioners (and thus practitioner-researchers), ethical dilemmas will still arise in research practice. In this context, dilemmas are especially likely to occur when researchers who are also practitioners recognize the need to acknowledge relevant multiple responsibilities and sensi-tivities. These will include perceived responsibilities towards clients/ service users, fellow practitioners and organisational bodies, other researchers, and (in the case of students) meeting academic/university agendas relating to student assessment, or complying with regulations or 'competences'[1] specified by agencies controlling professional education.

One key concern for practitioner-researchers is therefore how to 'manage' all these responsibilities in practice, in ways that all parties would consider 'ethical'. Such 'self-regulatory' research processes (in which these responsibilities need to be actively managed) will have their counterpart, we would suggest, in the rhetoric of 'reflexive'/ 'reflective' professional practice which is currently found in much professional education relating to health and social care (Ashford et al., 1998; Reed and Proctor, 1993; Schon, 1987; Tsang, 1998). We also suggest that such reflexivity connects with other more 'individualised' forms of researcher reflexivity, as found for example in feminist research (Mauthner, 2000). However, it is partly the reflexive positioning of different professional practitioners (e.g. social workers and nurses vis-a-vis each other) as well as those following different research or professional paradigms within the same profession (Holland, 1999) which encourages such 'self-regulation'[2] in both professional practice and in research practice.

In this chapter we will explore issues of 'confidentiality' and 'negotiation' within the research process. We will also consider issues around 'access' and seeking 'informed voluntary consent' from participants. These areas will be illustrated through our substantive examples, in which we show how a focus on all these issues ties together research and professional practice in ways that we think may be different from other researchers' concerns. One of us (Linda Nutt) has worked as a practitioner-researcher whilst the other (Linda Bell) has been closely involved in practitioner-education including research supervision. In attempting to 'stand outside' practitioner-research in order to reflect on and discuss research ethics concerns, we are aware of the difficulties involved in speaking simultaneously to professional and 'other' researcher audiences, such as sociologists. Even the languages used by these varied kinds of researchers about research and research ethics may differ; however, we are attempting here to present practitioner-research and the ethical dilemmas it raises in ways which would be recognizable to practitioner-researchers as well as to a wider audience.

We suggest that the necessary 'self-regulation' of the practitioner-researcher means s/he may also have to choose whether or not to emphasize the role of 'practitioner' when carrying out research. This involves making professional as well as research judgements within specific research settings, and our examples will show that potential conflict or tensions between these roles needs to be acknowledged. For example, the practitioner-researcher may make initial decisions about separating or connecting these roles, which may then be difficult to achieve in practice. In addition, some professional guidance may recommend a particular course of action when practitioners are dealing with a research role and with professional (clinical) obligations (RCN, 1998: 19, see below).

Whilst ethics are clearly bound up closely with research as well as with professional practice, we suggest further that these elements cannot be unravelled in a simplistic way rendering one kind of methodological research approach 'ethical' and another not. However, some of the literature emanating from 'practitioner research' suggests that particular methodological approaches to research should be more ethically acceptable to practitioners, because they either take a participatory and inclusive stance towards research participants (Everitt et al., 1992), or provide more reliable 'evidence' on which to base professional practice (Macdonald and Macdonald, 1995). We end the chapter by exploring some of these debates, since clearly these claims are based in different epistemological positions.

Approaches to practitioner research ethics

Many professional bodies issue guidelines for their practitioners relating to professional conduct and in some cases to appropriate research practice. As Wise (1987: 187) points out:

> most professional groups whose jobs bring them into contact with members of society tend to have a set of guidelines, which carry varying degrees of authority, to guide their practice: social workers and doctors are two examples that come immediately to mind . . . (See also BASW, 1996; UKCC, 1992; National Institute of Medical Herbalists.)

Nursing with its focus on holistic care and management of 'risk' for patients (Reed and Proctor, 1993) also produces research guidelines for practitioners that emphasize safety and the carrying out of acceptable procedures (Royal College of Nursing, 1998). Nurses carrying out research are expected to be appropriately qualified, and also to be willing to publish and thus share their findings with other practitioners (Schrock, 1991: 34). As noted above, there is also acknowledgement by the Royal College of Nursing of potential tensions between clinical (professional) and research roles. Nurses are specifically advised that 'nurses who have a research role in a clinical area should seek clarification about the division between their research role and their professional obligations' (RCN, 1998: 19). It is necessary to consider, however, how easy or difficult this clarification might be to accomplish in practice. These nursing Research Ethics guidelines effectively 'mesh' with the nursing UKCC 'Code of professional conduct' (UKCC, 1992) to which all nurses should adhere. This Code similarly emphasizes 'the interests, condition or safety of patients and clients' whilst instructing nurses to protect all confidential information concerning patients and clients obtained through professional practice. The UKCC Code also requires that nurses should report to an 'appropriate person or authority' any circumstances under which safe and appropriate patient care could not be provided.

This professional example surely raises a first, key dilemma for practitioner-researchers from all professions/occupations. Whilst all approaches to research ethics may emphasize 'confidentiality' as an important element, for a health or social care practitioner-researcher there may be circumstances in which this assurance does not preclude reporting something discovered in the course of research practice to an 'appropriate' recipient (as noted above, UKCC, 1992). 'Absolute' confidentiality within the research setting would therefore be precluded in certain risky situations. Some researchers who are not health or social care practitioners may feel that this compromise over confidentiality strikes at the heart of 'ethical research' itself. As discussed further below, this dilemma can run through the process of constructing ethical research guidelines for student-practitioners, and is also a theme picked up through the account below of research into foster care.

Like nursing, social work has its own professional Code of practice ethics (as distinct from research ethics, BASW, 1996).[3] This Code is an interesting document due to the degree of 'reflexivity' used in explaining and discussing the reasons for inclusion of the different clauses making up the document. The code has a clear emphasis on a value-base of anti-discriminatory professional practice[4] (Thompson, 1997), and also discusses confidentiality in similar terms to the nursing practice code. It is suggested that confidential information should only be disclosed with the consent of the client, except where there is clear evidence of serious danger to the 'client, worker, other persons or the community', when it should be disclosed appropriately. This professional practice Code clearly has implications for social work practitioners who are also doing research.

When considering 'informed' voluntary consent and questions of access to participants from the point of view of practitioner-researchers, many of the same issues will be raised as in other kinds of research (see Miller and Bell in Chapter 3). However, there may be explicit recognition, which varies from one profession/occupation to another, that in working with clients/service users as research participants, the practitioner-researcher will need to clearly acknowledge specific aspects of the relationship between the practitioner and client/service user. The BASW (social work) code, for example, recognizes the idea of a power imbalance between social workers and their clients, and also recognizes the disadvantages suffered by social work 'clients' in society more generally. The theoretical implications of this recognition for research are explored, for example, by Boushel's discussion of 'race' (Boushel, 2000: 71) in which she 'identifies some of the political, personal and technical challenges an anti-racist approach presents' for social welfare research. Similarly, feminist approaches to professional practice or practitioner research will need to acknowledge the same kind of issues as identified below in the foster care research example (see also Langan and Day, 1992).

In a broader sense, nursing and other 'health' research is usually acknowledged to be locked into a 'medical' model requiring the sanction of research ethics committees, whether in universities or in hospital trusts (see Miller and Bell in Chapter 3). It may be implied that, in this context, research usually involves pre-determined, outcome-based 'clinical' projects, and so importance may thus be attached to gaining 'informed consent' from participants in clinical procedures. This implies gaining access and obtaining consent at the initial stage of the research from clients/service users especially where these people are perceived as in any way 'vulnerable' (e.g. people who are older, or who have mental health problems). In a methodological context, these ethics committee processes may thus have significant implications for practitioner-researchers conducting qualitative research who apply to such committees. For example, issues of 'negotiation' during the research process, including re-negotiation at different stages, have already been highlighted in this volume as an aspect of 'ethics' (Miller and Bell, see Chapter 3). However, continuing to re-negotiate may not be considered acceptable by an ethics committee. 'Confidentiality' may also be addressed in a formal way at this early stage, through required production of consent forms or information sheets concerning the planned research, even though this may not always be appropriate (as noted by Miller and Bell).

In terms of re-negotiation during the research process, it may be that practitioner-researchers are thrown back onto their own guidelines for professional ethics; although in practice a degree of professional 'reflexivity' or 'reflective practice' would seem to be what is most useful in these circumstances (Ashford et al., 1998: 11) there may in fact be tensions between this reflective practice and the competence-based practice framework currently underpinning professional education in social work, nursing, or other occupations. As both of our examples below reveal, effective negotiation may be considered a key aspect of 'ethics' in relation to qualitative practitioner-research, since it relates in complex ways to professional competence, reflective

practice/reflexivity and to the multiple responsibilities and sensitivities indicated at the start of this chapter.

'Ethical' practitioner research in practice?

We now explore these key themes around confidentiality, access,
informed consent and negotiation through our two substantive examples. These two examples illustrate situations in which different
approaches to acknowledging the role of 'practitioner' are taken
(whether by design or necessity) by practitioner-researchers themselves. We explore these ethical issues in relation to differing contexts
of expectations and agendas surrounding practitioner-researchers. We
illustrate these contexts by drawing on different parts of one
practitioner-researcher 'spectrum', namely student social work practitioners doing research projects, and a fully experienced and qualified
social work practitioner undertaking a research degree (doctorate).

Professional practice and doctoral research on foster care: separate or connected?

The research topic Linda Nutt has explored concerns foster care. Her
research uses a broadly qualitative, feminist approach to investigate
how foster carers make sense of their everyday lives in relation to
their own families and to the 'extra' children for whom they care. The
study aims to understand the lives of foster carers in and on their own
terms. Linda N completed the study, outside her work time, as part of
her doctorate when simultaneously employed by the National Foster
Care Association (NFCA). Her paid post involved providing a social
work consultancy service to foster carers registered with six local
authorities – authorities from which she also drew her research sample. Here we examine the complexities of this situation, particularly in
relation to the mix of professional and academic statuses of the
researcher. We explore how Linda N attempted to conceptualize her
research and her work as separate entities within different worlds,
and how the research journey exposed the practical problems of
achieving this. She found there were too many crossovers, and eventually reflects that she could not avoid being the same person who
wore both hats.

Linda Nutt's professional training was as a social worker; schooled
in the use of the 'case work relationship', she expects to help clients

understand their personal situations and take decisions as to what change, if any, they wish to effect in their lives (Biestek, 1961; Ferard and Hunnybun, 1962). Before commencing this research she decided that she would not be a 'social worker' in the research interviews as she wanted to conduct them in a very different manner. For her this was new, less sure ground and she wanted to keep separate the two experiences of 'doctoral researcher' and 'social work practitioner'. As a feminist researcher she addressed the power relations between herself and interviewees and planned that the foster carers she would interview should remain 'in control'. She did not want the foster carers to feel in any way 'subordinate' (as they might in a social worker-client relationship) but as a researcher she aimed for equality and an interview schedule that was sufficiently loose to allow the carers to explore their own agendas.

Linda Nutt naively believed that, if she interviewed foster carers who were not known to her, that they would not identify her as the worker employed by NFCA to provide a social work service in their area. In fact, her name was well known in foster care networks and the fact of her NFCA post must have affected the creative process of the interview. Interviews are interactional events, constructed as they happen (Hammersley and Atkinson, 1983: 15), they are the product of a particular time and place (Gubrium and Holstein, 1995) which means that Linda Nutt, as interviewer, was intimately involved in creating the data and, more importantly, in organising the meanings via her analysis. For some carers this information would have provided a commonality of knowledge (Finch, 1984) and could therefore be viewed not so much as problematic but more as an additional resource. However, when interviewed, all the foster carers, even those who were so new that they awaited the placement of their first foster child, used a social services vocabulary. They used a professional discourse which provided a professional shorthand and which Linda N recognized and found immediately seductive and impossible to ignore. Interviewer and interviewee were both immersed in the foster care world. Reflecting back on this situation, Linda N now feels that too often she nodded in complicity – assuming that her understandings were their understandings when, in fact, 'shorthand' risks misunderstandings which could discredit the data and invite problematic, ethical implications on analysis. The following example is one carer's description of a baby's family visits to the foster carer's home:

> With one baby I had contact three times a week. Here – sometimes more when Grandma came and you are, you know, trapped and the house is invaded but the, they say that it is best for the children but what about our children? But I suppose it is, for them you know. But they don't tell you or

explain just say that her mum has – and it was better than the screams when they took her to the Family Centre and then I could give the guardian the detail of it all which I couldn't have if they took her off each time – you know.

Conversations depend upon cultural assumptions, and in this example there are a number of expressions and assumptions involving this shorthand – 'contact', what is 'better' and for whom, the 'guardian', 'Family Centre' and interpreting 'they'. Together with the foster carers, Linda N was actively involved in constructing an understanding of foster care, but were interviewees responding to Linda as a researcher, or Linda as the NFCA social worker with official social services links?

This is relevant to how the carers felt about the interview, about her and about the material that they produced. This 'intrusion' was particularly clear in three interviews. Two male carers requested specific advice and information. Linda therefore turned off the tape, discussed their problem and once this formal business was completed, switched on the tape and resumed the study. In another interview with a female carer she instinctively commented on the social service process of dealing with allegations against foster carers in response to the carer's particular experience. Upon reflection she considers this inappropriate. She had commenced the study with particular judgements concerning what did and did not constitute 'research'. One of these judgements was that she would 'just listen' to the carers rather than actively contribute to the data. She had not thought through that this is untenable: that the interview is always a social interaction. These three interviews reveal some of the practical difficulties of keeping separate the identities of researcher and practitioner. For Linda N the boundaries proved fragile.

Except for the many expressions of 'you know'[5] so as to involve Linda N in the interaction, none of the foster carers sought any personal information from her. If there was uncertainty about how to 'place' her (Edwards, 1993), foster carers did not appear to allow this to inhibit the stories they wished to tell. Did they see her position as an 'insider' or an 'outsider' – or perhaps as identified by Song and Parker (1995) as ambiguous and therefore not readily definable? There was, apparently, no interest in her as a person but we do not believe, as posited by Edwards (1993), that a more equal exchange would have elicited more information – though it might have produced different data. Edwards argues that an exchange of information, particularly personal information, aids the informants to 'place' the researcher and this encourages disclosure. Perhaps, on some occasions, some of the foster carers were reassured that they could 'place' Linda N within their foster care world.

Reflecting on the 'snowballing' sampling techniques used in this study, Linda Nutt believed that, if the contacts were made via the foster carers' own networks, this would ensure that carers had a choice not to participate. However, as she has no information about how she and the study were described by each contact foster carer, she cannot know if the added dimension of her official post (if known) acted as a pressure to ensure compliance with the request – one thing she sought to avoid. Perhaps the use of snowballing may have inadvertently exacerbated the dilemma, as she used the implicit power of her work position, so that the ethical intention of 'voluntary' consent was contaminated.

It is also possible that the way the research was conducted may have influenced some foster carers' use of the NFCA service Linda Nutt was paid to provide. For example, in several interviews, although she thought she understood what the carers were saying, because she wanted them to be more explicit, wanted their words on tape, she played the naive researcher requesting description and explanation. Did this undermine their confidence in her as a NFCA foster care 'expert' whom they could contact for advice and information? Moreover was this response, in fact, actual deception, as she was, in a sense, giving dishonest messages to the carers by feigning non comprehension and how ethical was this practice (see also Punch, 1994)?

Due to the intimate nature of their interviews, it is also possible that some carers may have been inhibited from using her NFCA social work service. Brannen (1988) has suggested that it is safer for participants if they never again meet the researcher as this minimizes any gossip and maximizes the chances of secrecy and anonymity. It also frees them to speak with emotion. Over time, five of the 27 fostering households have contacted Linda Nutt in her NFCA capacity to seek social work advice and support about fostering problems. Four acknowledged her as also a researcher but one male carer seemed not to realise that he already knew her. He related the facts of his problem and described the foster children as though she had never visited his house. For him, the researcher and the NFCA worker were two separate people; he now sought the professional social worker.

Throughout the year that Linda Nutt was conducting her research interviews she was concerned to keep apart what she conceptualized as two 'separate' identities. She was aware that the information that the foster carers shared in their research interviews was frequently very intimate and given in the belief that she would not divulge it to their local authority – with whom her other identity worked. She also harboured ideas, probably irrationally, that researchers behaved differently from social workers. One way that she attempted to put boundaries around her 'separate' practitioner and researcher worlds was in her decisions about which note-paper she used. Initially she decided to send letters and notes to the carers on home-headed stationery (Linda as independent researcher), rather than NFCA business paper (Linda as social work practitioner). She also sent Christmas cards updating them on the progress of the research. This posed a problem one year when NFCA audited her role and sent questionnaires to random carers who had used her paid service. Three of the foster carers Linda Nutt had interviewed were also selected by NFCA for their sample and she then felt (ethically) unable to send them cards in case they interpreted her action as some sort of bribe to say that she had given them 'good' advice. On another occasion NFCA required volunteer foster carers who would be interviewed for the media. Linda Nutt decided to write to her study sample with the details. She then found it a dilemma as to whether this should go out on NFCA paper (as work) or on personal stationery (because her links with them were forged through the research). In the end she sent those carers who definitely knew about her NFCA post the letter on work stationery and used home paper for the others.

The ways in which issues around confidentiality, negotiation and professional competence are interwoven and complex are illustrated in the following example where professional social work responsibilities conflict with the demands of research. As noted above, Linda Nutt was a paid professional social worker bound by general social work codes of practice. This example illustrates not only the difficulties arising when social work dilemmas impact upon research, but the practical impossibility of separating the two worlds:

As she was leaving the home of a new carer following the research interview Linda Nutt noticed an unambiguously sexually explicit picture in the hallway. For most researchers this would not be an issue: art is a matter of personal taste. But Linda Nutt wasn't just a researcher she was also a practitioner. Frequently when children are placed in foster homes little is known about their life experiences so new carers are instructed to assume that all children have been sexually abused unless specifically told otherwise. It is thus always considered essential not to give fostered children messages that could be interpreted as in any way sexual. As noted earlier, confidentiality is an absolute for researchers but cannot always be for practitioners. There is a statutory responsibility to disregard confidentiality where children are at risk. Nonetheless, because she wanted to keep the roles clear and separate – to act as a researcher (and be in receipt of information) and not as an employee of the NFCA (who would give them information), Linda Nutt chose not to tackle this issue with these new carers but spent several days considering this ethical dilemma. In the end the NFCA social worker practitioner identity overcame that of the researcher identity and Linda Nutt informed the local authority of her unease regarding the picture and its potential impact upon the foster children. Her reaction to its subject matter was guided by her professional training and the fact the painting was displayed in a house that offered refuge to children who could have been sexually abused. She did not mention this to the carers but left the social services department to make their own assessment.

Following this incident, Linda Nutt had felt obliged, as a practitioner-researcher, to recognize and act on her professional social work code of ethics which puts the safety of children above all confidentiality assurances. Linda Nutt, against her best endeavours, acted as 'research worker as helper' (Sainsbury et al., 1982), by contacting the local authority. We recognize that there may be divergent views about what, for her, was a dilemma. This would probably not have been an issue for an 'academic' researcher – people's art preferences being their own individual and private choices. Linda Nutt's action leaves her open to the criticism of, at the very least, making too many assumptions and, at worst, an abuse of power and an exploitation of the relationship between herself and her interviewees. Nonetheless, as a practitioner-researcher and therefore bound by social work practice ethics she could not deny her overriding responsibility towards the foster children. But in doing what she did, she breached any researcher (ethical) understandings of confidentiality and principles of anonymity. All the participants had been assured that their local authorities were not being formally notified as to which carers were participating in the study. In this case not only did she identify the carers but she raised cautions regarding their foster care practice leaving them with possible consequences.

This particular dilemma was symptomatic of a confusing situation caused by the insoluble problem of balancing transparency of action (and ensuring that all the carers who participated in the research study knew about Linda Nutt's professional post); and the knowledge that this risked the production of a more 'public' description of their lives-as-foster carers with the recognition of her official NFCA status. Full disclosure would have risked a changed, and more restricted and possibly less emotional set of data.

Although enabling people to behave in an emotional manner is familiar territory to a social worker or counsellor, Linda Nutt decided not to reflect back to carers in their interviews any statements in a way that might encourage them to examine strong and painful emotions concerned with their fostering. The way a story is told can reveal how the teller knows her/himself (Birch and Miller, 2000). Linda Nutt wanted interviewees to tell her about issues which were important to them; however, she chose not to demonstrate empathy which might encourage them to reveal more than they wished (see also Duncombe and Jessop in Chapter 6). She witnessed great pain in some foster carers as they talked about their experiences but, although acknowledging this, she remained intent not to encourage further painful disclosure: not to 'social work' them. Although some revealed their inner lives, there was no reciprocal exchange: there was, whatever the original intention, no equality of relationship. Linda is unsure how she would conduct herself if she were to start her research again, but she is aware that different social worker or feminist 'techniques' might have helped some of the carers live more peacefully with some very painful emotions. The retelling of past experiences can in itself help to make sense of the past and redefine elements more positively (Birch and Miller, 2000). One carer whose interview recounted a series of personally felt sad and frustrating events telephoned upon receiving her tape (after it had been transcribed), to thank Linda Nutt for the interview and 'memories of happier times'.

All researchers have to be self-regulating in their standards of ethical behaviour. It may be that, as illustrated above, the role of the social work practitioner-researcher is in some ways clearer than that of the 'academic researcher'. For practitioner-researchers, an important part of their ethical codes and of their concepts of ethics is to act 'responsibly'. In some cases, ethical commitment may go beyond the research participants to include significant others such as in this study, looked-after children. Linda Nutt began her study with a particular set of theoretical and 'ethical' research guidelines in mind which attempted to separate practitioner and researcher; but despite this, she found that, in practice, qualitative practitioner research cannot be totally managed and controlled by taking this approach.

Production of ethical guidelines for university student-practitioners embarking on final projects and dissertations as part of the Diploma in Social Work

The guidelines discussed below bring together ethical issues already raised, such as confidentiality and negotiation during the research process, with other perspectives relating to individual 'private' research, 'public' professional expectations and University assessment requirements which are all relevant to student-practitioners doing research. Crucially these different expectations relate to power and control both within, and over, the research setting. The student-practitioner is not therefore seen as a 'free agent' who can construct his or her own research agenda, and then carry it through without reference to others. Wise (1987) notes that: 'The issue of potential exploitation is crucial, since ethical guidelines tend to address themselves to the fact that differential power exists for the different actors within the research setting and ethical guidelines help guard against the potential abuse of that power which could lead to harm resulting from professional practice'. This point would apply to situations involving simply the 'researcher' and the 'researched'. However, in practitioner-research, the 'researched' may be assumed to be a service user/client on the receiving end of professional practice of some kind. Where research is done between practitioners of different kinds, the power relations in the research encounter may be somewhat different.

Dilemmas about 'exploitation' relating to the above mentioned multiple responsibilities and sensitivities will, however, be magnified due to the complex nature of expectations encountered when carrying out, as in this example, a final year project or dissertation as part of professional education and training. Such research projects relate to both professional and practice-based (placement) situations and to academic requirements. The student is considered to be 'responsible' as a trainee practitioner for adhering to and applying ethical practice guidance[6] and also any wider ethical framework of her/his profession and/or professional body (BASW, 1996).

There are also differing agendas relevant to ethical research practice with which the student may be expected to comply. Academically, the student will be expected to produce a piece of work which is 'academically sound' with the implication that this will mean it is 'ethically' acceptable, although the nature of this 'academic/ethical soundness' may be unclear except in so far as it successfully/ unsuccessfully meets criteria for assessment. We could ask, in this situation, who is being 'exploited'? Might the student find her/ himself in an ethically and academically untenable position during project work if they were to mis-read others' agendas? In these circumstances the interests of the student-practitioner, as well as those of the service user research participant, the 'professional' participant, and all those with a 'stake' in the student's research project, need to be carefully balanced. Paradoxically, a set of ethical guidelines, though seemingly constraining, may also act to free student practitioners to carry out certain kinds of work and follow agendas which are significant to them (for example, feminist agendas).

In 1998, due to issues raised by students themselves as well as academic staff on a professional education programme in social work (Diploma in Social Work) in a higher education institution, it was decided to construct a set of guidelines[7] which would try to balance all the differing agendas referred to above. In the initial drafting, the first over-riding principle was that students should adhere to the value principles taught as part of their professional training; these were outlined in the programme 'planner', a document issued to all the institution's Diploma in Social Work students (DipSW) annually.

The BASW practice guidelines are also referred to specifically in the ethical guidelines. These were also common to all sets of students, who were being trained in three 'strands': DipSW (two year) BA; BA (Hons) with DipSW; Postgraduate Diploma/MA with DipSW. The academic requirements for each set of students therefore differed, although all were expected to produce a final project related to their specialist social work 'pathway' (working with children and families; adults with specific needs; palliative care; criminal justice).

Other key issues raised in the initial draft guidelines included:

- seeking informed voluntary consent from participants (with a caveat that it is expected students will find greater difficulty in conducting research with their own clients/service users);
- not naming participating agencies or individuals in the student's final report;
- negotiating effectively both with participating agencies/individuals outside the university and with academic tutors;
- confidentiality – with the previously noted dilemma concerning 'absolute' confidentiality highlighted;
- issues around the ownership and dissemination of research findings, which sought to balance the rights of student, the university and research participants (including individuals and organisations).

In revising this initial draft in consultation with colleagues, two key issues came to light, one concerning 'generalized' ethical research principles and the second methodological approaches to research. The previous draft guidelines had rightly emphasized the significance of professional ethics and professional practice in this context, and this emphasis was retained in the final guidelines. However in the second draft we suggested a stronger connection with more generalized 'research ethics' and principles such as 'beneficence', 'justice' and 'respect' were also listed in the revised guidelines. The possibility of needing to obtain the approval of a relevant research ethics committee was also raised. Ethics committees within higher education will vary in the way that they have been established, although as noted in Miller and Bell (see Chapter 3) many will take as a model the ethics committees established in hospital or health trusts (see also Tierney, 1995). We suggest that this model has broader implications for research in social care and the social sciences, since where 'evidence based' approaches to practice are emphasized specifically, this can raise methodological issues around the perceived status of 'qualitative' research approaches (see next section, below).

In this context, the intention of the revised guidelines was to set the work of student social work practitioners into a broader 'research' context as well as a 'professional' one, and so to balance these agendas in some way. However, some might argue that appeals to these 'broader' principles, not strictly focused on professional concerns, might seem to be adding to the 'idealism' surrounding research practices noted earlier.

Of significant concern when constructing the guidelines, was that this 'idealism' might pre-suppose assumptions favouring particular methodological approaches to research. It was noted during consultation with colleagues that some people tended to favour specific models of research, including participatory approaches. These concerns were specifically related to 'ethics'; for example there was debate about the 'ethics' of participant observation and particularly about covert observation. It therefore seemed necessary to spell out to student-practitioners that whilst 'ethics' were indeed closely bound up with 'research' as well as with 'professional practice', this could not be unravelled in a simplistic way rendering one kind of research approach 'ethical' and another not. Again the intention was to ensure that whilst the agendas of the university, professional practitioners and their organisations, clients/service users and the students themselves were addressed (particularly with regard to adequate negotiation and reporting of findings), students were not going to be unnecessarily constrained in undertaking interesting and worthwhile research projects. Being able to take up approaches emphasizing anti-racism (as noted by Boushel, 2000), or feminism albeit in a professional context might depend upon the careful balancing of such constraints. We therefore advised:

> Remember that although some approaches to research specifically aim to involve service users (e.g. action research), this does not mean some kinds of research project are automatically more 'ethical' than others. You still need to pay attention to ethical principles whether you are doing an experiment, a survey or a piece of qualitative research.

Whilst methodologically and sociologically these statements might still raise more questions than they answer (not least, what is meant here by 'ethical'?) the underlying message was conveyed: as a practitioner-researcher the student is not unduly restricted in the choice of methodology and methods despite any connections which may be drawn in the literature between professional practice and 'participatory' or 'evidence based' approaches to research (as discussed further below). However, they are expected to negotiate fully with others and to act 'responsibly' in both professional practice and research activities. (The implication of this may be, de facto, to rule out such activities as 'covert' work.) To this extent, student-practitioners should then be in a position to actually 'do research' as 'self regulating' practitioner-researchers; to acknowledge and grapple with at least some of the kinds of research dilemmas experienced by practitioner-researchers such as those discussed earlier by Linda Nutt.

Ethics and evidence: The significance of methodology as an aspect of practitioner research

Although there is little space here to discuss the broader implications of 'evidence-based practice', particularly in health (see for example Gomm and Davies, 2000; Kendall, 1997), we note below the broader idea that 'ethical' research can be perceived as 'justifiable' research, which produces clear and effective answers to questions about 'outcomes' (however these may be defined; see for example Macdonald and Macdonald, 1995). The application of 'evidence based' approaches to professional practice and therefore to the commissioning of 'appropriate' research have often been discussed elsewhere in health literature (Rosenberg and Donald, 1995; Sackett et al., 1996), including growing discussions in the field of complementary and alternative health care. As noted by other commentators (Jordan et al., 1998; Kendall, 1997) heavy emphasis is placed by 'evidence-based' adherents on research 'evidence' taken from specific kinds of research which are deemed more 'reliable' than others (especially randomised, controlled trials). This in itself raises important issues around the perceived status of qualitative research, although health researchers have also pointed out the difficulties of using RCTs to evaluate health care (Bowling, 1997: 200–201).

As we noted at the beginning, some literature emanating from 'practitioner research' does, on the other hand, suggest that particular methodological approaches to research should be more 'ethically acceptable' to practitioners. The implications of this are, therefore, that research methodology itself relates in complex ways to issues of research ethics, professional practice, and practitioner research. For example, an emphasis on the underpinning, 'enabling' 'value base' of social work research is developed in advice given to practitioner researchers by Everitt et al. (1992), who suggest, both methodologically and ethically, that 'participatory' forms of research are the most acceptable forms of research for social work practitioner-researchers. Although not necessarily made explicit, the emphasis in Everitt et al. (1992) seems to be on 'qualitative' research approaches.

Linda Bell's experience of working with student social work practitioners certainly suggests these students tend to favour 'qualitative' approaches to research. However they do not necessarily choose 'participatory' research that would fully involve research participants (although this is probably related more closely to professional and academic requirements than to any student views about the 'ethics' of particular research methodologies). Furthermore, research carried out with fellow practitioners rather than with social work clients may be preferred by students, partly as a way of avoiding 'ethical' research dilemmas. So perhaps 'participatory' research remains an 'ideal' rather than a reality for these students? As noted earlier by Linda Nutt, the power imbalance remains, de facto, between the social worker and the client; and will surely remain during research unless definite steps are taken to shift it.

Macdonald and Macdonald (1995) however seem to be taking a slightly different line and challenging any apparent 'ideal' emphasis on 'participatory' research by pointing out that social workers do actually need to find out 'what works' for their clients. They thus emphasize an approach to research which involves testing out interventions so as develop 'evidence based' practice. Their view is that finding 'what works' is almost impossible, without rejecting what they call a 'take your pick' approach to social work intervention. In practical research terms this could mean assigning clients randomly to different interventions, collecting the 'evidence' and comparing the results (in an RCT). Macdonald and Macdonald (1995) appear to take an essentially 'ends justifies the means' approach by pointing out that most current social work interventions are not 'tested' anyway, and that not all clients receive the same service either. They ask: 'how ethical is it to operate a programme, with little rationale, and no inbuilt attempt to make sure we are not doing more harm than good?' (1995: 48).[8]

Developing complementary and alternative medicine (CAM) professions, such as medical herbalism, whose practitioners are becoming increasingly involved in research, may also, like Macdonald and Macdonald, emphasize the ethical necessity of using 'appropriate' forms of research, methodologically speaking. For some, this may mean an emphasis on randomized controlled trials or other experimental designs (Ernst, 1996) rather than qualitative research approaches which could emphasize 'holistic' approaches to research participants. However this may be disputed between practitioners of different persuasions or regulating bodies (Bell, L. et al., 1999; Stone, 2000). Stone's comments interestingly suggest an intertwining of issues around ethics and methodology in this CAM research context based on 'patient-centredness', in which 'the patient is an active participant in his or her healing process' (2000: 208):

There is no reason to assume that the autonomy-focussed ethics of Western, liberal democracies should automatically provide the theoretical under-pinnings of CAM any more than assuming that the empirical, rational scientific mode is the most appropriate way of establishing the efficacy of CAM therapies. As with research methodologies, so a wider array of ethical theories (such as care-based ethics, feminist ethics and narrative ethics) might need to be invoked in order to adequately capture the subtleties of the CAM relationship. (Stone, 2000: 208)

'Evidence-based' approaches to practitioner research might suggest favouring a movement away from 'listening to people (clients)' when conducting research as a practitioner-researcher. However, as dis-cussed above, Linda Nutt was very keen to continue to listen to research participants, although this led her in some senses to 'play down' her role as a practitioner (except in circumstances where she perceived that this practitioner role had to take precedence over that of 'researcher').

Conclusions

In this chapter we have used two examples from different parts of one practitioner-research 'spectrum', student practitioners and an experi-enced social worker taking a research degree, to explore various issues defined as relevant to practitioner research ethics: these include 'con-fidentiality', and 'negotiation' of the research process in 'professional' contexts. We have tried to demonstrate how these issues translated into actual research situations, including the issues around developing a set of ethical guidelines for student practitioner-researchers. We conclude that since practitioner-researchers have to negotiate a range of responsibilities, these in themselves could be seen to constitute an 'ethics of caring' (see Edwards and Mauthner in Chapter 1). Therefore decisions about emphasizing or 'playing down' the role of 'practi-tioner' may be an important part of such negotiation. As suggested in our final section, the broader methodological context of differing epistemological positions within practitioner-research is also relevant. For student-practitioners with multiple responsibilities towards aca-demic, professional and client audiences, ethical guidelines can help to emphasize the 'practitioner' role whilst allowing practical decisions about research to be taken by 'self-regulating' individuals as they interpret both the guidance and the actual research situation. For experienced practitioners, decisions about the presentation of self may be an overriding element in allowing research to be conducted 'ethically'.

Notes

[1] These competences will include aspects of professionally and theoretically based knowledge, skills (for example, in communication with clients/service users) and values (such as taking an anti-oppressive approach). Competences may be formally grouped into an overall framework relevant for professional education, as in the current Diploma in Social Work (2001), which details six core competences: 'Communicate and Engage', 'Promote and Enable', 'Assess and Plan', 'Intervene and Provide Services', 'Work in Organisations', 'Develop Professional Competence'. For a discussion of tensions between 'competence' and 'reflection' see Ashford et al. (1998).

[2] 'Self regulation' may be considered an important concept underlying aspects of reflexive practice 'competence' *within* specific professions and is reflected in professional education e.g. the current Diploma in Social Work. It is a separate issue from official 'regulation' and registration of some practitioners, as currently proposed by the Dept of Health. See also DOH Research Governance Framework for Health and Social Care (2001).

[3] The new General Social Care Council will in future also produce codes of practice for social care.

[4] For example, the Code states: '[Social workers] will not discriminate against clients, on the grounds of their origin, race, status, sex, sexual orientation, age, disability, beliefs, or contribution to society, they will not tolerate actions of colleagues or others which may be racist, sexist or otherwise discriminatory, nor will they deny those differences which will shape the nature of clients needs and will ensure any personal help is offered within an acceptable personal and cultural context'.

[5] Implications of tacit knowledge, as Altheide and Johnson (1994) explain, may be significant but also problematic.

[6] Student social workers must currently meet practice requirements for the Diploma in Social Work in six core competences as laid down currently by the Central Council for Education and Training in Social Work. (See footnote 1). (CCETSW was superceded by the General Social Care Council in 2001.)

[7] I produced the final set of guidelines during 1999 and acknowledge the support of colleagues Dr Oded Manor, who began the work, Ms Lesley Oppenheim and other colleagues working on the DipSW programmes at Middlesex University.

[8] 'Empiricism does not provide an escape route from "theory" to "truth" – observation is never theory free, it cannot be. However it offers a way of making explicit the theoretical underpinnings of our conceptualisations, hypotheses or assumptions about problems (and solutions), and the possibility of controlling for some of these influences when seeking to test their relative usefulness' (Macdonald and Macdonald 1995: 48).

References

Altheide, D.L. and Johnson, J.M. (1994) 'Criteria for assessing interpretive validity in qualitative research', in N.K. Denzin and Y.S. Lincoln (eds), *Handbook of Qualitative Research*. London: Sage.

Ashford, D., Blake, D., Knott, C., Platzer, H. and Snelling, J. (1998) 'Changing conceptions of reflective practice in social work, health and education: an institutional case study', *Journal of Interprofessional Care*, 12(1) Feb: 7–19.

Bell, L., Bell, C., Chevallier, A., McDermott, A. and Adams, R. (1999) 'Herbalism and Osteo-arthritis; a study investigating herbal treatment outcomes, patient and practitioner view-points'. Paper given at the *British Sociological Association Medical Sociology Conference*, York, September.

Biestek, F. (1961) *The Casework Relationship*. London: George Allen and Unwin.

Birch, M. and Miller, T. (2000) 'Inviting intimacy: the interview as therapeutic opportunity', *International Journey of Social Research Methodology*, 3(3): 189–202.

Boushel, M. (2000) 'What kind of people are we? "Race", anti-racism and social welfare research', *British Journal of Social Work*, 30: 71–89.

Bowling, A. (1997) *Research Methods in Health: Investigating Health and Health Services*. Buckingham: Open University Press.

Brannen, J. (1988) 'The study of sensitive subjects', *Sociological Review*, 36(3): 552–63.

British Association of Social Workers (BASW) (1996) *The Code of Ethics for Social Work*.

Edwards, R. (1993) *Mature Women Students: Separating or Connecting Family and Education*. London: Taylor and Francis.

Ernst, E. (1996) 'The ethics of complementary medicine', *Journal of Medical Ethics*, 22: 197–8.

Everitt, A. et al. (1992) *Applied Research for Better Practice*, British Association of Social Workers. London: Macmillan.

Ferard, M.L. and Hunnybun, N.K. (1962) *The Caseworker's Use of Relationships*. London: Tavistock.

Finch, J. (1984) ' "It's great to have someone to talk to": the ethics and politics of interviewing women', in C. Bell and H. Roberts (eds), *Social Researching: Politics, Problems, Practice*. London: Routledge and Kegan Paul.

Fuller, R. and Petch, A. (1995) *Practitioner Research – the Reflexive Social Worker*. Buckingham: Open University Press.

Gallagher, B., Creighton, S. and Gibbons, J. (1995) 'Ethical dilemmas in social research: no easy solutions', *British Journal of Social Work*, 25: 295–311.

Gomm, R. and Davies, C. (eds) (2000) *Using Evidence in Health and Social Care*. Sage and Open University.

Graham, H. (1984) 'Surveying through stories', in C. Bell and H. Roberts (eds), *Social Researching*. London: Routledge and Kegan Paul.

Gubrium, J. and Holstein, J. (1995) *The Active Interview*. Thousand Oaks, California: Sage.

Hammersley, M. and Atkinson, P. (1983) *Ethnography: Principles in Practice*. London: Tavistock.

Holland, R. (1999) 'Reflexivity', *Human Relations*, 52(4): 463–84.

Jordan, L., Bell, L., Bryman, K., Maxim, J. and Newman, C. (1998) 'Evaluating communicate: organisational issues and their relevance for clinical evaluation', *International Journal of Language and Communication Disorders*, 33: 60–5, Supplement.

Kendall, S. (1997) 'What do we mean by evidence? Implications for primary health care nursing', *Journal of Interprofessional Care*, 11(1): 23–34.

Langan, M. and Day, L. (1992) *Women, Oppression and Social Work: Issues in Anti-Discriminatory Practice*. London: Routledge.

Macdonald, G. and Macdonald, K. (1995) 'Ethical issues in social work research', in R. Hugman, and D. Smith, *Ethical Issues in Social Work*. London: Routledge.

Mauthner, M. (2000) 'Snippets and silences: ethics and reflexivity in narratives of sistering', *International Journal of Social Research Methodology*, 3(4): 287–306.

National Institute of Medical Herbalists (n.d.) *Code of Ethics. Code of Professional Practice.*

Oakley, A. (1981) 'Interviewing women: a contradiction in terms', in H. Roberts (ed.), *Doing Feminist Research.* London: Routledge and Kegan Paul.

Punch, M. (1994) 'Politics and ethics in qualitative research', in N.K. Denzin and Y.S. Lincoln (eds), *Handbook of Qualitative Research.* London: Sage.

Reed, J. and Proctor, S. (1993) *Nurse Education: a Reflective Approach.* Edward Arnold.

Robson, C. (1993) *Real World Research: a Resource for Social Scientists and Practitioner Researchers.* Oxford: Blackwell,

Rosenberg, W. and Donald, A. (1995) 'Evidence based medicine: an approach to clinical problem-solving', *British Medical Journal,* 310: 1122–6, April.

Royal College of Nursing of the United Kingdom (RCN) (1998) *Research Ethics: guidance for nurses involved in research or any investigative project involving human subjects.* Standards of care series.

Sackett, D., Rosenberg, W., Muir Gray, J., Haynes, R.B. and Richardson, W.S. (eds) (1996) 'Evidence-based medicine: what it is and what it isn't', *British Medical Journal,* 312: 71–2.

Sainsbury, E., Nixon, S. and Phillips, D. (1982) *Social Work in Focus: clients' and social workers' perceptions in long-term social work.* London: Routledge and Kegan Paul.

Schon, D. (1987) *Educating the Reflexive Practitioner: Towards a New Design for Teaching and Learning in the Professions.* San Francisco: Jossey Bass.

Schrock, R. (1991) 'Moral issues in nursing research', in D. Cormack (ed.), *The Research Process in Nursing.* Oxford: Blackwells.

Song, M. and Parker, D. (1995) 'Commonality, difference and the dynamics of disclosure in in-depth interviewing', *Sociology,* 29(2): 241–56.

Stone, J. (2000) 'Ethical issues in complementary and alternative medicine', *Complementary Therapies in Medicine,* 8: 207–13.

Thompson, N. (1997) *Anti-discriminatory practice.* British Association of Social Workers.

Tierney, A. (1995) 'The role of research ethics committees', *Nurse Researcher,* 3(1): 43–52.

Tsang, N.M. (1998) 'Re-examining reflection – a common issue of concern in social work, teacher and nursing education', *Journal of Interprofessional Care,* 12(1): 21–31.

UKCC (1992) *Code of Professional Conduct.*

Vass, A. (ed.) (1995) *Social Work Competences: Core Knowledge, Values and Skills.* London: Sage.

Wise, S. (1987) 'A framework for discussing ethical issues in feminist research: a review of the literature', in V. Griffiths et al. 'Writing feminist biography? Using life histories', *Studies in Sexual Politics,* 19: University of Manchester.

CHAPTER 5

ENCOURAGING PARTICIPATION: ETHICS AND RESPONSIBILITIES

Maxine Birch and Tina Miller

'Ethics is in origin the art of recommending to others the sacrifices required for co-operation with oneself' Bertrand Russell (1976).

Introduction

In many areas of social research the term 'participant' is used to describe the role undertaken by individuals invited to take part in a research project. The shift in terminology from research subject to research participant is reflected in academic professional discipline codes of conduct, such as the British Psychological Society (1996) and British Sociological Association (1993). In feminist qualitative research the term 'research participant' reflects many positive developments in how the researcher approaches, understands and maintains the research relationship. In this chapter we explore how this notion of participation coincided with our understanding of 'being good researchers' and forming 'good research relationships'. When we examined our experiences of encouraging research participation we found that a dissonance had occurred between the ideal of 'participation' presented in ethical codes of behaviour, our hopes of encouraging the research respondent to feel part of the process and what actually occurred during the research process itself. These experiences lead us to argue that there is a need for researchers to return to the concept of participation from a personal/political perspective and to nurture the very seeds of a feminist perspective. We also advocate that the doing of ethically responsible research requires the researcher to negotiate participation at the outset of a research project and be sensitive to the dimensions of participation that have been agreed – which may indeed be partial participation and which may shift.

We argue that two aspects of qualitative methodology, participant observation and longitudinal interviews construct a specific type of research relationship characterized by sharing personal and private

experiences over a long period of time. We have demonstrated elsewhere that this type of research relationship may involve acts of self
disclosure, where personal, private experiences are revealed to the
researcher in a relationship of closeness and trust (Birch and Miller,
2000). It is precisely the quality of such a relationship that can provide
access to the rich, deep data, that the qualitative researcher seeks. The
focus on the research relationship as a social relationship is indebted
to the many creative researchers in the development of a feminist
perspective during the 1980s and after. Feminists have identified
notions of friendship, rapport, interpretation, and power in the interview setting. From researchers such as Ann Oakley (1981), Janet Finch
(1984), Catherine Reissman (1987), Dorothy Smith (1987), Jane Ribbens
(1989), Margaret DeVault (1990) to Pam Cotterill (1992), we have
inherited a comprehensive examination of the research interview relationship. This accumulated knowledge illuminates the many components of the research relationship and highlights certain imperatives
to assess and guide research relationships. This knowledge in turn has
led to the emergence of a 'moral high ground' that guides the feminist
researcher towards 'good' quality research relationships (Price, 1996).
In planning and executing the first stages of our respective research
we found that we wished to position ourselves within this feminist
'moral high ground' and ensure 'good' relationships. For us, the
notion of participation embodies specific ideals of how the researcher
and researched should co-operate with each other in order to form a
'good', honest and reciprocal relationship. Within our research negotiations we used the term research 'participant' in order to create
reciprocal feminist research relationships. However, the ideal of fully
involving research respondents, for example by inviting comments on
our interpretations of the research data, was hard to maintain over the
different stages of the research process. We found that the research
ideals of participation that we embraced at the outset eventually came
into conflict with our personal goals of completing our projects and
fitting into the requirements of the academic world. This conflict led
us to desert the 'moral high ground' and re-interpret our earlier
understanding of what participation should involve.

When reflecting upon our experiences we found we both shared
feelings of guilt and worrying reminders of 'I should have done this'
and 'I promised that'. At the end of our projects we felt dissatisfied
that we had never fully achieved 'real' participation in the research
process. We felt that we had deserted our original ethical stance and
moved towards an instrumental position, where meeting academic
deadlines and obtaining a PhD became paramount. We had theoretically argued for, entered into and explicitly and/or implicitly promised 'participation' as a characteristic of our research relationships.
However, during our projects we found that we renegotiated our

interpretation of how participation could be achieved at different stages of the research. In this chapter we describe how the ideal of participation can be difficult to achieve in research relationships and we identify particular ethical concerns that can arise as a result when undertaking qualitative work. From this we develop research strategies that in the context of research practice can help to identify these ethical concerns. We argue that the need to provide spaces for all research participants to consider the ethical dimensions of the research and how to address them constitute an 'ethics of responsibility'. We can use this framework to challenge and change our research practices.

Why participation?

In order to embrace the complexity of understanding individuals and the social lives we construct and maintain, today's researcher is called upon to create reflexive and innovative research designs. As PhD students in the 1990s we inherited the reflexivity of feminism, the deconstruction of post-structuralism and the uncertainty of post-modernism. Our key influences at this time were: feminist reflexivity developed into an auto/biographical perspective (Ribbens, 1993; Stanley, 1990, 1992), the reflexive project of the self and constructing a gendered sense of self-identity (Giddens, 1991, 1992; Griffiths, 1995), the deconstruction of a postmodern self (Benhabib, 1992; Lather, 1991) and the growing awareness of narrative and stories in understanding lived experiences (Denzin, 1996; Frank, 1995; Josselson and Lieblich, 1997; Plummer, 1995). These influences enabled us to build a model of the individual as a reflexive, relational matrix of self-awareness and understanding. This model is illustrated in Benhabib's words, 'Identity does not refer to my potential for choice alone, but to the actuality of choices, namely to how I, as a finite, concrete, embodied individual, shape and fashion the circumstances of my birth and family, linguistic, cultural and gender identity into a coherent narrative that stands as my life's story . . . The question becomes: how does this finite embodied creature constitute into a coherent narrative those episodes of choice and limitation, agency and suffering, initiative and dependence?' (Benhabib, 1992: 161). In gathering coherent narratives or life stories from an individual, the researcher must acknowledge their own part as a co-producer in such stories (Corradi, 1991). And it is this recognition of the dynamic and constituent nature of the research encounter in which data is generated that necessitates the need for all participants to be visible in the research process.

The present challenges of postmodernist feminist research are to bring together the contradictions, previously held in many modernist perspectives, such as agency and structure, objectivity and subjectivity, distance and involvement in to the research relationship (Lather, 1991). Here participation is perceived to be a methodological resource to bring together dualities and recognize the plurality of realities. Patti Lather argues that research designs can be 'interactive, contextualised and humanly compelling, because they invite joint participation in the exploration of research issues' (1991: 52). An active research relationship then involves the exchange of ideas and understanding, and is a shared enterprise.

Participating in an ethical model of responsibility

Using the methodological strategies of participant observation and longitudinal interviews, we tried to explore the life stories of others while at the same time acknowledging the construction of our own coherent narratives as researchers. It is the reflexive analysis of personal research experiences that is central to the development of an ethical feminist model, which we propose here. This model is based on an 'ethics of responsibility' adapted and developed from the work of Margaret Urban Walker (1997). Walker proposes that an 'ethics of responsibility' provides an alternative framework for appreciating ethical dimensions against the 'ethics of care' present in some feminist debates. Walker argues that an ethics of care may unintentionally reinforce essentialist notions of being a woman whereas the assessment of responsibilities broadens our ethical awareness beyond gendered constructions (1997). The ethics of responsibility model involves identifying three levels of what Walker calls 'ethical narratives': the narratives which firstly present the individual's sense of moral identity, that is the presentation of a 'good self', secondly the narrative which seeks to maintain this ethical 'good self', when relating to others, and thirdly a recognition of narratives concerned with representing moral values dominantly held in the public sphere. Importantly, Walker argues that these three narrative layers constitute the *ethical components* of our life stories. For us it is the second level of ethical narrative, the self in relation to others that is essential in helping us to understand ethical issues in the research process. This is because it encompasses the dynamic connection between a sense of being good and upholding beliefs in public moral values. If researchers use this model of ethical responsibility to reflect on their research, they can begin to identify ethical narratives in the research process and related ethical concerns. For example, our feelings of guilt as our own research goals became more instrumental as we finished our PhDs could have been openly reflected upon and discussed at the time with those participating in our projects. But what expectations did those who participated in our projects have? What did participation mean to them? In order to explore this in more detail we discuss Walker's ethics of responsibility model (1997) in relation to our specific projects.

Maxine's examples arise from 'the therapy study' (Birch, 1996, 1998; Birch and Miller, 2000) and illustrate her experiences of trying to achieve joint participation in an ethnography, which attempted to develop an auto/biographical position in participant observation. The therapy study involved Maxine's membership in four therapy groups advertised and promoted in the context of alternative health. All the groups shared the explicit promise to enable members to discover and uncover dimensions of their sense of an inner self, which may have been hidden or masked as a result of the complexities of social life. Interviewing both the facilitators and other group members complemented data gathered from the researcher's membership of the groups. To maintain our focus in this chapter on the experiences of trying to achieve a participatory research style in participant observation, we direct the reader to other publications for further information on the project (Birch, 1996, 1998; Birch and Miller, 2000). In our discussion Maxine also draws on her study of the relationship between three urban friendship groups of young people and their smoking and non-smoking life style stories. She gathered these stories from interview settings and we explore them in relation to the model of ethical responsibility proposed here.

We also draw on two of Tina's studies to analyse research respondent's participation in the interview process. The first study explored take-up of antenatal care amongst Bangladeshi women living in southern Britain (Miller, 1995). This small-scale study employed an ethnographic approach involving Tina accessing and joining a language group established to teach English to Bangladeshi women. The second study documented women's experiences of transition to first-time motherhood (Miller, 1998, 2000a, 2000b). This was a longitudinal study. Both these projects illustrate the differing perceptions of participation that can co-exist in research. This focus prompts Tina to question whether 'participants' want to participate in every aspect of the research process and to consider the ethics of imposing a particular research relationship that is not sought. (For more details about these last two studies see Miller and Bell, Chapter 3.)

Developing an ethics of responsibility: tracing ethical narratives in field notes

During the 'therapy study' Maxine recorded her field notes in two sections: one page for the observed actions of others, 'the concrete record' and the other page for Maxine's personal reflections on the events that had occurred, 'the intuitive, feeling record'. Keeping two sections of field notes has been reported in ethnographic studies from the discovery of Malinowski's diaries (1967) to the retrospective analysis of the research relationship (Okely and Callaway, 1992). In the therapy study the concrete record provided the data for the analysis of storytelling that went on in the group. The 'intuitive, feeling record' provided the ethical narratives, which are analysed here. These ethical narratives were produced in relation to Maxine's sense of what is right and wrong in relation to others – the second level of ethical narrative identified in Walker's model (1997). It is these ethical narratives that present the ethical dimension in the research process. Throughout the intuitive, feeling record of the field notes questions were raised on what, how and why certain interactions had occurred and what, how and why certain interactions had not. When Maxine went into the field as a member of the alternative therapy groups she went equipped with the methodological term 'auto/biographical ethnography' adapted from the works of Jane Ribbens (1993) and Liz Stanley (1992, 1993). For Maxine this hyphenated connection of auto/biography appeared to represent the 'me and you' in the research process and so offered the potential to encourage joint participation as described previously in the work of Patti Lather (1991) and Tyler (1986). Tyler's case for a postmodern ethnography calls for the participation of all those involved in order to demonstrate the various realities that are encountered in the research process (1986). Maxine hoped that the methodological tool of auto/biography would enable her to explore the research relationship whilst engaged in the research process.

In the early stages of negotiating access to the alternative therapy groups Maxine found that the descriptive term 'auto/biography' gave her a tool which appeared sympathetic and conducive to the group's objective of discovering one's self. The facilitators of the groups warmed easily to the description of auto/biography as a methodological style. An unforeseen research 'bargain' occurred as the facilitators immediately detected a potential tool and wanted to participate in order to learn about this research style and use it to explore their work. However the explanation at this stage of negotiation did not explicitly state the more complex academic understanding of auto/biography where the hyphenated connection could be reinterpreted to mean the story of others. A particular example of how auto/biography was presented and interpreted differently is illustrated in the following extract from Maxine's corresponding pages of field notes:[1]

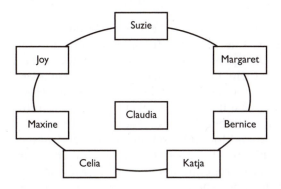

The group started with all the women introducing themselves. Summary of the round: Apart from Suzie we were all mothers, with Bernice and I being single parents. Five members worked in the alternative health fields with skills ranging from Astrology, Alexandra technique, Massage, Yoga, Acupuncture, Counselling. One woman was a psychologist and the other a secretary. We were all white. All of them had previous contact with the facilitator Claudia. During my turn to introduce myself I talked about my research, about autobiography and the other two groups involved. Claudia asked if the others were happy with this. All agreed but one.

I sat there in this candle lit room with all the other women looking at me. It was my time to explain my research role in the group. I felt quite uneasy. I tried to explain to the group how my research role would involve my own experiences in the group for the research. Had I deliberately underestimated how my research style would also be looking at the experiences of the group? I felt embarrassed to say. I could feel myself not saying everything. Too afraid that they would say no? After all the facilitator had agreed for my involvement to take place. Funny group they gave nothing away, they did not look pleased or interested. Slowly they went round most of them quietly agreeing this would be OK until . . . She said she was a psychologist and that she was pregnant. Firstly from her background she did not want to be the subject of any research! God she had said it, the truth! Secondly she did not know if she could commit herself to the group due to the baby.

When Maxine discovered that one member of the group was also an 'academic' she felt that her presentation of an auto/biographical methodology had not disguised the actuality that participation in this project would not be exactly as Maxine had suggested. Maxine would be collecting the stories of *others* more than telling her own story. After this initial introduction the woman never returned to the group and Maxine felt that her decision not to participate was based on knowing more about the potential research relationship than the others who had agreed to participate. Indeed, how ethical had it been for Maxine to 'disguise' the various interpretations of the term 'auto/biography'?

Maxine's field notes on her feelings subsequently record how her research role was never really discussed beyond this initial introduction in all the groups she attended. When Maxine was involved in the self-disclosure therapeutic activities as a group member she occasionally raised her role as a researcher in the group. However this felt uncomfortable, as if the research role took away the authentic claim of being a group member. Maxine experienced tensions being a participant observer and found herself unable to perform the two competing roles within the therapeutic activities practised in the groups. Outside of these therapeutic activities, when Maxine stopped being an active group member, she was able to concentrate on her research role once again and construct her field notes. In this way the field notes recorded the ethical narratives that arose from the two competing roles. The lack of reference to Maxine's research role was not the result of a planned strategy, but the way that being a member of the group evolved. The research role could re-emerge during breaks from the self-discovery activities undertaken. However, this felt like the research role being separated by a great sense of being 'real' in the different contexts of a therapy group member and a researcher. Maxine found that being a member of the group involved an ethical commitment to remain 'true' to her group membership. This may have been related to the precise character of the groups, where techniques of self-disclosure promoted this feeling of showing your 'real', 'true' self. Therefore the hyphenated connection in the textual representation of auto/biography began to symbolize the movement from being a 'Me' and sharing the present experiences of those being researched to being an 'I', the researcher who recorded stories about the other 'Me's. The two roles continued to provide an ethical tension, as the more private and intimate aspect of the researcher's experiences could remain hidden from the public account of the research process, the field notes, whereas the private and intimate aspects of others could become the data. Ironically then Maxine's own participation was only partial in this context when compared to the other participants. The term auto/biography hid the researcher's task to record the stories of others and these others may not have fully appreciated whose experiences formed the research.

Some researchers argue that the possibility of practising a feminist ethnography is continually evasive as 'equality with research subjects in the ethnographic approach masks a deeper, more dangerous form of exploitation' (Stacey, 1988: 22). The examples taken from Maxine's study could be seen to support this explanation of exploitation. On the other hand they illustrate the complexity of ethical issues. In order to develop an approach that embraces an ethics of responsibility as advocated by Walker (1997) the situational and trans-situational characteristics of ethical concerns in the field must be appreciated. The practice of ethnography is said to lead to a swamp, a 'murky quagmire' (Price, 1996) where you can never predict what issues become important. The boundaries of qualitative research concerned with narrative are constantly remapped and renegotiated as the process unfolds (Birch and Miller, 2000; Josselson, 1996). Therefore if we are to fully embrace feminist ideals of participation, the participants in the research must be included and invited to take part in this remaking and renegotiation.

In order for Maxine to meet an ethics of responsibility her research design should have identified *processes of participation*. For example, one strategy could be to increase the visibility of field notes and use them as an ethical research tool. Field notes from the other group members could complement the 'field notes' of the researcher. The field notes could have been shared and discussed, which would have raised the research role within the more immediate setting. Regular slots could be timetabled for 'ethical talk' so both the researcher and the participant disengage from the research topic and talk openly about the research process. In this way, ethical narratives could be produced jointly in the spirit of full participation. It would be this model of 'ethical talk sessions' or what Seyla Benhabib refers to as an 'open-ended moral conversation' (Benhabib, 1992: 9) that could promote the practice of joint participation. In this way the relativity of situational and trans-situational ethical concerns could be addressed by applying a regulatory procedure at all times. As Benhabib has noted, 'In ethics, the universalizability procedure, if it is understood as a reversing of perspectives and the willingness to reason from the other's (others') point of view, does not guarantee consent: it demonstrates the will and the readiness to seek understanding with the other to reach some reasonable agreement in an open-ended moral conversation' (Benhabib, 1992: 9). If this interpretation of a 'universalizability procedure' is taken into the research relationship, this means not only presenting the 'knowing' of the area being researched from joint participation, but also the understanding of the research relationship from each other's point of view.

Yet the call for an understanding of the research relationship from the perspectives of participants together with the researchers' own reflexive account of the research process, can pose further dilemmas. Whilst it is good research practice to reflect on and acknowledge the differing perspectives of all those involved it is also necessary to question how far those we gather data from actually want to participate. In her qualitative research on take-up of antenatal care amongst Bangladeshi women, Tina experienced difficulties accessing this largely hidden group (Miller, 1995). Eventually a small group of women were 'volunteered' into the research by a powerful gate-keeper (see Miller and Bell, Chapter 3). Although they could be argued to have 'participated' in the research that took place over several months, their participation was limited in a variety of respects. Even though Tina entered the research embracing feminist notions of reciprocity (see discussion of this in Mauthner, 2000), sensitivity and power sharing for example, the initial problems of access led to women participating in the study who would almost certainly not identify themselves as 'participants'. 'Reluctant respondents' would more accurately convey their perception of their role in the research.

This raises the ethical concern of how far participation in any fully participatory sense is actually desired by those we research and how far we may be imposing a particular relationship on those we seek to collect data from. Whilst it can be argued that we can and should operate within a feminist 'ethics of responsibility' this does not auto-matically mean that those whose lives we wish to research will share, or embrace, our vision. Any notion of 'open-ended moral conversa-tions' (Benhabib, 1992) or ethical talk sessions as suggested earlier would almost certainly have not been recognized and/or welcomed by the Bangladeshi women who Tina interviewed. Their perceptions of Tina were as an interviewer who was there to collect information. These perceptions persisted in spite of Tina's efforts to attend their language group, join in sewing activities and help with the crèche [helping organise the crèche had been part of the research bargain struck with the gate-keeper]. Eventually a number of the women agreed to be interviewed, some individually and some in a group, but Tina felt they participated *reluctantly*. It was also apparent that their expectations, as with many of the people we research, were that the process of being interviewed involved responding to a set of questions and that once the interview was over so too was their involvement in the research. Indeed, on reflection, it may be that the women finally agreed to be interviewed in order to bring to an end the research relationship that Tina had sought to establish. Tina had no further involvement or communications with the group once the data had been collected.

Learning from these experiences Tina included an end-of-study questionnaire in her longitudinal research on women's experiences of transition to first-time motherhood (Miller, 2000a, 2000b). The ration-ale behind this questionnaire was to ask the mothers about their experiences of *being* participants in the study. This piece of longitudi-nal research had involved the women participating in three interviews over the course of approximately a year during which they first became mothers. The longitudinal dimension of the research together with the particular focus on mothering and motherhood – an experi-ence that Tina shared with the women – led Tina to feel that fuller participation was possible in this study. Yet the longitudinal element only served to highlight the ways in which goals can shift as the research process unfolds. Tina found that whilst her feelings of gratitude to the women who agreed to participate remained throughout the study – and continue today – her notion of what participation should involve shifted as academic pressures took precedence. At the outset, Tina made two distinct commitments to the women who participated. The first was to return the tapes of the interviews to them once they had been fully transcribed, which she did. The second was to send them the findings of the study, and this commitment has recently been met. However, good intentions of sending accessible forms of the research and its findings were not realized. Shortage of time and work demands resulted in Tina sending them an unedited version of her 'Findings' chapter from her thesis. In practice, participation was limited to the data collection phase in both Tina's studies and the women who were interviewed/participated appeared to have had no other expectations. Again this prompts us to consider the ways in which we may be in danger of imposing research relationships, based on particular notions of participation, that are not sought by those whose lives we set out to study.

Similarly, in Maxine's therapy study, ethical concerns arose once she came to the analysis of her fieldwork data and the interview transcripts. In the later stages of analysis and writing up, Maxine's ethics of responsibility were transposed to the academic field where it was easier not to keep the research participants informed. The significance of the ethical research relationship was altered. It was in the later stages of the analysis and the final production of the report that Maxine chose not to maintain communication or participation with the research respondents. To meet Walker's model of an ethics of responsibility, Maxine should have maintained communication and invited joint interaction at all stages. But, as both Maxine and Tina found, attempting to achieve a feminist ethics of responsibility in combination with meeting institutional and academic demands can involve many tensions. Tina's research experiences lead her to both acknowledge the *ideal* of participation represented in Walker's ethics of responsibility model, and to question its applicability in all research settings. Tina would argue that whilst we should never enter into what could be seen as exploitative research relationships, we must be clear at the outset about the commitments we are making to those who take part. Our aim then should be to honour those commitments – which may not necessarily involve participants in anything more than the data collection phase. Further clarity is needed so that particular interpretations of 'participation' are transparent from the outset. This is not to say that researchers must slavishly adhere to prescriptive guidelines but rather they should be encouraged to reflect upon the dimensions of participation that they wish to invite and promote during their research. The aim then is not to prescribe one particular form of ethically responsible research but to acknowledge the need to embrace an ethics of responsibility in the context of diverse and shifting research settings and relationships.

Ethical terms and practical guidelines

We could then identify ethical narratives produced in the research process in order to develop an ethics of responsibility guide for researchers. This guide could be used to promote opportunities for ethical reflection by all involved and to acknowledge the co-production of certain elements – and the power of the researcher to produce the final research story. This guide could also provide the researcher with a choice of terms to indicate certain practical decisions and strategies followed. The qualitative research glossaries that are used in higher education need to be constantly updated. For example the term 'research covenant' can be used alongside the terms of research bargain and/or research contract. The 'research covenant' signifies an agreement by coming together rather than a contractual bond (Denzin and Lincoln, 1998b). In areas of feminist biographical and narrative qualitative research, this coming together would have to be negotiated and renegotiated throughout the research process.

In her research with young people and their 'smokey stories' (Birch, 2001) Maxine is still hoping to achieve ethical research strategies. She has used her role of 'being' a mother of teenage children and belonging to a local neighbourhood as a route to access three friendship groups of young people. Clearly, in this study, ethical concerns are immediately raised as she has access to a much broader framework of situated knowledge than usually available in an interview setting. Maxine is familiar with the areas where these young people live; she has heard other stories about their housing estates, and information about their families. This 'insider' knowledge places the information gathered in the interviews in a richer context. However, it also necessitates the need for a clearer guide for ethical responsibility. Being in the 'field', whether this is before or during the research implies a particular aspect of being, belonging and participating in social life, such as 'being a mother and belonging to a community' or 'being a member of a therapy group and belonging to a friendship network'. This suggests that when researching life experiences that are shared, the need to be more ethically reflexive becomes essential. The constant re-negotiation and re-mapping of ethical judgements is vital when researching familiar, intimate and sensitive areas of social life.

A further possible addition to the qualitative researcher's glossary is the term 'bricoleur' (Denzin and Lincoln, 1994: 3–4). The description of the qualitative researcher as a 'bricoleur', a professional do-it-yourself person, succinctly conveys the many dimensions of the qualitative researcher role. For example, the bricoleur could be encouraged to develop a set of close-knit practices specific to the 'situational and trans-situational' ethical problems we discuss here. We suggest that these close knit set of practices could then be linked to a framework of ethical responsibilities that demands close attention be paid to the process of participation. Yet an ethics of responsibility must also acknowledge the different interpretations of participation that are possible and within this the potential power of the researcher to impose on-going participation that is not sought or wanted.

To seek full and active participation from our research participants – throughout a project – demands that not only we, but also those whose lives we research, share a common interest and understanding of the research enterprise. For many this would require a fundamental shift in the ways in which research is conceptualized. Yet to not embrace the possibility of full participation may mean that particular positions become reinforced. If we constantly permit interpretations to depend upon the researcher and the academic community and ignore the participation of the 'research participant' we may be in danger of reinforcing particular ways of knowing and particular forms of knowledge. Why are 'we', as white, academic women being so secretive, especially when we are researching areas of familiar experiences? Are we fearful of being marginalized if we challenge existing academic conventions? Researchers must be encouraged to look for flexible research practices and different ways to produce the final research story. Against the demands for academic conformity, feminists must continue to seek to produce different writing strategies such as those argued for by Laurel Richardson (1990, 1992). Regrettably, it appears that the production of feminist research knowledge is still trapped in the structures of academic credibility as identified by Dorothy Smith in the 1980s (1987). In the context of increasing pressures from a hierarchical higher education system, where research funding and quality assurance define particular measures of academic prestige these debates have become even more important.

Conclusion

Our argument is for closer attention to be paid to the various dimensions of participation in qualitative research if participation is to represent more than just a semantic shift. We have acknowledged the need as feminist researchers to work from a position that is continually, ethically sensitive, to those whose lives we investigate, honouring research commitments made. We have discussed our difficulties in maintaining participation in our research projects and we have noted the need for research designs to identify the processes of participation. If research participants are willing (and able) to take a fully participatory role then researchers must develop different styles of writing that may challenge academic conventions but will reflect the *co*-production of research accounts. Such an enterprise depends upon the negotiation of an active research relationship where the exchange of ideas and understanding forms a rich seam that runs throughout the research. Our aim here then, is not to prescribe one particular form of ethically responsible research, but to insist on the need to embrace an ethics of responsibility in the context of diverse and shifting research settings and relationships.

Note

[1] All names have been changed.

References

Benhabib, S. (1992) *Situating the Self: Gender, Community and Postmodernism in Contemporary Ethics.* Cambridge: Polity Press.

Birch, M. (1996) 'The Goddess/God within: The construction of self identity through alternative health practices', in K. Flanagan and P. Jupp (eds), *Postmodernity, Sociology and Religion.* London: Macmillan.

Birch, M. (1998) 'Re/constructing research narratives: self and sociological identity in alternative settings', in J. Ribbens and R. Edwards (eds), *Feminist Dilemmas in Qualitative Research.* London: Sage.

Birch, M. and Miller, T.A. (2000) 'Inviting intimacy: the interview as 'therapeutic opportunity', *International Journal of Social Research Methodology, Theory and Practice,* 3(3): 189–202.

Birch, M. (2001) 'Smokey stories: an exploration of young people's narratives in the maintenance of smoking and non-smoking lifestyles'. Unpublished paper. School of Health and Social Welfare: Open University.

British Psychological Society (1996) *Code of Conduct, Ethical Principles and Guidelines.* Leicester.

British Sociological Association (1993) *Statement of Ethical Practice.* Mountjoy Research Centre: Durham.

Corradi, C. (1991) 'Text, context and individual meaning: rethinking life stories in a hermeneutic framework', *Discourse and Society,* 2(1): 105–18.

Cotterill, P. (1992) 'Interviewing women: issues of friendship, vulnerability and power', *Women's Studies International Forum,* 15(5/6): 593–606.

Denzin, N. (1996) *Interpretive Ethnography.* Thousand Oaks, CA: Sage.

Denzin, N.K. and Lincoln, Y.S. (eds) (1994) *Handbook of Qualitative Research.* Thousand Oaks, CA: Sage.

Denzin, N.K. and Lincoln, Y.S. (eds) (1998a) *Collecting and Interpreting Qualitative Materials.* Thousand Oaks, CA: Sage.

Denzin, N. and Lincoln, Y.S. (eds) (1998b) *The Landscape of Qualitative Research: Theories and Issues.* Thousand Oaks, CA: Sage.

DeVault, M. (1990) 'Talking and listening from women's standpoint: feminist strategies for interviewing and analysis', *Social Problems,* 37(1): 96–116.

Finch, J. (1984) ' "It's great to have someone to talk to": the ethics and politics of interviewing women', in C. Bell and H. Roberts (eds), *Social Researching: Politics, Problems, Practice.* London: Routledge and Kegan Paul.

Frank, A. (1995) *The Wounded Storyteller.* Chicago: The University of Chicago Press.

Giddens, A. (1991) *Modernity and Self-Identity.* Cambridge: Polity Press.

Giddens, A. (1992) *The Consequences of Modernity.* Cambridge: Polity Press.

Griffiths, M. (1995) *Feminisms and the Self. The Web of Identity.* London: Routledge.

Josselson, R. (ed.) (1996) *Ethics and Process in The Narrative Study of Lives.* Volume 4. Thousand Oaks, CA: Sage.

Josselson, R. and Lieblich, A. (eds) (1997) *The Narrative Study of Lives.* Vol. 5. Thousand Oaks, CA: Sage.

Lather, P. (1991) *Getting Smart.* London: Routledge.

Malinowski, B. (1967) *A Diary in the Strict Sense of the Term.* London: Routledge and Kegan Paul.

Mauthner, M. (2000) 'Snippets and silences: ethics and reflexivity in narratives of sistering', *International Journal of Social Research Methodology, Theory and Practice,* 3(4): 287–306.

Miller, T.A. (1995) 'Shifting boundaries: exploring the influence of cultural traditions and religious beliefs of Bangladeshi women on antenatal interactions', *Women's Studies International Forum,* 18(3): 299–309.

Miller, T.A. (1998) 'Shifting layers of professional, lay and personal narratives: longitudinal childbirth research', in R. Edwards and J. Ribbens (eds), *Feminist Dilemmas in Qualitative Research.* London: Sage.

Miller, T.A. (2000a) 'An exploration of first time motherhood: narratives of transition'. PhD dissertation, Warwick University.

Miller, T. (2000b) ' "Losing the plot". Narrative construction and longitudinal childbirth research', *Qualitative Health Research,* 10(3): 309–23.

Oakley, A. (1981) 'Interviewing women: a contradiction in terms', in H. Roberts (ed.), *Doing Feminist Research.* London: Routledge and Kegan Paul.

Okley, J. and Calloway, H. (eds) (1992) *Anthropology and Autobiography.* London: Routledge.

Plummer, K. (1995) *Telling Sexual Stories.* London: Routledge.

Price, J. (1996) 'Snakes in the swamp', in R. Josselson (ed.), *Ethics and Process in The Narrative Study of Lives.* Vol. 4. Thousand Oaks, CA: Sage.

Reissman, C.K. (1987) 'When gender is not enough: women interviewing women', *Gender and Society,* 1(2): 172–207.

Ribbens, J. (1989) 'Interviewing: an "unnatural situation"?', *Women's Studies International Forum,* 12(6): 579–92.

Ribbens, J. (1993) ' "Fact or Fictions?" Aspects of the use of autobiography written in under-graduate sociology', *Sociology*, 27(1): 81–92.

Richardson, L. (1990) *Writing Strategies: Reaching diverse audiences*. Newbury Park, CA: Sage.

Richardson, L. (1992) 'The consequences of poetic representation: Writing the other, rewriting the self', in C. Ellis and M.G. Flaherty (eds), *Investigating Subjectivity: Research on Lived Experience*. Newbury Park, CA: Sage.

Smith, D. (1987) *The Everyday World as Problematic: A Feminist Sociology*. Milton Keynes: Open University Press.

Stacey, J. (1988) 'Can there be a feminist ethnography?', *Women's Studies International Journal*, 11(21): 227.

Stanley, L. (ed.) (1990) *Feminist Praxis. Research, Theory and Epistemology in Feminist Sociology*. London: Routledge.

Stanley, L. (1992) *The Auto/biographical 'I': The Theory and Practice of Feminist Auto/biography*. Manchester: Manchester University Press.

Stanley, L. (1993) 'On auto/biography in Sociology', *Sociology*, 27(1): 41–52.

Tyler, S.A. (1986) 'Postmodern Ethnography', in J. Gifford and G.E. Marans (eds), *Writing Culture: The Poetics and Politics of Ethnography*. Berkley: University of California Press.

Walker, M. Urban (1997) 'Picking up pieces lives stories and integrity', in D. Tietjens Meyers (ed.), *Feminists Rethink the Self*. London: HarperCollins.

CHAPTER 6

'DOING RAPPORT' AND THE ETHICS OF 'FAKING FRIENDSHIP'

Jean Duncombe and Julie Jessop

... the irony I now perceive is that [the feminist] ethnographic method exposes subjects to far greater danger and exploitation than do more positivist, abstract, and "masculinist" research methods. The greater the intimacy, the apparent mutuality of the researcher/re-searched relationship, the greater is the danger. (from 'Can There Be a Feminist Ethnography?' Stacey, 1988: 21)

Introduction

This chapter centres on discussion of some of the ethical, feminist, emotional, and methodological issues associated with how rapport is gained, maintained, and 'used' in qualitative interviews. Our interest in rapport was stimulated by our own research,[1] where we found that in order to persuade some of our women interviewees[2] to talk freely, we needed consciously to exercise our interviewing skills in '*doing* rapport' with – or rather *to* – them. Uncomfortably, we came to realize that even feminist interviewing could sometimes be viewed as a kind of *job* where, at the heart of our outwardly friendly interviews, lay the instrumental purpose of persuading interviewees to provide us with data for our research, and also (hopefully) for our future careers.

Our discomfort in our research interviews has broader analogies and deeper roots. For example, there are strong parallels between 'doing rapport' and the kinds of 'emotion work' that women, in particular, perform in their relationships by simulating empathy to make others feel good (Hochschild, 1983). Hochschild has argued that the spread of jobs where women are paid to simulate empathy represents the 'commercialisation' of human feeling, and those who do such work run the risk of feeling, and indeed actually *becoming*, 'phoney' and 'inauthentic' (Hochschild, 1983). Seen in this light, feelings of 'insincerity' which we sometimes experience as interviewers can be linked to the pressures of commercialisation in the 'job' of qualitative interviewing; even within feminist research.

An obvious starting point for a discussion of ethical issues associated with rapport is the early seminal article by Ann Oakley, which
has played a large part in opening up feminist discussion of this
'commonly used but ill-defined term' (Oakley, 1981: 35). Oakley criticized the model of 'rapport' advocated in methods textbooks for being
instrumental, hierarchical and non-reciprocal, qualities she characterized as would-be 'professional' and 'scientific', and basically mas-
culine. By aiming to suppress the role of gender and individual
personality in interview relationships, this model failed to engage
with major feminist and ethical issues. As an alternative, Oakley
advanced the now familiar argument that feminist researchers and
their women subjects participate as 'insiders' in the same culture,
where the 'minimal' social distance between them offers the basis for
an emotionally empathetic, egalitarian and reciprocal rapport. However, she warned that the closer rapport that permits the feminist
researcher to gain a deeper understanding of women's intimate lives
and feelings also brings greater ethical problems:

> 'Frequently researchers . . . establish rapport not as scientists but as human
> beings; yet they proceed to use this humanistically-gained knowledge for
> scientific ends, usually without the informants' knowledge' (Sjoberg and
> Nett, 1968: 215–16). These ethical dilemmas are greatest where there is least
> social distance between the interviewer and interviewee. Where both share
> the same gender socialisation and critical life experiences, social distance
> can be minimal . . . (from 'Interviewing Women: A Contradiction in Terms',
> Oakley, 1981: 55)

Somewhat ironically, Oakley has recently criticized feminist propo-
nents of qualitative methodology, on the grounds that their eagerness
to claim 'preferentially to own the qualitative method' has become
part of their own 'professionalising agenda' within academia (Oakley,
1998: 716). However, we would suggest that this criticism distracts
attention from two important but rather different trends, the first of
which has taken place largely outside feminism. We believe that the
expansion of 'consumer research' and various other interviewing jobs
both in commerce and government, has highlighted the value of
research methods which persuade interviewees to disclose their more
private and 'genuine' thoughts. As a result of which, the ability to 'do
rapport' by 'faking friendship' in relatively less-structured[3] qualitative
interviews has become a set of 'professional' and 'marketable skills',
and generally with a training sanitised of any concern with broader
ethical issues. In order to tap into wider debates, we would suggest
that the skills of 'doing rapport' have become commodified, with little
discussion of the function of rapport in 'agenda setting' and 'the
management of consent' in the interview situation – terms used by

Lukes to describe the hidden use of power in relationships (Komter, 1989; Lukes, 1974).

The second trend has been within feminism (although not exclusively), where the earlier, relatively uncritical acceptance of feminist claims for a special rapport between women has been challenged by a much more sceptical debate concerning the limits and ethical problems of 'feminist' qualitative research methods (see Edwards and Mauthner, Chapter 1).

These broad trends will now be outlined and examples from our own research will be drawn upon to illustrate and explore some of the ethical dilemmas associated with the concept and practice of rapport. We hope to convey how ethical problems emerge, overlap, and change unpredictably during interviews, and also to indicate how our awareness of these ethical dilemmas has changed as our 'careers' have developed from interviewing on behalf of other researchers, to interviewing for 'our own' research.

The commodification of rapport: 'agenda setting' and 'the management of consent'

We have suggested that there has been a trend towards the professionalisation, or more accurately, the commercialisation or 'commodification', of the skills of 'doing rapport' in less-structured qualitative interviews. We now explore in more detail what we mean, and how this trend differs from the 'would-be professionalism' criticised by Oakley. Nevertheless, both these trends are alike in their neglect of the broader ethical issues integral to the inequalities of power in the interviewing process. Chief among these issues in relation to rapport is the 'management of consent'.

The most important difference in approach between the two models of rapport that we have discussed so far, is well summarized in the following description of what is involved:

> Rather than trying to expunge the personality of the interviewer and to standardise interviews, this [more personalised] approach demands that interviewers should *manage* their appearance, behaviour and self-presentation in such a way as to build rapport and trust with each individual respondent. [our emphasis] (O'Connell Davidson and Layder, 1994: 122–3)

There are close parallels here with Hochschild's discussion of the 'management of emotion' (Hochschild, 1983), as a passage from another methods text makes clear:

> *Rapport is tantamount to trust* [our emphasis], and trust is the foundation for acquiring the fullest, most accurate disclosure a respondent is able to make . . . When you are warm and caring, you promote rapport, you make yourself appealing to talk to, and, not least, you communicate to your respondents, 'I see you as a human being with interests, experience, and needs beyond those I tap for my own purposes' . . . In an effective interview, both researcher and respondent feel good, rewarded and satisfied by the process and the outcomes. The warm and caring researcher is on the way to achieving such effectiveness. (Glesne and Peshkin, 1992: 79, 87, quoted in O'Connell Davidson and Layder, 1994: 123)

We would argue that, in equating the process of 'doing rapport' with trust, and failing to question the insincerity of 'faking friendship', this passage exhibits a disturbing ethical naivety.

In order to achieve good rapport, however, interviewers are sometimes advised to adopt a special kind of naivety (Kvale, 1992), or what Glaser and Strauss (1967) characterise as a pretence awareness, where they convey overall ignorance about what interviewees say, whilst at the same time promoting rapport by giving the occasional knowing glance. Interviewers also learn that they should consciously dress and present themselves in a way that sends the correct messages to the interviewee. That is, they must seat themselves not too far away but not too near; maintain a pleasant, encouraging half-smile and a lively (but not too lively) interest. They should keep eye contact, speak in a friendly tone, never challenge, and avoid inappropriate expressions of surprise or disapproval; and practice the art of the encouraging but 'non-directive "um" '. If this is 'friendship', then it is a very detached form of it.

The development of techniques for 'doing rapport' has been reinforced by the adoption of counselling skills and language into the repertoire of the qualitative interviewer: 'Rogers's writings on therapeutic interviews have been a source of inspiration for the development of qualitative interviewing for research purposes' (Kvale, 1992: 24). Writings about counselling stress the need to minimize social distance and establish rapport and trust, by projecting an air of genuineness and empathy with the client. Counselling interviewers are trained to listen to 'what is said between the lines' as well as to the 'explicit description of meanings . . . The interviewer may seek to formulate the "implicit message", "send it back" to the subject, and obtain an immediate confirmation or disconfirmation of the interviewer's interpretation of what the interviewee is saying . . .' (Kvale, 1992: 32). Apart from this process of 'reflection', training in counselling discusses the use of pauses and how to be comfortable with (the 'sound' of) silences.

The skills of doing rapport also supposedly include the ability to draw boundaries around the range of subject matter and to limit the emotional depth of the interview; this is the 'purpose' in the apparently informal 'conversation with a purpose'. Kvale, for example, employs a mining metaphor to distinguish between 'qualitative research' interviews whose aim is to gather knowledge, and 'therapeutic interviews' that attempt to change subjects' lives: 'knowledge is understood as buried metal and the interviewer is the miner . . . The interviewer researcher strips the surface of conscious experiences . . . the therapeutic interviewer mines the deeper unconscious layers' (1992: 3).

This process of qualitative interviewing is generally seen as benign, leading the interviewee to valuable personal insights and enabling the researcher to contribute to a wider understanding of individual's lives and problems. Indeed this is the image of interviewing cherished by most qualitative researchers. However, the goals and potential outcomes of the interview are not the sole ethical issue to be considered. If interviewees are persuaded to participate in the interview by the researcher's show of empathy and the rapport achieved in conversation, how far can they be said to have given their 'informed consent' to make the disclosures that emerge during the interview?

It is clearly impossible for interviewees to give their *fully informed* consent at the outset of an essentially exploratory qualitative interview whose direction and potential revelations cannot be anticipated (Wise, 1987). Some researchers have suggested that consent requires an ongoing process of discussion, reflection, and re-negotiation of trust throughout the interview. However, as Kvale (1992: 115) has pointed out, this approach depends on unrealistic assumptions of equality and 'rationalism' in research relationships, particularly where the interviewee may not share the interviewer's goals. We would also suggest that such *continual* intervention would inhibit the development of rapport and give the interviewer too intrusive a 'voice' in the construction of the interview dialogue. Under commercial (or professional) pressure to obtain results, there is a danger that, rather than engage in such complex negotiations which might entail the risk of refusal, interviewers will find it more convenient to rely on their skills in 'doing rapport' to persuade interviewees to disclose the information they seek.

Unfortunately, the process of 'doing rapport' may lead the interviewer into some of the serious ethical and emotional difficulties that can develop unanticipated during the interview. For example, as Kvale warns, there is a danger that 'close personal rapport . . . may lead to the research interview moving into a quasi-therapeutic interview', and indeed 'some individuals may [deliberately] turn the interview into therapy', although Kvale also confidently claims: 'The interviewer feels when a topic is too emotional to pursue in the interview' (1992: 149, 155). However, in practice even skilled interviewers may find it difficult to draw neat boundaries around 'rapport', 'friendship' and 'intimacy', in order to avoid the depths of 'counselling' and 'therapy' (Birch and Miller, 2000). With deeper rapport, interviewees become more likely to explore their more intimate experiences and emotions. Yet they also become more likely to discover and disclose experiences and feelings which, upon reflection, they would have preferred to keep private from others (Finch, 1984; Oakley, 1981; Stacey, 1988), or not to acknowledge even to themselves. Indeed, by doing rapport 'too effectively' interviewers run the risk of breaching the interviewees' 'right *not* to know' their own innermost thoughts (Duncombe and Marsden, 1996; Larossa et al., 1981).

Ethical issues must inevitably arise where, increasingly, relatively unsuspecting interviewees are confronted by qualitative interviewers who are armed with a battery of skills in 'doing rapport' in interview relationships in order to achieve disclosure. In effect, by 'doing rapport' the interviewer 'sets the agenda' of the encounter and 'manages the consent' of the interviewee. This can work to close down or obscure any opportunities for the interviewee to challenge part or the whole of the interviewing process because this would appear a breach of the interviewer's ('faked') friendship. Under these circumstances, rapport is *not* 'tantamount to trust'. Instead, *'doing rapport'* becomes the ethically dubious substitute for more open negotiation of the interviewee's fully informed consent to participate in the interviewing process (see Birch and Miller, Chapter 5, and Miller and Bell, Chapter 3).

The limitations of woman to woman rapport

As Hey (2000) points out, the literature on 'doing rapport' often conveys the curious impression that interviewers (and counsellors) are being trained to do through artifice what most women supposedly do 'naturally' and 'spontaneously' as a consequence of their gendered subordination and socialisation: for example, expressing empathy and tuning in to the moods of others (Miller, 1986); doing 'emotion work' to make others feel good (Hochschild, 1983); seeking communication through 'rapport talk' (Tannen, 1991); and listening to, and understanding, what remains unsaid 'between the lines' (Devault, 1990) (although see Duncombe and Marsden, 1998). However, this somewhat over-generalized picture is becoming increasingly challenged by a number of feminist researchers in differing ways. Significantly, rather than explore how to 'do rapport' by 'faking friendship', some researchers are focusing on the conditions and ethical problems where rapport does *not* occur because the social and emotional distance between researcher and interviewee proves too great (see Hey, 2000).

This shift in emphasis can be seen as a result of wider feminist debates centred around the role of research (see Gillies and Alldred, Chapter 2). Initially, through disagreement about their goals and approaches, feminist researchers encountered dilemmas concerning the kinds of 'rapport' and 'openness' to be negotiated in the research relationship. Such dilemmas have worked to highlight the tensions between achieving an openness that enables women to speak 'in their real voices' (Ribbens, 1998: 17) and an 'openness to complete trans-formation . . . [that] lays the groundwork for friendship, shared struggle, and identity change' (Reinharz, 1992: 68). All qualitative interviewers inevitably play a part in the construction of the inter-view, yet it seems to us that the explicit goal of transformation impliesa more active analytical and interventionist role for the femin-ist researcher, whose voice may come to 'overlay' that of her subject. In fact, McRobbie (1982) doubts whether feminist researchers have either the capacity or the right to attempt to transform their subjects' lives.

Even in research with the more limited goal of understanding women's lives, differences of power arise almost inevitably from the researcher's ability to shape the interview 'dialogue' and to put together her version of the subject's lived reality, which, however, the subject herself may reject (Stacey, 1990; Wise, 1987). In addition, Wise (1987) and Phoenix (1994) have doubted whether shared womanhood can bridge differences of social class, ethnicity, sexual orientation and so on. Indeed, other feminists have pointed out that failures of empa-thy and rapport in the course of researching power may be evidence of important differences of perspective that need to be explored and defined rather than negotiated away (Cain, 1990; Smart, 1984).

Similar issues concerning rapport arise where researchers attempt to negotiate with interviewees the subsequent production of reports, data analysis and publication. Ideally, it is sometimes suggested, consent should be renegotiated at each stage (Kelly, 1988; Luff, 1999; Stacey, 1990). Yet some feminists argue that such negotiations are merely attempts to enlist interviewees' help in their own 'objectifica-tion' (Cain, 1990), since even the feminist (sociological) researcher must inevitably control the analysis (Ramazanoglu, 1989; see also Doucet and Mauthner, Chapter 7).

A consequence of these various differences between researchers and interviewees is that rapport in actual interviews may be less encompassing than the 'feminist ideal' outlined above. For example, when Luff interviewed potentially anti-feminist women from a pow-erful 'moral lobby', she sometimes experienced the expected lack of empathy, yet she was also surprised to feel what she described as 'moments of rapport' with women she expected to dislike (Luff, 1999). She stresses that feminist interviewers should reflect on both what is going on *but also how they feel about such moments*, as evidence of how aspects of women researchers' 'fractured' subjectivities and identities may sometimes mirror those of interviewees but, equally importantly, sometimes clash (Harding, 1987: 8). However, in describing her own feelings, Luff confesses:

> Listening to views, nodding or saying simple 'ums' or 'I see', to views that you strongly disagree with or, ordinarily, would strive to challenge, may be true to a methodology that aims to listen seriously to the views and experiences of others, but can feel personally very difficult and lead to questioning of the whole research agenda. (Luff, 1999: 698)

Luff worried that simulated friendliness might appear to support views irredeemably opposed to her own feminist beliefs. In practice, she found she could 'do rapport' (as we have called it) in relationships where she felt no empathy, but she guiltily suspected that her research was semi-covert. Her interviews with 'powerful' women offer a useful reminder that the balance of power is not always tilted mainly in the interviewer's favour. For example, after interviewing lone fathers, McKee and O'Brien (1983) have commented on men's tendency to take control, and how as women they had to assume a 'professional' asexual social distance in order to discourage unwanted male advances (McKee and O'Brien, 1983).

The above outlines the two trends we identified earlier: the 'commodification' of the skills of 'doing rapport', and feminist discussions of the limitations of what might be called the 'ideal feminist research relationship'. Luff's description in particular echoes our own ethical dilemmas as researchers, and we now explore our own research experiences in more detail.

Our own research experience of ethical problems with rapport

With hindsight, our own early attitudes to research were influenced by 'feminist' expectations that rapport would be easily achieved with women interviewees, but also (via graduate methodology training) by the 'professional' literature on 'doing rapport'. From both perspectives, rapport appeared ethically unproblematic and we pictured a 'good interview' as a reciprocal exchange, where our (genuine or simulated) expressions of empathy would ensure that interviewees would willingly make intimate disclosures. We were therefore unprepared for the disjunctures between these expectations and the ethical and emotional dilemmas that we experienced in practice – the feeling that we were intruding or even inflicting pain, or the way that pressures to collect data for our employers or our own research sometimes clashed with our sense of ethics.

Initially we were keen to establish ourselves as good interviewers, so although we often empathetically 'heard' our subjects' reluctance to be interviewed, we also felt (like salespersons) that to do our *jobs* properly we must deploy all the charm we could muster to get ourselves through the door so we could ask our questions. But once inside, to gain a 'good interview' we would have to work harder at doing rapport to get our interviewees to 'open up' more fully. However, we were unprepared to discover how widely many of these encounters could vary, or to experience the complexity of our personal reactions to doing rapport.

Hardly surprisingly, we found it more difficult to achieve rapport where we did not spontaneously feel empathy with our interviewees. For example, in an early study of Youth Training Schemes (YTS), Jean felt she established a 'genuine', if shallow, rapport with the YTS trainees and with the more conscientious employers who took training seriously, because she was 'on their side'. But with the more exploitative employers and trainers (who provided neither jobs nor training), she knew she was faking rapport to 'betray' them into revealing their double standards; and sometimes whilst smiling at them she also smiled to herself, thinking: 'What a revealing quote'. However, in analogous situations, Julie felt uncomfortable and personally compromised when she found that, in order to gain a 'good' interview, it seemed necessary to smile, nod, and appear to collude with views she strongly opposed.

In later research on household finances, Jean disagreed profoundly with the would-be 'scientific' detachment adopted by her employer and colleagues. Yet she discovered that establishing close rapport could bring disclosures that were outside the scope of the research and occasionally beyond her capacity to handle. For example, one aggrieved wife showed Jean the knife she said she planned to use to kill her husband, whom she described as a confidence trickster who had deceived her. Another wife confided that, despite an injunction against her pathologically violent husband, she still allowed him back into the house to sleep with her, unknown to her children, or to the police and social services who were trying to protect her and her family. 'Doing rapport' had gained Jean the confidences of 'friendship', yet she felt bound by the ethics of confidentiality not to call on others to intervene. More minor dilemmas arose where interviewees asked Jean to switch off the tape, inviting her collusion in concealing what they had to say from 'her boss' and 'the outside world', but setting Jean the temptation still to use the material.

In Julie's first interview as a paid research officer, she too was confronted with ethical dilemmas resulting from the 'over effective-ness' of her attempts at doing rapport. Her interviewee was a man whose wife had recently left him after 22 years, and he immediately protested that he did not know why he had agreed to participate because he did not feel comfortable in talking about his feelings. Nevertheless, prompted by her training and the desire to establish herself as an interviewer, Julie tried all the harder to put him at his ease, smiling, empathizing, and stressing that participation was vol-untary. Eventually, he was persuaded to reveal experiences from 20 years before that he had never even told his wife – the disclosure of which was emotionally upsetting and resulted in tears. Although Julie had alerted him to the fact that she was not a counsellor, she felt she had betrayed him into revealing more of his feelings than he would have wished, and more than she could handle (although after agree-ing to further interviews, he felt he had been helped). Overall, Julie recognized that her reactions were a complex mixture of guilt and sympathy for her interviewee, and worries over the power her tech-nique had given her, but nevertheless edged with a sense of satisfac-tion that she had gained a level of self-disclosure her employer would welcome.

As contract researchers, both Julie and Jean sometimes felt resent-ful and even possessive that the hard-won insights from their inter-views might then be appropriated by their employers and misinterpreted, misused or even discarded. Julie, in particular, felt she knew which 'good quotes' her employer would take up, but regretted how much of the deeply emotional content the employer would then regard as outside the remit of 'her' research. Both Julie and Jean felt there was inevitably loss or distortion when someone else attempted to analyse data abstracted from the emotional context of the rapport through which it had been generated. (There are echoes here of debates concerning attempts to archive qualitative data for re-analysis; see Mauthner et al., 1998.)

The differences accruing to specific interviewer positions were emphasized for Julie when she realized how, as a paid research assistant, her sense of 'doing a job' had relieved her from taking full responsibility when interviewees were upset by what she regarded as 'her employer's' research. Once conducting her own research, how-ever, she felt personally responsible, and consequently tended to steer interviewees away from potentially sensitive areas and to stop the interview at signs of distress, although she was then faced with the fact that her interviews might not achieve the degree of emotional disclosure that characterised the 'good interview'.

Ethical problems also arose in Jean's attempt to explore the 'inte-rior' of marriage by probing the disagreements and 'secrets' that couples keep from the outside world, and sometimes from one another and even themselves. Fully informed consent could not be negotiated in advance, but Jean hoped that by maintaining good rapport, interviewees would feel comfortable enough to participate. However, she later recognized that by using rapport in this way, she was disguising rather than solving the ethical problems that remained integral to her research.

Such problems were less pressing where Jean found it more diffi-cult to establish good rapport: some working-class husbands, in par-ticular, were reluctant to discuss their emotions, and their wives in turn seemed to fear their husbands would condemn them for any disclosure of 'marital secrets'. After keeping a child in the room to inhibit the development of rapport, one working-class mother con-cluded, almost triumphantly: 'There, I don't suppose you found out much, did you!' However, there was an illuminating moment of rapport in an otherwise sticky interview with another working-class woman, when she discovered that Jean (like herself) had suffered post-natal depression and she trusted Jean enough to become more open and vulnerable, although social distance returned when the discussion moved to other areas.

The value of shared experience in promoting rapport was more evident to Jean in interviews with liberal middle-class women whose tastes and lives seemed closer to her own. These interviews became enjoyable conversations, where intimate emotional disclosures came so easily that the boundaries between research and friendship seemed to blur. Yet Jean came to realize that again such 'over easy' rapport entailed pitfalls. For example, when interviewees said: 'You know what I mean', she tended to reply: 'I know', partly deliberately to build rapport but also intuitively because she felt she genuinely *did* know. Only on listening to the tapes later did she realize how 'reading between the lines' brought the risk that she might project her own understanding onto the interviewees' relationships.

Such 'over rapport' sometimes created more obvious ethical (and methodological and feminist) problems in joint interviews where cou-ples who were nursing grievances against one another were still comfortable, or aggrieved, enough to argue in Jean's presence. Some wives invited Jean to ally herself with them in condemning their husbands, who naturally then became hostile and reluctant to partici-pate. With such interviews Jean experienced very mixed feelings: satisfaction in capturing such revealing data on tape, yet (particularly on re-hearing the tapes) guilt that her presence might have fuelled conflicts she should have tried to smooth over or silence.

More subtly, Jean also began to worry that probing about love and intimacy might disturb relationships where couples (usually wives) had 'worked hard' emotionally to achieve a balance. For example, whenever Jean asked one wife about her husband's views, the wife began by saying, 'We think . . .' but then hesitated and switched to, 'Well, *I* think', until she reluctantly began to realize during the interview how little her husband ever disclosed to her. Similarly, in response to a question on displays of affection, she began by saying, 'Oh yes, we like to cuddle . . .', but then she corrected herself as she realized she was always the initiator, 'Well, *I* like to cuddle', adding thoughtfully, 'I'd never thought of that before'. Although the interviews ended with Jean engaging in 'repair work' to re-affirm that such couple relationships were 'all right, really', she could not dispel the thought that some couples or individuals might be betrayed by the rapport that she had established into learning too much about the imbalances of affection and power in their relationships.

The fact that interviews restricted to one visit might leave interviewees with unresolved pain, was brought home to Jean when some time after one interview she encountered a woman who had cried bitterly about intimate events in her personal life. Yet although they came face to face and she started visibly, obviously recognizing Jean, the interviewee walked past without a nod, perhaps now feeling that she had revealed too much of herself and recognizing that Jean was not, after all, a 'friend'.

Indeed, for both of us, later chance encounters with former interview subjects provided illuminating insights into how far there had been a blurring of boundaries between the temporary 'faked friendship' that we had induced by doing rapport, and 'real' friendship characterised by emotional empathy and continuity over time. For example, in repeated interviews with one subject, Julie felt a lot of effort was required in order to 'do her job' and establish rapport. However she persevered over several months and eventually gained sufficient trust for the interviewee to disclose incidents and emotions that were extremely painful to her. Yet the disparity of this relationship (from Julie's perspective) was revealed soon after, when this participant rang Julie at home to suggest meeting up for coffee. Although Julie chatted politely and talked about how the woman was now feeling, she felt she did not 'have time' to meet; she had 'done her job' in relation to that particular piece of research, and she was now too busy cultivating new 'friends' on the next research project.

Jean had a similar experience when someone whom she did not immediately recognize rushed over and embraced her in the street, and began chatting in a most friendly way about Jean's family and job. It took Jean several minutes to realize who this was, and she was left feeling slightly affronted by the 'assumption of familiarity' that was evident. Jean remembered that the interview (two years earlier) had been difficult, with little real rapport or 'reward' so that, in an effort to put the interviewee at her ease, she had disclosed more about herself than usual. In effect, she had begun to engage in what was supposed to be the behaviour of a 'real' friend, although now, at a distance from the interview, it no longer seemed appropriate to make the effort of expressing a friendship she did not feel.

This kind of blurring of boundaries between real and faked friendship seems more likely to occur in research where the interviewing process involves repeated visits. For example, Julie interviewed one woman five times over a ten-month period after her husband and friends had abandoned her, and listened empathetically to experiences that they sometimes had in common. In the last interview, when Julie asked her what she had gained from the research, she replied, 'Well, apart from anything else, I've made a friend'. However, this claim only brought home to Julie the falseness of the situation where the interviewee did not recognize how Julie's 'faking of friendship' had been part of her job. Julie's strong personal discomfort was later compounded when she could not immediately recall the interviewee's name when they met in the street. This, and similar experiences, in which it becomes apparent that a 'role' is being played, highlights the falsity of interview 'friendships' and leads to reflection on how interviewees themselves may be projecting a 'self' that is specific to the situation.

These later encounters with former interviewees offer intriguing insights about our different individual understandings of the unspoken interview 'contract', that is, how much of 'ourselves' we were prepared to give by way of 'doing rapport', and what we expected our interviewees to give us in return. In some interviews, Jean felt uncomfortable because her participants could feel that her research on intimacy might be intrusive and potentially exploitative; yet at the same time she wondered how far her interviewees might be acting a part to conceal their 'real' selves, as she felt that she herself was doing. In contrast, Julie experienced almost the reverse reaction with some of her interviewees, feeling that they were 'intruding' upon her when they 'called her bluff' by trying to take up and pursue the rapport she had established in the interview as if it had been real rather than 'faked' friendship.

Another way of looking at these episodes is that they provide further illustrations of how interviewees may exercise power in their relationships with interviewers, not only through withholding the data that interviewers want, but by transgressing (or failing to recognize) the hidden 'rules' or 'cues' as to how interview relationships are 'supposed' to develop. In our interviews such 'transgressions' took the form of participants rejecting our faked offers of 'friendship', or alternatively taking up the offer too enthusiastically as if it were genuine. Our contrasting personal responses to such 'transgressions', both as interviewers and *individuals*, highlight how the insights that we gain from research are influenced by both personal and social differences, and how ethical dilemmas permeate the whole experience of research interviewing.

Conclusion

Our discussion of the ethical issues associated with rapport started with what we called the 'ideal feminist research relationship' where spontaneous and genuine rapport supposedly leads more naturally to reciprocal mutual disclosure. We have contrasted this ideal with research relationships where the interviewer is influenced by commercial pressures to 'do rapport' by 'faking friendship' in order to encourage the interviewee to open up. In practice, of course, all interviewing relationships, including women's interviews with women, are situated somewhere along a spectrum between the extremes of more genuine empathy and relationships with an element of 'faking'. However, interview relationships raise common ethical problems, to the extent that they encourage or persuade interviewees to explore and disclose experiences and emotions which – on reflection – they may have preferred to keep to themselves or even 'not to know'.

These ethical tensions are associated with the misuse of the interviewer's power of persuasion, exercised through the ideologies of shared 'womanhood' or alternatively shared 'friendship'. We have shown how claims for a special status for shared womanhood have been challenged even from within feminism. Feminist researchers must, therefore, inevitably face ethical dilemmas concerning the balance between the possibly adverse individual emotional consequences of their interviews for their interviewees, as against the more abstract gains to feminism and public education that may result from their research. We have also argued that in this 'ethical equation' we need to take into account the influence of professionalisation, as a specific instance of a more general trend towards the 'commercialisation' or 'commodification' of rapport.

It was our sense of alienation from the kinds of rapport that we felt we needed to establish in our interviews that led us to this exploration of the ethics of rapport. On further reflection, we became aware that some aspects of our graduate training, and the literature on the skills of qualitative interviewing, tapped into a more general trend towards seeing such skills in terms of their marketability, with a consequent neglect of their ethical implications. In short, the skills of 'doing rapport' are becoming 'commodified'.

We have suggested that the commodification of the skills of 'doing rapport' raises ethical questions concerning how far interviewers are able to 'set the agenda' for the interview and to 'manage the consent' of interviewees to participate in disclosing more or less private and intimate information. Our advice is that interviewers should continue to worry about these issues as they emerge in each piece of research and each individual interview. However, interviewers should remember that interviewees are not totally powerless, and that they can withhold their participation – as long as interviewers do not 'do rapport' too convincingly.

Notes

[1] Julie has interviewed husbands and wives (not couples) between separation and divorce, and has recently interviewed divorced mothers, divorced fathers and their new partners as part of her PhD on post-divorce parenting. Jean has researched Youth Training Schemes, and has more recently interviewed wives, husbands (and other kin), for studies of household finances, and of love and power in couple relationships.

[2] We use the term 'interviewee' because we feel that 'subject' claims too much and 'respondent' claims too little participation in the research.

[3] Confusion arises because the term 'qualitative' is now used indiscriminately to refer to fairly structured interviews intended for quantitative computer analysis, which have virtually nothing in common with flexible ('unstructured' or 'semi-structured') 'conversations with a purpose' that rely at most on topic guides. Whereas Oakley deplored attempts to depersonalise and structure relationships in what she argued should be personal and flexible research relationships, our concern is with the spread of a commercial and phoney 'personalisation' in the realm of more flexible methods.

References

Birch, M. and Miller, T. (2000) 'Inviting intimacy: the interview as "therapeutic opportunity" ', *Social Research Methodology, Theory and Practice,* 3: 189–202.

Cain, M. (1990) 'Realist philosophy and standpoint epistemologies or feminist criminology as a successor science', in L. Gelsthorpe and A. Morris (eds), *Feminist Perspectives on Criminology.* Buckingham: Open University Press.

Devault, M.L. (1990) 'Talking and listening from women's standpoint: feminist strategies for interviewing and analysis', *Social Problems,* 37: 96–116.

Duncombe, J. and Marsden, D. (1996) 'Can we research the private sphere?', in L. Morris and E. Stina Lyon (eds), *Gender Relations in Public and Private.* London: Macmillan.

Duncombe, J. and Marsden, D. (1998) ' "Stepford wives" and "hollow men"? Doing emotion work, doing gender and "authenticity" in intimate heterosexual relationships', in G. Bendelow and S.J. Williams (eds), *Emotions in Social Life.* London: Routledge.

Finch, J. (1984) 'It's great to have someone to talk to: the ethics and politics of interviewing women', in C. Bell and H. Roberts, *Social Researching.* London: Routledge and Kegan Paul.

Glaser, B.G. and Strauss, A. (1967) *The Discovery of Grounded Theory.* Chicago: Aldine.

Glesne, C. and Peshkin, A. (1992) *Becoming Qualitative Researchers: An Introduction.* New York: Longman.

Harding, S. (ed.) (1987) *Feminism and Methodology*. Milton Keynes: Indiana University Press and Open University Press.

Hey, V. (2000) 'Troubling the auto/biography of the questions: re/thinking rapport and the politics of social class in feminist participant observation', *Genders and Sexualities in Educational Ethnography*, 3: 161–83.

Hochschild, A.R. (1983) *The Managed Heart: The Commercialization of Human Feeling*. Berkeley, CA: University of California Press.

Kelly, L. (1988) *Surviving Sexual Violence*. Cambridge: Polity.

Komter, A. (1989) 'Hidden power in marriage', *Gender and Society*, 3: 2.

Kvale, S. (1992) *InterViews*. London: Sage.

Larossa, R. et al. (1981) 'Ethical dilemmas in qualitative family research', *Journal of Marriage and the Family*, vol. 13.

Luff, D. (1999) 'Dialogue across the divides: "Moments of rapport" and power in feminist research with anti-feminist women', *Sociology*, 33(4): 687–703.

Lukes, S. (1974) *Power: A Radical View*. London: Macmillan.

Mauthner, N.S., Parry, O. and Backett-Miburn, K. (1998) 'The data are out there, or are they? implications for archiving and revisiting qualitative data', *Sociology*, 32(4): 733–45.

McKee, L. and O'Brien, M. (1983) 'Interviewing men: taking gender seriously', in E. Garmarnikov et al. (eds), *The Public and the Private*. London: Heineman.

McRobbie, A. (1982) 'The politics of feminist research: between talk, text and action', *Feminist Review*, 12: 46–57.

Miller, J.B. (1986) *Towards a New Psychology of Women*. Harmondsworth, Middlesex: Penguin.

Oakley, A. (1981) 'Interviewing women: a contradiction in terms', in H. Roberts (ed.), *Doing Feminist Research*. London: Routledge and Kegan Paul.

Oakley, A. (1998) 'Gender, methodology and people's ways of knowing: some problems with feminism and the paradigm debate in social science', *Sociology*, 32(4): 707–31.

O'Connell Davidson, J. and Layder, D. (1994) *Methods, Sex and Madness*. London: Routledge.

Phoenix, A. (1994) 'Practising feminist research: the intersection of gender and "race" in the research process', in M. Maynard and J. Purvis (eds), *Researching Women's Lives from a Feminist Perspective*. London: Taylor and Francis.

Ramazanoglu, C. (1989) 'Improving on sociology: the problems of taking a feminist standpoint', *Sociology*, 23: 427–42.

Reinharz, S. (1992) *Feminist Methods in Social Research*. Oxford: Oxford University Press.

Ribbens, J. (1998) 'Hearing my feeling voice', in J. Ribbens and R. Edwards (eds), *Dilemmas in Feminist Research: Public Knowledge and Private Lives*. London: Sage.

Sjoberg, G. and Nett, R. (1968) *A Methodology for Social Research*. New York: Harper and Row.

Smart, C. (1984) *The Ties That Bind: Law, Marriage and the Reproduction of Patriarchal Relations*. London: Routledge and Kegan Paul.

Stacey, J. (1988) 'Can there be a feminist ethnography?', in *Women's Studies International Forum*, 11.

Stacey, J. (1990) *Brave New Families: Stories of Domestic Upheaval in Late Twentieth Century America*. New York: Basic Books.

Tannen, D. (1991) *You Just Don't Understand: Women and Men in Conversation*. London: Virago.

Wise, S. (1987) 'A framework for discussing ethical issues in feminist research: a review of the literature', in V. Griffiths et al. (eds), *Writing Feminist Biography 2: Using Life Histories*. Studies in Sexual Politics. Manchester: Manchester University Sociology Dept.

CHAPTER 7

KNOWING RESPONSIBLY: LINKING ETHICS, RESEARCH PRACTICE AND EPISTEMOLOGY

Andrea Doucet and Natasha Mauthner

Introduction

Feminist discussions of ethics have tended to be separated into those that address research practice and those that concern knowledge construction processes as framed in philosophical or epistemological terms. On the one hand, feminist researchers who conduct qualitative research have documented the numerous ethical dilemmas that can arise during data collection and fieldwork, many of which revolve around issues of honesty and lying, power and privilege, and the overall quality of the relationships between researcher and researched (Hale, 1991; Patai, 1991; Reinharz, 1992; Wolf, 1996; Zavella, 1993; see also Jean Duncombe and Julie Jessop, Chapter 6)[1]. Parallel to this body of literature, there has been an enhanced focus by feminist philosophers and theorists on ethical issues surrounding the construction of knowledge (see Alcoff and Potter, 1993; Antony and Witt, 1993; Code, 1987, 1991; Duran, 1994; Lennon and Whitford, 1994; and Pam Alldred and Val Gillies, Chapter 8). These scholars, and many others, draw attention to the 'relations between knowledge and power' (Flax, 1992: 451; Tanesini, 1999: 3) as well as issues of advocacy (Code, 1995), subjectivity and objectivity (Code, 1993; Longino, 1993), and the political and ethical dilemmas involved in reconciling or choosing between relativism and/or realism (Lazreg, 1994; Seller, 1988; Smith, 1999). While methodological and epistemological discussions about ethics have made important contributions to feminist practice, theory and epistemology, our concern here is that they have largely remained separate and parallel discourses (but see Maynard, 1994). This chapter aims to find paths towards greater integration between feminist research that reflects on issues of ethics and methodology *and* feminist scholarship on epistemology and ethics.

We began our work for this chapter by searching for feminist scholars who link ethics, methods, methodologies and epistemologies in explicit terms. We found a noteworthy example in the work of Canadian philosopher Lorraine Code (1984, 1987, 1988, 1991, 1993, 1995; see also Burt and Code, 1995; Code et al., 1983). In connecting concrete discussions of innovative, alternative and experiential participatory research practice (i.e. Burt and Code, 1995) with abstract philosophical discussions about knowing, knowers, and knowledge production (i.e. Code, 1987, 1995), Code's work has centred on, among other things, a consistent concern with 'recognizing the ethical dimensions of knowing' (Griffiths and Whitford, 1988: 19), as framed in inter-twined methodological and epistemological terms. In her writing and theorising, she constantly interchanges the terms 'knowing well', 'knowing responsibly' and 'epistemic responsibility', thus underlining the weight of social and political responsibility attached to those who are involved in 'power-based knowledge construction processes' (Code, 1995: 14). She argues that the explanatory capacities of theories, and of policies based upon them, 'depend upon their having a basis in responsible knowledge of human experience' (1988: 187–8) and that '(k)nowing well, being epistemically responsible has implications for people's individual, social and political lives' (1987: 10). For Code, there are ethical issues involved in research *relationships*, as well as in being accountable within the varied sets of relations that comprise any given research project. Following on from Code, our chapter takes up her invitation to consider, in both methodological and epistemological terms, what it means to 'know well', to 'know responsibly' and to attain a high degree of 'epistemic responsibility'.[2]

Our chapter develops two arguments that point to concrete ways of conducting ethical research practice, as well as to dilemmas that occur while attempting to do so. Our arguments about linking ethics, methods, methodologies and epistemologies focus specifically on data analysis processes because, for qualitative researchers, these are significant sites where everyday accounts are translated or transformed into academic, theoretical and policy-related knowledges. Our chapter focuses on ethical dilemmas in analysis which revolve around issues of relationships and accountability in data analysis processes.

Our first argument focuses on research *relationships*. We underline the importance of attempting to maintain 'relationships' with our research respondents/subjects during data analysis processes, particularly with subjects who may not 'fit' our theoretical, epistemological and political frameworks. While pointing to the importance of attempting to do this, we also highlight inherent tensions. In recognizing a responsibility to research respondents, we also know that there are other research relationships that incorporate. As pointed out by Code, those who are involved in the processes of knowledge production have an ethical responsibility to those from whom/for whom knowledge is produced as well as to others who are involved in the production of theory, knowledge and policy. While ethical issues in research are most often, and with justification, centred on the researcher's relationship with and to *research respondents*, we argue that there are other research relationships that should also be attended to in ethical discussions. These 'other', often unmentioned, relationships include the ones we have, or create, with many different communities: our readers; the users of our research; and the varied knowledge communities that influence our work, including 'interpretive' (Fish, 1980), 'epistemological' (Longino, 1985; Nelson, 1993) and academic communities. That is, from the beginning of a research project and far after its completion, a researcher and their work exist in many complex sets of relationships (see also Linda Bell and Linda Nutt, Chapter 4). In recognizing these multiple contexts which influence our research processes, and within which research endeavours occur, we are inevitably drawing attention to potential conflicts of interests and possible ethical dilemmas. Our chapter is thus informed by a concept of 'ethics' that relates to a wide sense of 'acting responsibly' as researchers who have an obligation and commitment not only to research participants but also to those who read, re-interpret and take seriously the claims that we make.

Our second argument is about ethical issues of *accountability*. Here we suggest that one way of building ethical research relationships with readers, users and varied communities is to be as transparent, as is reasonably possible, about the epistemological, ontological, theoretical, and personal assumptions that inform our research generally, and our analytic and interpretive processes specifically. In this vein, we are employing a wide concept of reflexivity. Reflexivity is often configured as a methodological issue, where it is up to the researcher's discretion to decide how much and what to reveal about themselves. We argue that reflexivity holds together methodology, epistemology and ethics; and we conceptualize reflexivity not only in terms of social location, but also in terms of the personal, interpersonal, institutional, pragmatic, emotional, theoretical, epistemological and ontological influences on our research (see Mauthner and Doucet, in press). Moreover, in speaking about the ethical significance of reflexivity, we are referring to its relevance to issues of honesty, transparency and overall accountability in research.

Three case studies

In order to illustrate methodological and epistemological ethics in the context of data analysis processes, we draw on three case studies. The second and third are from our own doctoral research projects from which we have written several collaborative and individual pieces on knowledge construction processes with a particular emphasis on data analysis (Doucet, 1998; Doucet and Mauthner, 1999; Mauthner and Doucet, 1998, in press; Mauthner et al., 1998). Our studies, while separately conceived and carried out, shared a common focus in that they were both qualitative studies on women and men's parenting and employment lives; Andrea's was a study of heterosexual couples attempting to share housework and child care (Doucet, 2000, 2001) while Natasha's focused on women's experiences of motherhood and postnatal depression (Mauthner, 1999, 2002). Both studies involved multiple interviews, innovative and participatory methods of data collection, and 'the data' were analysed in the context of a research group while using a particular adaptation of the 'voice centred relational method' of data analysis.

In addition to our own work, we also draw on a case study that occurs in a completely different academic discipline and in another time in history. This is a case study on the work of American geneticist Barbara McClintock (1902–1987) as discussed by Evelyn Fox Keller (1983, 1985). We selected McClintock as an exemplary case of 'knowing well' for two reasons. First, we were initially drawn to her story by an intriguing paradox that remained at the centre of her work and her life. Second, we wanted to broaden out the dominant feminist way of reading this case study by highlighting it as an important example of 'knowing responsibly' and ethical research practice. Although McClintock's subjects of study were plants and not humans, we nevertheless argue that the wider implications of her work have relevance for feminist ethical discussions in both methodological and epistemological terms.

The central paradox that attracted us to the work and life of Barbara McClintock is well described by Keller. McClintock was a scientist who was able 'to make contributions to classical genetics and cytology that earned her a level of recognition that few women of her generation could imagine' (Keller, 1983: 158). Yet, paradoxically, her life was marked by both 'success and marginality' (Keller, 1985: 159). Even though she was named a Nobel Laureate, showered with numerous other awards, and was internationally praised for her research and her landmark discovery of genetic transposition,[3] for decades her work remained largely 'uncomprehended and almost entirely unintegrated into the growing corpus of biological thought' (Keller, 1985: 159). Keller maintains that one key explanation for McClintock's marginality was not that she was a woman but that she was 'a philosophical and methodological deviant' (1985: 159) because of her philosophical and methodological stance towards her subject matter. 'These were my friends', wrote McClintock, 'you look at these things, they become part of you. And you forget yourself' (McClintock, cited in Keller, 1985: 165). In a world characterized by positivist empiricist models of knowing and knowers as detached, distanced, and objective, McClintock's unconventional view of maize and corn plants as her 'friends' was clearly out of sync with the precepts and approaches of her scientific colleagues.

It is precisely this radical and unconventional way in which McClintock developed and maintained her *research relationships*, albeit with corn plants, that has attracted attention from feminist scholars, both in the realms of epistemology (Alcoff and Potter, 1993; Bar On, 1993; Belenky et al., 1986; Keller, 1985; Longino, 1990; Tanesini, 1999) and methodology (Reinharz, 1992: 234). A recurrent feminist reading of the significance of McClintock's work is that she developed 'feminist ways of knowing' (Belenky et al., 1986) through developing a close relationship with the plants that she was studying. This intimacy with her research subjects that allowed her to 'hear what the material has to say to you' and to develop a profound 'feeling for the organism' (Keller, 1983: 198) is often used as a metaphor for social scientists conducting responsive interviewing practice (e.g. Gilligan et al., 1990) and, for feminist philosophers interested in the role of emotions, feeling and connection in knowledge construction (e.g. Griffiths and Whitford, 1988). Returning to the words of McClintock:

> I start with the seedling and I don't want to leave it, I don't feel I really know the story if I don't watch the plant all the way along. So I know every plant in the field. I know them intimately and I find it a great pleasure to know them. (McClintock cited in Keller, 1983: 198)

We suggest that McClintock's story also represents a case study of 'knowing well' and 'responsibly' because it illustrates the ethics of research relationships in two ways. First, McClintock attempted to maintain relationships with subjects that did not 'fit' her theoretical frameworks and analytical concepts. Secondly, her work demonstrates a wide concept of theoretical, ontological and epistemological reflexivity. We now turn to examine these two issues through McClintock's work as well as through our own research.

Ethics and maintaining relationships with research subjects

Barbara McClintock

In her book *Reflections on Gender and Science*, Keller writes on McClintock:

> Her work on transposition in fact began with the observation of an *aberrant pattern* of pigmentation on a *few kernels of a single corn plant*. And her commitment to the significance of this *singular pattern* sustained her through six years of solitary and arduous investigation – *all aimed at making the difference she saw understandable*. (1985: 163; emphasis added)

Not only did McClintock develop and maintain a close and 'loving' relationship with her research subjects, but she also focussed in on the uniqueness of each research subject, even those subjects whose characteristics fundamentally challenged the theoretical, ontological and epistemological perspectives that she started out with. This is how McClintock describes the process of coming to challenge mainstream explanations:

> If the material tells you 'it may be this', allow that. Don't turn it aside and call it an exception, an aberration, a contaminant . . . The important thing is to develop the capacity to see one kernel (of maize) that is different and make that understandable . . . If something doesn't fit there's a reason, and you find out what it is. (cited in Keller, 1985: 162–3)

McClintock saw, heard and felt something that was not immediately comprehensible, at least within the dominant theoretical, ontological and epistemological frameworks of her field. Yet she maintained a relationship with her research subjects during on-going data analysis. The commitment to maintain, rather than cut off, the relationship during this prolonged analysis set her apart from her colleagues working in the same field of research. Speaking again through Keller, McClintock writes:

> 'I feel that much of the work is done because one wants to impose an answer on it . . . They have the answer ready and they know (what they want) the material to tell them'. Anything else it tells them they don't really recognize as there, or they think it's a mistake and throw it out . . . (cited in Keller, 1983: 179)

McClintock's apparent refusal to 'twist her data', particularly the aberrant patterns, to fit more acceptable mainstream scientific explanations constitutes an ethical issue because she faced the dilemma of

deciding what to incorporate or reject, what to emphasize, and ultimately what to disclose about her analysis processes. In the end, she
risked alienating herself from her scientific community by maintaining a close relationship with the research subjects that were otherwise
regarded as scientific 'misfits'. The ethical dilemma illustrated by
McClintock's story is that of honouring some relationships and cutting off others and the difficult choices over doing this within, or
against, certain 'epistemological communities' (Longino, 1993; Nelson,
1993). That is, will we alienate ourselves from a particular epistemological or scientific community, as McClintock did, if we pursue
certain explanations and make particular knowledge claims? And if
we know this is possible, what path will we choose and to whose
harm? This dilemma is especially profound in cases where established
scientific communities, at times with weighty mentors, have the
power to censure some stories and promote others (Haraway, 1991:
106).

McClintock's story tells of the courage and determination it takes
to 'stay with the data'; and the potential cost of remaining faithful to
one's data. It can be remarkably difficult to 'listen to the data' amidst
political, theoretical, epistemological, ontological or institutional pressures (Mauthner and Doucet, in press). Moreover, the often isolated
and invisible nature of the data analysis process compounds the
vulnerability of both researcher and research participants. The analysis of data usually takes place 'back in the office', in isolation from our
respondents, research users and colleagues. We often find ourselves
alone with our data and generally speaking few other people will see
this 'raw' data.[4] In the words of Miriam Glucksmann, these subdued
moments of the research relationship are rife with 'ethical considerations' and endowed with issues of 'trust':

> . . . ethical considerations enter equally, if not more, into the stage of
> processing the data as into the interview situation. Usually the researcher
> has sole access to and total control over the tapes or transcripts. No one else
> oversees which parts she selects as of significance . . . Each researcher is left
> on trust to draw the difficult line between interpreting the data in terms of
> its relevance to her research questions as opposed to twisting it in a way
> that amounted to a misrepresentation of what was said. (1994: 163)

Data analysis is where the power and privilege of the researcher
are particularly pronounced and where the ethics of our research
practice are particularly acute because of the largely invisible nature of
the interpretive process (Mauthner and Doucet, 1998). Looking back at
our research processes, we now realize that it was during our data
analysis processes that similar ethical dilemmas surfaced in our work.
It was there that we encountered moments of struggling to reconcile

dominant political or theoretical conceptions with contrasting accounts and emergent concepts that we were 'hearing' in our data.

Andrea

In Andrea's research, there is evidence of this ethical issue of maintaining research relationships with subjects or respondents who did not fit into her initial theoretical framework. Influenced by many excellent works on gendered divisions of domestic labour that were emerging in Britain in the early 1990s, Andrea began her data analysis work by looking for 'success stories' as represented in the accounts of women who successfully maintained autonomous identities as workers with their parenting practices and identities. As her analysis work progressed, however, she began to 'read' and 'hear' her data in different, at times contradictory, terms. Specifically, her increased reading of literature on the 'ethic of care', combined with the birth and care of her own children, saw her gradually coming to the view that many studies on gender divisions of domestic labour were underpinned by liberal feminist conceptions of autonomous self sufficient and individualistic beings (see Doucet, 1995). Subject accounts which did not fit into these liberal feminist theoretical frameworks were those that espoused more connected and relational ways of being and acting; these included accounts that prioritized domestic lives, particularly the care of children, over and above employment identities and practices. Indeed, in other research studies similar accounts as offered by research respondents were sometimes inadvertently treated as being either deficient or as trapped within gendered ideologies (see Doucet, 1995, 1998 for review).

Rather than seeing a 'problem' in and with women's accounts that articulated the value of care giving and the importance of challenging 'male stream' models of full-time work, Andrea attempted to hear her respondents accounts from within alternative theoretical frameworks informed by 'the ethic of care' and 'relational' ontologies; these included notions of 'selves in relation' (Ruddick, 1989: 211), of 'relational beings' (Jordan, 1993: 141), of human relations as 'interdependent rather than independent' (Tronto, 1995: 142), and of daily practices as embedded in a complex web of intimate and larger social relations (Gilligan, 1982).[5] That is, in contrast to employing an ontology of self-sufficient human beings which emphasized where women were successful in their attempts to achieve greater autonomy from their children and their household lives, the adoption of a relational ontology enabled Andrea to also hear how women and men defined domestic work and responsibility in intrinsically relational terms, between persons as well as between social institutions (see Doucet, 1998, 2000, 2001).

Yet dilemmas around this issue of maintaining research relationships were also raised. In analysing interview transcripts from 46 individuals and 69 interviews, it became clear, early on, that relationships could not be maintained with *each and every respondent*. Grouping respondents into heuristic categories where they shared some elements of daily practice or underlying ideological assumptions was a first way of dealing with the complexity of understanding respondents' diverse lives and accounts. Maintaining relationships with certain respondents allowed Andrea to find ways of articulating novel concepts that were not as clearly heard within academic discourses. Nevertheless it is also important to point out that while this can be conceived as ethical practice, in that certain relationships were valued and maintained, others were inevitably cut off and *not* given equal weight. In particular, when women and men espoused views on distinct and irreconcilable gendered differences between women and men, Andrea tended to play these down, as they were slightly outside of the analytical frameworks she was using.

Natasha

A prominent ethical dilemma Natasha faced in her research on motherhood and postnatal depression was how to make sense of women's attitudes towards medical diagnoses, explanations and treatments of their depression. The dilemma arose partly because of differences of opinion among the women, and partly because of conflicts between some of the women's beliefs, Natasha's views, and feminist theories. Taking any kind of position on these issues risked alienating the women and/or feminist research communities.

All of the women she interviewed expressed relief at having their experiences labelled and diagnosed 'postnatal depression'. They actively used this term to describe their feelings and were strong advocates of the label. This position conflicted with dominant feminist accounts which viewed postnatal depression as a medical construct not a medical condition. Most feminists criticized the label for medicalizing and pathologizing women's distress, and for reifying postnatal depression. They suggested replacing it with other, less-'loaded' terms such as 'unhappiness after childbirth'. Natasha was in agreement that the label 'postnatal depression' was a historically and culturally specific construct, and that its use implied the existence of biological abnormalities within individual women. However, she also believed it was important to recognize, understand, and reflect women's use of the label. She resisted the feminist view that in using such medical terms women were simply being *passively* regulated by and subjected to medical discourses of postnatal depression. Instead, she argued that women *actively* draw on the culturally dominant medical discourse to make sense of their experiences partly because there are few alternative ways for women to interpret their feelings; and partly because a medical explanation absolves women from feelings of guilt, blame, and responsibility. By locating their problems within their body – typically, hormonal changes – and therefore beyond their control, a medical diagnosis validates women's experiences of motherhood despite the fact that, in their eyes, they have fallen short of cultural ideals of motherhood (Mauthner, 2002). In staying with the women's accounts and using the term 'postnatal depression', however, she risked alienating, and indeed has alienated, some of the feminist researchers reading her work.

However, Natasha has also risked alienating at least some of the women she interviewed by questioning hormonal explanations and medical treatments of postnatal depression. Although, as noted above, Natasha puts forward an explanation of why many women embrace a medical diagnosis, explanation and treatment of their depression, she also argues that the hormonal basis of postnatal depression is, as yet, unproven; even if there is a hormonal basis, women's stories implicate a host of psychological, interpersonal, social, and cultural processes in their depression that cannot be ignored; and while antidepressants may help some women overcome depression, women are also calling out for other forms of treatment (namely, talking treatments) (Mauthner, 2002). While this position is in accordance with some of the women's views, others may feel it undermines their strong beliefs in, and advocacy of, a medical approach to their depression. In this instance, the ethical problem of how to retain relationships with each and every one of her respondents remains unresolved as some relationships are inevitably 'sacrificed' in favour of others.

While pointing to the importance of maintaining relationships with subject or respondents who do not initially fit ours, or our academic discipline's, dominant theoretical frameworks, it is also important to reiterate that we are not maintaining a thoroughly ethical position with *all* research subjects. Indeed it could be argued that in hearing some perspectives, we are cutting off others and thus perhaps acting unethically with some respondents. What we are highlighting here is the importance of recognizing that being uniformly ethical, in the sense of maintaining a close and connected relationship, is not possible with all respondents. This is partly because respondents are not a homogenous group, and partly due to the fact that in taking theoretical positions in our research, some accounts are heard with greater commitment and connection than others. The complexity of our multiple research relationships and commitments in research confounds our desire, however well intentioned we may be, to remain in relationship with *all* research respondents. This issue will become even more complicated in the next section.

Ethics, reflexivity and accountability in methodology and epistemology

Barbara McClintock

In her analysis of McClintock's life and work, Keller asks an intriguing question: 'What enabled McClintock to see further and deeper into the mysteries of genetics than her colleagues?' (1983: 197). Keller argues that McClintock's insights grew, not only out of the close relationships she maintained with her research subjects, but also from her realization and admission that the theoretical, ontological and epistemological dimensions of her work had radically altered as a result of her research. Keller points to a dialectical process between methodology and epistemology/ontology/theory whereby McClintock's observations shifted her 'gestalt', which in turn modified how and what she observed. As an example, Keller refers to how McClintock gives an 'account of a breakthrough . . . in analysis' pointing to how the geneticist 'describes the state of mind accompanying the shift in orientation that enabled her to identify chromosomes she had earlier not been able to distinguish' (1985: 165). In the process of utilizing innovative methods that allowed a certain 'listening' and 'responding' to the data, McClintock came to take on a changed conception of 'nature' and a different epistemological understanding of 'what counts as knowledge' (Keller, 1985: 166). These different epistemological, ontological and theoretical assumptions led, in turn, to radically different analytical questions to be asked of her subjects, and consequently to distinct readings of data, changed findings, and a thoroughly altered story.

Keller's interpretation of McClintock's knowledge construction processes is an excellent case in point of the wide and strong reflexivity we are calling for. In reflecting on how it was that McClintock came to the claims and discoveries that she did, Keller reasons that it is not the fact that she was a white middle-class female scientist working within a world of men. Nor was it only her relational and connected way of doing research – her 'feeling for the organism' – that mattered to her work. Rather, it was the ontological, theoretical and epistemological assumptions that informed her work, her realization that they changed part way through her research, and her ability to make these transparent. Keller writes:

> I am claiming that the difference between McClintock's conception of nature and that prevailing in the community around her is *an essential key* to our understanding of her life and work. (1985: 167; emphasis added)

What is striking about McClintock's experience and account is her honest rendering of these reflexive processes. As qualitative researchers confronted with differing ways of interpreting a story, it is not just staying close to the research participants or subjects that merits recognition as an ethical issue, but the naming of the assumptions that lead us to read and tell the stories that we do (Doucet, 1998; Mauthner et al., 1998). These are not just methodological and epistemological issues, but also ethical issues in that they involve being as honest, transparent and accountable as possible with our varied audiences, about the role our informing assumptions play in interpreting individual stories. This 'strong' and 'robust' reflexivity (Harding, 1992, 1998) within our research practice goes beyond situating ourselves in terms of gender, class, ethnicity, sexuality and geographical location. Indeed, as Daphne Patai points out, these locations, and their automatically associated power differentials, are often 'deployed as badges'; they are meant to represent 'one's respect to "difference" but do not affect any aspect of the research or the interpretive text' (Patai, 1991: 149). A robust conception of reflexivity means giving greater attention to the interplay between our multiple social locations and how these intersect with the particularities of our personal biographies *at the time* of analyzing data (Doucet, 1998; Mauthner et al., 1998). This strong reflexivity also means being cognisant and open about the epistemological, ontological and theoretical assumptions which inform our work, and particularly as they shape our data analysis processes. Just as ethical reflections in fieldwork concentrate on issues of honesty/lying, power and relationships (i.e. Wolf, 1996), these ethical issues of transparency and honesty in naming the influences on our knowing processes are also fundamental in providing responsible accounts of 'coming to know people' (Code, 1988).

In our own work, we have both become aware of how our theoretical and personal biographies affected our knowledge construction processes as well as the knowledges that we produced about women and men's lives. We would argue that a wide and robust concept of reflexivity should include reflecting on, and being accountable about, personal, interpersonal, institutional, pragmatic, emotional, theoretical, epistemological and ontological influences on our research, and specifically about our data analysis processes. We want to concentrate here on outlining how our respective backgrounds – personal, theoretical, ontological and epistemological – came to play a role in the analysis of our data and the findings we drew and made from our data. Moreover, as we highlight in the following section, it is with hindsight, as well as time and distance from our doctoral projects, that we have both been able to understand and articulate how our research was the product of these multiple influences (see Mauthner and Doucet, in press).

Andrea

It is with the benefit of hindsight that Andrea has become aware of the multiple influences – personal, institutional, theoretical, and epistemo-logical – that shaped her research. Diverse theoretical strands emerged from her varied academic studies in political science, sociology and international development studies, as well as from her four years as a participatory research trainer in South America. With a background in Marxism and critical theory and later influences from interpretivist qualitative traditions, symbolic interactionism, feminist standpoint theory, Andrea began her doctoral research with methods that attemp-ted to encourage people's 'voices' and to situate those accounts within theoretical explanations that would, she hoped, contribute to pro-gressive social change around gendered home and employment lives. Andrea's theoretical approach began to widen and change due to combined institutional, personal and theoretical influences. Institu-tional circumstances included the arrival of a well-known feminist academic who encouraged her to incorporate relational theory as a complement to the theoretical approaches she was already using. In terms of personal influences, Andrea's biography as a new parent and carer while writing about these topics deeply altered her choice of academic texts that framed her research and analysis. This combina-tion of her personal life, institutional context and choices of academic texts and theoretical frameworks then guided her toward particular ways of 'seeing' and 'hearing' respondents' accounts during her data analysis processes (Doucet, 1998). In particular, the inclusion of rela-tional theory enabled Andrea to 'hear' her respondents' accounts in more relational, rather than individualistic terms and this provided the basis for innovative thinking around domestic and community lives and processes (Doucet, 2000, 2001).

In terms of personal influences, it is also with retrospection that Andrea has become acutely aware of how her own biography affected her choice of academic texts that guided her research, and how this combination of personal life and academic texts led her to particular ways of 'seeing' and 'hearing' respondents' accounts during her data analysis processes (Doucet, 1998). Recognizing the liberal feminist conception of autonomous self-sufficient individuals that underlined much of the literature on gender divisions of domestic labour, Andrea aimed to balance out this perspective through the inclusion of a relational ontology as informed by feminist work on 'care' and the 'ethic of care' (Gilligan, 1982; Graham, 1983; Jordan, 1993; Ruddick, 1989; Tronto, 1993). Moving towards this inclusion was, however, very much affected by her own parenting practices and ontological connection with care and these processes, in turn, had a profound effect on her knowledge construction processes. In specific terms, research respondents who challenged mainstream and 'male stream' models of parenting and work were, in retrospect, accorded particular weight during data analysis processes, partly because they provided a balance to the well established liberal and liberal feminist inspired stories on women and parenting that dominated the literature on gender and domestic labour and also because their challenges resonated with Andrea's experiences and the theoretical literature she was exploring (see Doucet, 1998, 2000, 2001).

Natasha

For Natasha, personal, theoretical, ontological and epistemological influences also came to affect her knowing processes. While she initially approached her doctoral research from a positivistic background in experimental psychology, her disenchantment with the discipline and its positivist paradigm led her to move to a social and political sciences department in the first year of her PhD. Despite the physical move, she still felt intellectually caught between two paradigms. Whilst her explicit theoretical and methodological position was one in which she rejected notions of the detached, neutral, 'objective' researcher, she nevertheless felt a positivist pressure to render herself, her voice, and her influence, invisible in her research. This was compounded by the fact that, having not experienced motherhood herself, she viewed the women she was interviewing as 'experts' about motherhood and postnatal depression. Her tendency to prioritize the women's accounts also resulted from her desire to react against the dominant research traditions and theories in her field, in which mothers' views are devalued and disregarded (Mauthner, 1998, 2002). And here, she was influenced by feminist standpoint epistemology and the notion of 'giving voice' to marginalized groups such as women and particularly women with mental health problems. Her approach also reflected the epistemological and ontological assumptions underpinning the methodological and theoretical tradition she was using in analysing her data in which there is a tendency to romanticize women's 'voices' and 'subjectivities'.

Like Andrea, Natasha was also inspired to incorporate relational theory into her doctoral theoretical framework. This was partly facilitated through her discontent with existing theoretical explanations and partly through institutional influences in that she began to work with a visiting feminist academic who introduced relational theory and associated methodological approaches to her and her University department. Increasingly, she began to listen to the women's stories of depression and mothering through a 'relational' filter – listening for a relational 'self', prioritising her analysis on relational issues in women's accounts, and constructing a relational interpretation of postnatal depression. This shift in ontological and theoretical approaches meant that her understandings of postnatal depression altered radically and she began to posit alternate understandings to those that were dominant and publicly powerful.

In speaking about these processes together, and in looking back on our knowing processes, we (Andrea and Natasha) are now aware of the multiple influences that came to matter greatly in our work. Moreover, as in the McClintock case study, our theoretical and ontological concepts changed over the duration of our projects' evolution, partly due to personal and institutional influences in our research, and these changes profoundly affected the knowledges that we each produced. These changes were not fully known to us while we were in the thick of data analysis, and while under institutional pressure to complete our projects. It was only much later that the breadth and width of our reflexive processes was revealed to us. In this sense, we would argue that the theoretical and epistemological life of a project, and the knowledges it creates, live on long after the project work has been formally completed. When we speak about accountability in research, it is perhaps best configured in this very long-term way as a process through which researchers engage in a conversation with those who read, re-read, critique and utilize their work and also in relation to one's evolving thinking about theoretical, methodological, and epistemological issues. We argue that being reflexive with our readers in an ongoing and evolving way increases ethical research practice. It builds a closer relationship between the researcher and their readers, allows for greater accountability on the part of the researcher, and instils trust in the reader in that they know something about how knowledge was constructed.

One dilemma that is raised here is that since some of these critical assumptions affecting our knowledge production may not be readily available or known to us at the time of conducting our research, it may be that reflexivity and accountability are ultimately limited. That is, in spite of our attempts to be highly reflexive, we concur with Grosz (1995: 13) who maintains that 'the author's intentions, emotions, psyche, and interiority are not only inaccessible to readers, they are likely to be inaccessible to the author herself'. We have argued elsewhere that it may be more useful to think in terms of 'degrees of reflexivity', with some influences being easier to identify and articulate at the time of our work while others may take time, distance and detachment from the research (Mauthner and Doucet, in press). In a similar way, it may be that there are *'degrees of ethical accountability'* in that it may be that we can be as open and transparent as is reasonably possible at each stage of our knowing processes but that it may take time and engagement with varied academic communities – interpretive or epistemological – before we can actually clearly articulate the multiple influences on our research. One way of increasing the likelihood of this strong reflexivity and thus enhancing our ethical research practice along the lines of being accountable is to create dedicated times, spaces, and contexts within which to be reflexive. In our own case, a research group set up around data analysis assisted us in beginning to think critically about the assumptions informing our work and thus in acquiring some degree of reflexivity in our research.

A further dilemma arises through the fact that research respondents are not a homogenous group and saying too much about what influences our research at any given moment may hinder our projects' attempts at data collection. That is, in cases where we have differing world views and political assumptions than those held by some of our research respondents, we may risk their inclusion if we speak too much about the research's informing assumptions. Of course we can and should let research respondents know some of the assumptions which inform our work. Indeed many researchers have experimented with varied ways of involving their participants throughout the project's stages, especially during data analysis and writing up (Borland, 1991; Denzin, 1998; Edwards, 1993; Ribbens, 1994). While this is laudable, we would also maintain that with large samples of diverse research respondents, this is not always possible and the ethics of doing this very much depend on the project's overall purposes and focus. Moreover, we suggest that relationships with respondents cannot necessarily take precedence over other relationships and commitments, including with those persons and communities who will read, use and build on our knowledge. Ethical issues, we argue, need to be framed and considered in terms of these wider relationships that go beyond those we nurture and maintain with respondents.

In this section, we have pointed to a complex and wide conception of reflexivity as being an ethical issue that relates to being as transparent as possible about theoretical, ontological and epistemological conceptions, while also recognizing that this wide conception of reflexivity incorporates interpersonal and institutional contexts of research, as well as ontological and epistemological assumptions, and epistemological conceptions of subjects and subjectivities all of which can have a profound effect on our research (see Mauthner and Doucet, in press). We have also drawn attention to what we now regard as the limited extent of our reflexive processes at the time of our research. We point out how, with the benefit of hindsight, we have reached a greater understanding of the range of influences which shaped our research. We also want to suggest that the particular conceptions employed by researchers are less important than the *epistemological accountability* involved in making these conceptions as transparent as possible for the many communities who have a relationship to, and interest in, our work (Mauthner and Doucet, in press).

Conclusions

In this chapter, we attempted to follow Lorraine Code's initiative to reflect on the intertwined ethical, methodological and epistemological processes and to consider what it means to 'know well', to 'know responsibly' and to attain a high degree of 'epistemic responsibility'. Using, as illustrative case studies, the life and story of American geneticist Barbara McClintock as well as our own research studies, this chapter argued for the inseparability of ethics, research practice and the construction of knowledge. First, we argued that attempting to build 'responsible knowledge' involves maintaining relationships, or staying in relation, with research subjects, particularly those who may not fit our theoretical, epistemological and ontological models. We emphasized particularly the importance of these continuing relationships during data analysis processes. Secondly, we argued for a 'robust' concept of reflexivity that goes beyond the usual calls for researcher location. This is a reflexivity that includes reflecting on social as well as political and institutional locations but also involves transparency and accountability about the theoretical, epistemological, and ontological assumptions that inform and influence our knowledge construction.

Several implications emerge from the arguments made in our chapter. The first is that data analysis is an ethical issue because it exposes power and privilege in relationships, decision-making around maintaining or curbing relationships with research subjects, and the potential for profound relational violations. In arguing that data analysis processes are ethically infused, we also suggest that data analysis methods are not neutral techniques. Rather, they are methods that embrace both methodological and epistemological assumptions. In this vein, we challenge the distinction Sandra Harding (1987) draws between methods, methodology and epistemology. We argue that data analysis methods *are* epistemological and ontological issues because they carry epistemological and ontological assumptions with them, although these may alter in our own utilization of these methods. In arguing for the inseparability of ethics, epistemology and method-ology, data analysis processes are key sites for noting the deeply knotted quality of these strands of responsible knowledge construction.

The second key implication arising from this chapter is that reflex-ivity, as an integral part of knowing processes, is also an intensely ethical issue. While feminist researchers often draw attention to the importance of reflexivity as an ethical aspect of our commitment to the women from whose experiences we construct knowledges, we also have an 'epistemic responsibility' to the women (and men) who read our work and indeed to any person who takes our knowledge claims seriously. While we cannot always know or name the multiple of influences on our research at the time of conducting it (see Grosz, 1995; Mauthner et al., 1998), we can be as reflexive as possible in the very wide sense that we have outlined in this chapter. In recognizing that knowledge construction requires a range of commitments and relationships to large groups of knowers, both participants and read-ers alike, we then recognize the critical importance and ethical weight that 'robust' reflexivity plays in our knowing processes. '(I)f we are to ensure that we know responsibly and well' (Code, 1995: 43), greater sustained attention must be accorded to the ethical aspects of our data analysis procedures and to putting in place strong enactments of reflexivity throughout our knowing processes.

Thirdly, the arguments we are positing in this chapter lead to a wide concept of ethical practice, one that focuses on relationships and accountability and recognizes the importance of attending to these issues throughout and beyond the research process. Just as the meth-odological literature, including feminist contributions to methodo-logical debates, has concentrated overwhelmingly on data collection processes (see Mauthner and Doucet, 1998), it may also be the case that ethical discussions in methodology have concentrated heavily on research relationships with respondents during data collection. This partly mirrors the separate discourses on feminist ethics in method-ology and feminist ethics in epistemology. It also mirrors a continuing division in research which feminist empiricists have, to their credit, astutely tried to draw together: the 'context of discovery' and 'the context of justification' (see Longino, 1990, 1993). That is, while femin-ists have ably described the influences on data collection processes at the 'discovery' phase of the research, little attention has been accorded to the context of *justification*. That is, much greater attention should be given to the epistemological questions of justifying and validating one's knowledge claims and of building and maintaining relation-ships with the readers and users of our research, as well as the academic, interpretive and epistemological communities within which this research is conceived, carried out and reviewed. Our view is that ethical research practice must attend to the close connection between both the contexts of discovery and the contexts of justification by attending to the continuous, fluid and complex relationships that constitute qualitative research projects throughout the varied contexts and processes of knowledge construction. In order to actualise ethical research practice, there needs to be a wider understanding of the multiple commitments that research entails and the long-term quality of 'knowing well' and 'knowing responsibly'.

A final implication of what we are arguing is that, as argued in the Introduction to this book, research may be best served by 'situational' or contextualized ethics. That is, each research project will have to decide how to enact a process of attempting to include the per-spectives of research subjects who would seem to challenge our initial theoretical frameworks, which relationships to emphasize and which relationships to play down, how much and how far to be accountable and to whom. Being ethical in research practice may involve *varied degrees* of ethical responsibility and accountability. These processes can be greatly assisted through the creation of supportive 'knowing' com-munities that can aid us in our attempts to achieve what Code has referred to as 'responsible knowledge of human experience' and 'exemplary kinds of knowing' (Code, 1993: 39).

Acknowledgements

We are indebted to the mothers and fathers who agreed to take part in our respective research studies. We are grateful to Melanie Mauthner, Maxine Birch, Julie Jessop and Tina Miller for their critical commen-tary on this chapter as well as to the members of the Women's Workshop on Qualitative/Household Research. We also thank Carol Gilligan, Martin Richards and Robert Blackburn for the support, encouragement and insights they continue to give us in our work. Financial support for our research was provided by the Medical Research Council of the United Kingdom, and the Commonwealth Association and the Social Sciences and Humanities Research Council of Canada, respectively.

Notes

[1] More recently, increasing attention has been accorded by feminist researchers to ethical concerns or 'worry' that occur in the intersections between 'ethics, writing, and qualitative research' (Fine and Wies, 1996: 251; see also DeVault, 1999).

[2] While Code is one of the few feminist philosophers who actively engages with grounded methodological questions at the level of practice, the details of translating 'epistemic responsibility' into concrete methodological principles and practices still requires some attention. In her early attempts at this translation between epistemological concerns and methodological guidelines, Code argued cogently for constant links between knowledge and experience while simultaneously recognizing the structural contexts of this experience; she thus argued for 'finding appropriate ways of knowing women's experiences and the structures that shape them . . . and of developing theoretical accounts of knowledge that retain continuity with experiences' (1988: 187). She also drew on the work of Carol Gilligan (1982) and called for a 'methodological approach' that entailed 'listening responsively . . . and responsibly' to 'people's stories (to *women's* stories) as they recount their experiences' (1987: 197). More recently Code has gone further in calling for the use of 'vigilant methods' (1995: 33) including innovative alternative methods such as participatory, activist and experiential research practices (Burt and Code, 1995; see also Birch and Miller, Chapter 5).

[3] Put simply, genetic transposition is the view that 'genetic elements can move in an apparently co-ordinated way from one chromosomal site to another' (Keller, 1983: 199). Keller also writes about the significance of this discovery to McClintock: 'For her, the discovery of transposition was above all a key to the complexity of genetic organisation – an indicator of the subtlety with which cytoplasm, membranes and DNA are integrated into a single structure. It is the overall organisation, or orchestration, that enables the organism to meet its needs, whatever they might be, in ways that never cease to surprise us' (Keller, 1983: 199).

[4] This situation might be different in the case of collaborative research where researchers might analyse their data together.

[5] In addition, this view can be viewed as akin to sociological accounts that highlight the self in symbolic interactionist terms (Blumer, 1969; Mead, 1934; Smith, 1999).

References

Alcoff, L. and Potter, E. (eds) (1993) *Feminist Epistemologies*. London and New York: Routledge.

Antony, L.M. and Witt, C. (1993) *A Mind of One's Own: Feminist Essays on Reason & Objectivity*. Boulder, Colorado: Westview Press.

Bar On, B-A. (1993) 'Marginality and epistemic privilege', in L. Alcoff and E. Potter (eds), *Feminist Epistemologies*. London and New York: Routledge.

Belenky, M.F., Clinchy, B.M., Goldberger, N.R. and Tarule, J.M. (1986) *Women's Ways of Knowing: The Development of Self, Voice, and Mind*. New York: Basic Books.

Blumer, H. (1969) *Symbolic Interactionism: Perspective and Method*. Berkeley: University of California Press.

Borland, K. (1991) "That's not what I said': interpretive conflict in oral narrative research', in S. Gluck and D. Patai (eds), *Women's Words: The Feminist Practice of Oral History*. London: Routledge. pp. 63–75.

Burt, S. and Code, L. (1995) *Changing Methods: Feminists Transforming Practice*. Peterborough, Ontario: Broadview Press.

Butler, J. (1995) 'Contingent foundations', in S. Benhabib, J. Butler, D. Cornell and N. Fraser, *Feminist Contentions: A Philosophical Exchange*. London: Routledge.

Code, L. (1984) 'Toward a "responsibilist" epistemology', *Philosophy and Phenomenological Research*, 45(1): 29–50.

Code, L. (1987) *Epistemic Responsibility*. Hanover and London: Brown University Press.

Code, L. (1988) 'Experience, Knowledge and Responsibility', in M. Griffiths and M. Whitford (eds), *Feminist Perspectives in Philosophy*. Bloomington and Indianapolis: Indiana University Press. pp. 187–204.

Code, L. (1991) *What Can she Know? Feminist Theory and the Construction of Knowledge*. Ithaca, NY: Cornell University Press.

Code, L. (1993) 'Taking subjectivity into account', in L. Alcoff and E. Potter (eds), *Feminist Epistemologies*. New York and London: Routledge. pp. 15–48.

Code, L. (1995) 'How do we know? Questions of method in feminist practice', in S. Burt and L. Code (eds), *Changing Methods: Feminist Transforming Practice*. Peterborough, Ontario: Broadview Press. pp. 13–44.

Code, L., Ford, M., Martindale, K., Sherwin, S. and Shogan, D. (1983) *Is Feminist Ethics Possible?* Ottawa: CRIAW/ICREF.

Denzin, N.K. (1998) 'The art and politics of interpretation', in N.K. Denzin and Y.S. Lincoln (eds), *Collecting and Interpreting Qualitative Materials*. London: Sage. pp. 313–44.

DeVault. M. (1999) 'Speaking up carefully: authorship and authority in feminist writing', in M. DeVault, *Liberating Method: Feminism and Social Research*. Philadelphia: Temple University Press. pp. 187–91.

Doucet, A. (1995) 'Gender equality and gender difference in household work and parenting', *Women's Studies International Forum* 18(3): 271–84.

Doucet, A. (1998) 'Interpreting mother-work: Linking methodology, ontology, theory and personal biography', *Canadian Woman Studies*, 18(2&3): 52–8.

Doucet, A. and Mauthner, N. (1999) 'Subjects and Subjectivities in Feminist Theory and Research'. Paper presented to the British Sociological Association Conference, Glasgow, Scotland.

Doucet, A. (2000) ' "There's a huge difference between me as a male carer and women". Gender, domestic responsibility and the community as an international arena', *Community, Work and Family* 3(2): 163–84.

Doucet, A. (2001) 'You see the need perhaps more clearly than I have: exploring gendered processes of domestic responsibility', *Journal of Family Issues* 22(3): 328–57.

Duran, J. (1994) *Knowledge in Context: Naturalized Epistemology and Sociolinguistics*. London: Rowman and Littlefield.

Edwards, R. (1993) *Mature Women Students: Separating or Connecting Family and Education*. London: Taylor and Francis.

Fine, M. and Wies, L. (1996) 'Writing the "wrongs" of fieldwork: confronting our own research/ writing dilemmas in urban ethnographies', *Qualitative Inquiry* (2, 3): 251–74.

Fish, S. (1980) *Is There a Text in this Class?: The Authority on Interpretive Communities*. Cambridge, MA: Harvard University Press.

Flax, J. (1992) 'The end of innocence', in Judith Butler and Joan W. Scott (eds), *Feminists Theorise the Political*. London: Routledge. pp. 445–63.

Gilligan, C. (1982) *In a Different Voice*. Cambridge, MA: Harvard University Press.

Gilligan, C., Brown, L.M. and Rogers, A. (1990) 'Psyche embedded: a place for body, relationships and culture in personality theory', in A.I. Rabin, R. Zucker, R. Emmons and S. Frank (eds), *Studying Persons and Lives*. New York: Springer. pp. 86–147.

Glucksmann, M. (1994) 'The work of knowledge and the knowledge of women's work', in M. Maynard and J. Purvis (eds), *Researching Women's Lives from a Feminist Perspective*. London: Taylor and Francis. pp. 149–65.

Griffiths, M. and Whitford, M. (1988) 'Introduction', in M. Griffiths and M. Whitford (eds), *Feminist Perspectives in Philosophy*. Bloomington and Indianapolis: Indiana University Press. pp. 1–28.

Grosz, E. (1995) 'Sexual Signatures: Feminism after the Death of the Author', in E. Grosz (ed.), *Space, Time and Perversion*. London: Routledge. pp. 9–24.

Hale, S. (1991) 'Feminist method, process and self criticism: interviewing Sudanese women', in S.B. Gluck and D. Patai (eds), *Women's Words; the Feminist Practice of Oral History*. London: Routledge. pp. 121–36.

Haraway, D. (1991) *Simians, Cyborgs and Women*. New York: Routledge and Kegan Paul.

Harding, S. (1987) 'Is there a feminist method?', in S. Harding (ed.), *Feminism and Methodology*. Bloomington, Indiana and Milton Keynes: Indiana University Press and Open University Press. pp. 1–14.

Harding, S. (1992) *Whose Science? Whose Knowledge?* Milton Keynes: Open University Press.

Harding, S. (1998) *Is Science Multicultural? Postcolonialism, Feminisms and Epistemologies*. Indiana: Indiana University Press.

Jordan, J. (1993) 'The relational self: a model of woman's development', in J. van Mens-Verhulst, K. Schreurs and L. Woertman (eds) *Daughtering and Mothering: Female Subjectivity Reanalysed*. London: Routledge.

Keller, E.F. (1983) *A Feeling for the Organism: The Life and Work of Barbara McClintock*. New York: W.H. Freeman.

Keller, E.F. (1985) *Reflections of Gender and Science*. New Haven and London: Yale University Press.

Lazreg, M. (1994) 'Women's experience and feminist epistemology: a critical neo-rational approach', in K. Lennon and M. Whitford (eds), *Knowing the Difference: Feminist Perspectives in Epistemology*. London: Routledge.

Lennon, K. and Whitford, M. (eds) (1994) *Knowing the Difference: Feminist Perspectives in Epistemology*. London: Routledge.

Longino, H. (1990) *Science as Social Knowledge: Values and Objectivity in Scientific Inquiry*. Princeton: Princeton University Press.

Longino, H. (1993) 'Subjects, power and knowledge: description and prescription in feminist philosophies of science', in L. Alcoff and E. Potter (eds), *Feminist Epistemologies*. New York: Routledge. pp. 101–20.

Mauthner, N.S. (1999) ' "Feeling low and feeling really bad about feeling low": Women's experiences of motherhood and postpartum depression', *Canadian Psychology*, 40(2): 143–61.

Mauthner, N.S. (2002) *The Darkest Days of My Life: Stories of Postpartum Depression*. Cambridge, MA: Harvard University Press.

Mauthner, N.S. and Doucet, A. (1998) 'Reflections on a voice centred relational method of data analysis: analysing maternal and domestic voices', in J. Ribbens and R. Edwards (eds), *Feminist Dilemmas in Qualitative Research: Public Knowledge and Private Lives*. London: Sage.

Mauthner, N.S. and Doucet, A. (in press) 'Reflexive Accounts and Accounts of Reflexivity in Qualitative Data Analysis'. Submitted to *Sociology*.

Mauthner, N.S., Parry, O. and Backett-Milburn, K. (1998) ' "The Data are Out There, or Are They?" Implications for Archiving and Revisiting Qualitative Data', *Sociology*, 32: 733–45.

Maynard, M. (1994) 'Methods, practice and epistemology', in Mary Maynard and Jane Purvis (eds), *Researching Women's Lives from a Feminist Perspective*. London: Taylor and Francis.

Mead, G.H. (1934) *Mind, Self and Society*. Chicago: University of Chicago Press.

Nelson, L.H. (1993) 'Epistemological communities', in Linda Alcoff and Elizabeth Potter (eds), *Feminist Epistemologies*. London: Routledge.

Patai, D. (1991) 'U.S. academics and Third World women: is ethical research possible?', in S.B. Gluck and D. Patai (eds), *Women's Words; the Feminist Practice of Oral History*. London: Routledge. pp. 137–54.

Reinharz, S. (1992) *Feminist Methods in Social Research*. Oxford: Oxford University Press.

Ribbens, J. (1994) *Mothers and their Children: A Feminist Sociology of Childrearing*. London: Sage.

Ruddick, S. (1989) *Material Thinking: Towards a Politics of Peace*. Boston: Beacon.

Seller, A. (1988) 'Realism versus relativism: towards a politically adequate epistemology', in M. Griffiths and M. Whitford (eds), *Feminist Perspectives in Philosophy*. Bloomington and Indianapolis: Indiana University Press. pp. 169–86.

Smith, D. (1999) 'Telling the truth after post modernism', in D. Smith, *Writing the Social*. Toronto: University of Toronto Press.

Tanesini, A. (1999) *An Introduction to Feminist Epistemologies*. Oxford: Blackwell Publishers.

Tronto, J. (1993) *Moral Boundaries: A Political Argument for an Ethic of Care*. New York and London: Routledge.

Tronto, J. (1995) 'Care as a basis for radical political judgements' (Symposium on care and justice), *Hypati*, 10: 141–9.

Wolf, D.L. (1996) 'Situating feminist dilemmas in fieldwork', in D.L. Wolf (ed.), *Feminist Dilemmas in Fieldwork*. Boulder, Colorado: Westview.

Zavella, P. (1993) 'Feminist insider dilemmas: constructing ethnic identity with "Chicana" inform-ants', in L. Lamphere, H. Ragone and P. Zavella (eds), *Situated Lives: Gender and Culture in Everyday Life*. London: Routledge. pp. 42–62.

CHAPTER 8

ELICITING RESEARCH ACCOUNTS: RE/PRODUCING MODERN SUBJECTS?

Pam Alldred and Val Gillies

Introduction

The research interview is not a clear window onto the interviewee's experience, rather it is the joint production of an account by inter-viewer and interviewee through the dynamic interaction between them. This is now widely accepted among qualitative researchers, particularly those informed by feminist research debates, but what are the implications in terms of the responsibility the researcher bears for the performance elicited or for the account produced and how it functions politically?

This interaction in the research interview tends to elicit presenta-tions of self which largely conform to dominant cultural forms because of the implicit expectations that shape the interview process. At a general level, this is because strangers who seek to connect with each other will adopt an established mode of communication, but in more particular ways, it is also about the 'space' constructed for an interviewee to occupy, given the presumptions about research that both interviewee and researcher bring to the interview. It is some of the more particular layers of expectation about research interviews that we will explore here. Research interview practices must be seen as 'helping' or 'suggesting' that participants employ conventional modes of self-expression and so perform as (or within a narrow range of difference from) the 'standard' subject. This standard subject is of course an historically particular model of individual who, within Western cultures, is understood through modernist principles as bounded, rational and autonomous. What if, therefore, research inter-views do not merely look in upon, but actively serve to produce modern subjects? That is, provide a particular social experience through which we experience and in some ways are active in produc-ing ourselves as modernist individuals. What are the ethical implica-tions of research practices exerting a pressure to conform to cultural expectations? And what are the political implications of research accounts that then serve to reinforce the centrality and superiority of this Western model of the self?

The research interview has been a key tool for feminist and other critical researchers in the social sciences. As we argued in Chapter 2, such researchers have sought either to enable muted or marginal perspectives to be validated and more widely acknowledged in the public sphere, or have aimed to empower research participants through consciousness raising or action research. Research embodies modernist principles, at least embracing notions of progress and enlightenment which have attracted feminist theorists' and philosophers' criticisms of its epistemology. Another consequence of the modernist foundation of social research is that it, unsurprisingly, rests on a modernist model of the subject. This model is critiqued by feminist and psychoanalytic scholars for its mythical rationality, boundaried and radical independence, and by cultural and political theorists for the way it has functioned to bolster a sense of the superiority of the Western subject against the inferiority of its Others. Its hegemonic status is corroborated by the understanding of the subject in social research. Our research practice is usually located in a framework that assumes and enforces particular conditions of subjectivity, irrespective of the sensitivity with which we strive to recognize difference at later analytic stages. Therefore, as researchers, we elicit performances of self in which radical difference is suppressed by virtue of contemporary understandings of research, of ethical practice, of rapport and of the consenting, self-speaking subject.

We will explore the ethical implications of our argument that interviews elicit performances of the modernist subject on two levels. The first level concerns those who take part in the research. For some, being interviewed might be constraining or prescriptive, extending everyday pressures to be 'normal', while for others, or at other times, it might be a comforting affirmation of one's 'normality' or sociability. We will discuss some of the subtle, unintentional ways in which interviews can be normalizing for participants. The second level relates to ethical concerns associated with broader political relations. If, as feminists (or social and cultural theorists), we are critical of the cultural norms of Western subjectivity, are we justified in reinforcing this model of the self in our accounts, even when we believe the research has a progressive impact locally? But how else do we make powerful claims to know that can have any influence today? And, how can we conceive of ethical research practice without founding it on the modernist subject? This tension arises from the attempt to build feminist/critical research on the foundations of modernist understandings of knowledge and the subject, and the impossibility of escaping understandings through which we are ourselves formed.

This chapter explores some of the implicit ways in which ethical research practice relies on this modernist notion of the subject. Feminists such as Erica Burman (1992) and Elspeth Probyn (1993) have urged that researcher reflexivity should concern relations not only 'in the field', but also 'in the academy and beyond' and so we discuss the presence of assumptions about the subject at different stages of the research process. We argue that ethical scrutiny of research must consider its impact on a cultural, not only an individual level. We hope to contribute to feminist debates about research by highlighting the way in which even when presuming the modernist subject is not unethical at the immediate or individual level, by eliciting and representing this mode of subjectivity, we bolster its arrogant normativity and perpetuate its exclusions. Identifying the modernist subject as a culturally particular ideal at least interrupts its naturalization.

The modern subject(s) of research

The production of knowledge in the social sciences is a modernist project that rests on empirical realist understandings of truth and reality, which are core features of the Western epoch identified as modernity. If research is a modernist knowledge practice, it is not surprisingly based on a modernist notion of the subject. This is the Cartesian subject, whose cognitive processes operate independently of emotion and according to the rules of abstract rationality (Henriques et al., 1998). Also referred to as the psychological subject, the individual celebrated in liberal humanism is the model of personhood presumed in post-Enlightenment thought. Historically there have always been those who failed to live up to this ideal for reasons attributed to their own inadequacy or pathology: it was women's 'emotionality', 'mad' people's 'irrationality', children's 'instability' and 'immaturity' and the colonial subject's supposed cognitive inferiority. Attributing failure to match the 'ideal' to the psychology or make-up of particular groups, meant the normality of the model itself went unquestioned.

However, critiques from many perspectives have shown this unitary, rational subject to be untenable. Feminist scholars have long identified its presumption of masculinist ideals, and post-colonial theorists, postmodernists and post-structuralists have developed critiques of its 'independence' and cognitivism, and questioned assumptions about 'development' and rationalism. This Cartesian subject 'whose self-consciousness acts as guarantor of meaning', is challenged 'both by versions of psychoanalysis (Althusser, 1971; Frosh, 1987) and discourse analysis (Parker, 1992), which see the subject as being fragmented and constituted within language' (Marks, 1996: 115). Michel

Foucault emphasized the modernity of the notion of the subject as the self-centred, constitutive agent of history and of its own biography (Henriques et al., 1998). His work has been central in showing how discourses and practices function to constitute subjectivities in historically specific ways and how power operates through processes that produce subjectivity. This is why for many feminists and others, post-structuralist approaches offer not an abandonment of a political subject, but a better way of understanding the operation of power than seeming acquiescence to hierarchical power relations and adoption of 'false consciousness'. This affords us a more complex understanding of the relationship between culture and the psyche, but also explains why the subjectivity constituted through Western modernity is not vanished by deconstruction in academic seminar rooms. Since we are ourselves subjects of its formation, we are materially and psychologically invested in it. As feminist post-structuralists have shown, the idea that our desires would fall in line with our politics is itself rationalist (Walkerdine, 1990; Weedon, 1987).

The very idea of interviewing someone is rooted in particular understandings about what being a person is, about communication between two people and about how knowledge can be generated by the posing of questions by one and recording of responses by another. The account an individual provides in an interview is seen as a snapshot of their perspective. The expectation is that they are responsively reflexive and can 'represent' themselves to us. 'Giving primacy to interviewees' talk about their experience ... suggests that their speech may refer to themselves as a unified, authentic subject' whereas social constructionist theory has warned that 'giving our "subject" a "voice" involves the fantasy that it is possible to have unmediated direct knowledge of experience (James and Prout, 1990)' (Marks, 1996: 115). Social research interviewing is viewed here as a practice that rests on and reiterates the dominant construction of the individual, so that even research which tries to introduce broader ethical considerations and a degree of reflexivity into its practice, tends to construct the interviewee as the rational, self-reflexive modernist subject (e.g. David et al., 2001; Marks, 1996).

Those who were historically excluded from full (modern) subject status were not viewed as potential research subjects (Blackman, 1996; Hogan, 1998; Hood et al., 1999; Rose, 1985) because they are seen as unable to participate in the (polite, rational, reflexive, 'middle-class') interaction required to negotiate an interview 'contract', or because communication might fall outside the bounds of expected interaction, where transgressions of that mode of being might be experienced as so disruptive as to breach the implicit 'contract' between interviewer and interviewee. However, in the second half of the twentieth century, the in-depth interview has been an important tool for progressive social researchers from the Chicago school and left-wing sociologists of the 1960s onwards, as a way of allowing marginalized perspectives greater recognition. Feminist theorists and activists and 'race' theorists and multiculturalists have shown that dominant (white, European, androcentric) ways of seeing the world are not the only ways and have used it to gain some recognition of other perspectives by the mainstream and for validating them amongst marginalized groups. More recently it has provided a tool for researchers to hear the views of children and young people.

However, some feminist and post-structuralist writers have pointed out that even progressive, reflexive and ethically well thought through research can prompt interviewees to narrate them-selves through the dominant discourses of subjectivity, ultimately reinforcing the implicit rules of subjectivity by which contemporary individuals are expected to govern and regulate ourselves. Deborah Marks (1996) argues this and illustrates it through her own interviews with young people who had been excluded from school. She hoped to provide a supportive ear as someone not associated with the school regime. However many of the young people narrated themselves through discourses of repentance and 'responsibility' for their 'bad behaviour'. Reluctantly, she recognized that the interviews functioned as yet another site for these pupils to produce themselves as reformed characters, as reflexive, self-regulating (and therefore now trustwor-thy) individuals. She employed the Foucauldian notion of Govern-mentality to understand how her interviews functioned in a regulatory way, not only in a restrictive sense, but also in a productive sense (Foucault, 1988; Rose, 1989, 1993). They were performative in that pupils performed, and thereby actively 'produced' themselves as subjects within the dominant meanings of 'bad behaviour' and legit-imate sanction. The interviews were therefore normalizing in that they allowed/invited/suggested that pupils regulate themselves in line with the school's discourse of responsibility and justice.

The notion of performativity, from Butlerian queer theory, maps the same collusive and resistive possibilities for subjects, but helpfully, the term (unlike 'normalizing' and 'regulation') does not foreclose the question of whether this is against the interests of the subject (Butler, 1990). The complexity of such an evaluation is suggested by Marks' (1996) example, where accepting the school's discourse of justice might help a particular pupil avoid further sanctions at this particular time. Interviews can therefore function to 'invite' people to occupy particular subject positions which can function in normalizing and regulatory ways, through their own will and through the production of certain desires, rather than in a coercive or sanction-threatening way (Foucault, 1988; Henriques et al., 1998; Rose, 1993).

Not only may interviewing function to reinforce a particular model of subjectivity for those who participate in research, but because it elicits performances of the modern subject and then represents these in authoritative accounts, it reinforces this model as the cultural norm. Research participants who might be seen as marginal subjects face particular risks because any indications of straying from the ideal subject are more likely to be attributed to their own failings or developmental limitations, rather than pointing to the limitations, or fabrications of the model of research. As Burman (1994) argues 'descriptive' norms when presented authoritatively come to function prescriptively, and eventually as normal in the sense that deviation from them becomes problematized or pathologized. The fact that interviews elicit a narrow range of expressions of subjectivity becomes a problem when, as public representations, they exert a normative effect due to the value explicitly and implicitly accorded to the status of research accounts. Just as eliciting a modernist performance is not necessarily damaging to the individual, the wider political implications associated with bolstering such cultural norms whilst undesirable generally, might be positive for particular groups. We discuss the dilemma this raises about our use of research in the next section.

Thoroughly Modern Millies?

Feminist theorists (Haraway, 1990; Hollway, 1989; Lather, 1991) have described how our knowledge practices are so predicated on modernist understandings that one can scarcely avoid using metaphors of light and vision or the 'further up the mountain' narrative of progress towards the Truth (Kitzinger, 1987; Rorty, 1980). The modernist understanding of how we come to know something constructs perceiving as a neutral, objective process and so obscures and negates the role of the researcher in constructing knowledge. We inevitably perceive through the lens of our own cultural perspective, and feminists and anthropologists in particular (see Nencel and Pens, 1991) have agonised about how we can hear and represent the views of those from perspectives different to our own, considering the compromises others make to be understood on (and literally in) the researcher's terms (Grossberg, 1989). At the same time as the particularity of perspective is under-recognized, the researcher is, implicitly, centre-stage. Our skill and insight are seen as allowing us access to 'knowledge', but our perspective and points of reference are naturalized, bolstering the centrality of the (modernist) self who 'knows' and the marginality of those (who are often Other in some way) who are known, in their (sometimes quirky) objectified states (Probyn, 1993). Feminists and others have problematized this subject/object split, and post-colonial and psychoanalytic theorists critique the (political and intra-subjective) violence of the hierarchical relation between self and Other (Venn, 1985).[1]

The knowledge relations this produces between researcher and researched is so inevitably hierarchical that some (e.g. Patai, 1991: 139) believe that it is not possible 'in the actual conditions of the real world today – to write about the oppressed without becoming one of the oppressors'. Whilst we may not accept her conclusion that when the research relation overlays existing structural inequalities research can never be ethical, her argument highlights how even critically considered work might still bolster particular dominant understandings or power relations. James Scheurich (1997) describes how the 'Western modernist imperium is constituting our common, everyday assumptions about researchers, research, reality, epistemology, methodology, etc.' and identifies what we might call the institutionalized racisms and imperialisms of the unintended political consequences of how research functions on a cultural level:

> Even though we researchers think or assume we are doing good works or creating useful knowledge or helping people or critiquing the status quo or opposing injustice, we are unknowingly enacting or being enacted by 'deep' civilizational or cultural biases, biases that are damaging to other cultures and to other people who are unable to make us hear them because they do not 'speak' in our cultural 'languages'. (Scheurich, 1997: 1)

The implication is that despite the political intentions of researchers, research can reinforce not only the particular and narrow range of ways of being a 'modern subject', but the broader political relations that stem from the modernist foundation of the research enterprise. However, research attempting to move beyond conventional, positivist assumptions to allow for a model of subjectivity as unfixed and performative, would itself generate another set of ethical issues. What does a radical openness to different 'ways of being' look like in practice, given that researchers too are formed as modern subjects? And if we could imagine it, enacting it would probably be compromised by understandings of good practice in research, as is embodied in professional bodies' codes of conduct and standards asserted by university research ethics committees, as well as, in all probability, by our common-sense understanding of (and commitment to) treating interviewees decently.

In current good practice around 'informed consent' it is now expected that researchers take responsibility for informing would-be participants of the aims, methods and funders of a study and the use to which the findings will be put, before they are asked to decide if they will participate. Standard good practice also involves asking if an interview can be taped and explaining the practice of anonymous write-ups, the use of pseudonyms where case studies or quotations are used etc. This is the explicit research 'contract'. But there is also an implicit 'contract' regarding the ways in which both parties are expected to act, and next we discuss aspects of this that relate to the interview interaction. As Burman (1992) highlighted, the parts of this that are concerned with the relationship once back 'in the academy', including, significantly, the researcher's right to interpret participants' words, is seldom made explicit, even in participatory or collaborative research. With the increasing significance of legal discourse, the research 'contract' is moving towards a more literal one. The legal framework is founded on the modern subject – to whom individual rights are accorded and from whom rational, cognitive agency is expected. The paradox is that it would be unethical in current conditions not to adopt practices that assume the modernist subject, and yet we can see how the ideas underpinning these practices are not ultimately ethical themselves.

Thus, while research may be considered ethical if it results in recognition or respect for individual subject status, reinforcing this status in itself can be seen as raising serious ethical concerns. Ethical considerations are more tangible when research can be recognized as impacting directly on people's lives, rather than indirectly through the cultural politics of representation. As researchers we are accustomed to considering the former, but far less the latter. Nevertheless, this ethical tension is often evident. For instance, research which seeks to 'hear the views of Black women' might (albeit unintentionally) reinforce the centrality and 'normality' of white women in contrast to whom Black women's difference marks them as Other. The dilemma we face as researchers is that in making powerful claims to 'know' in order to effect desirable social change, we inevitably bolster such hierarchical and normative political relations.

As researchers we occupy a position that rests upon and reinforces modernist knowledge practices and the commodification of knowledge. We elicit particular kinds of responses from research participants because the social 'space' of the interview is not as open to diverse ways of being as we might hope, but we might judge that the political gains for a particular group of being represented outweigh performative and/or representative compromises, either despite normalization or perhaps because of what inclusion in full modern subject status means for them. Thus, the modernist foundations of research limit radical political intentions, requiring us to hold in tension realizable but often reformist aims with more radical aspirations.

Recognizing these compromises can help us identify when there are strategic gains in modernity's own terms for those still marginalized within them, and when we want to challenge the frameworks that result in such exclusions, competition and individualism. Discussions of feminist research strategies (Alldred, 1996; Burman, 1998; Ribbens and Edwards, 1998) echo debates about the merits of the human rights framework, for instance, where the specific potential impact may be progressive, but the framework as a whole is Western and naturalizes the Western subject. Similar points have also been made about the way the liberal humanist individual is exported along with aid packages to 'developing' countries, with globalization functioning as cultural imperialism (Burman, 1995). The risk of unintentionally reifying particular meanings or agendas might create tensions even on the pragmatic level, amongst those involved. For instance, doing research about sex education can promote the shared aim of raising its status within schools, but it can be diverted by a national policy emphasis which justifies it narrowly in terms of reducing teenage pregnancy into a restricted focus on heterosexual sex, contraception and tacitly supporting the unqualified problematization of teenage pregnancy (David, 2001). Similarly, as one of us found, research which aimed to question the dominant discourse of parental involvement in education, functioned to reinforce it when teachers used the research itself to reinforce this message (David et al., 2001) and because asking parents' permission to interview young children probably fuelled guilt or anxiety about how involved they were in their children's education. Both cases risked reinforcing an agenda, when the intention was to open it up for questioning.

Prompting this chapter is the tension we each experience between a belief in the potential political gains of feminist interview-based research, and yet recognition of the limitations and unintended corollaries of our own practice. This tension derives from a rethinking of key modernist beliefs in which researchers are schooled: first, that research knowledge is Truth, and second, that 'the truth' is necessarily progressive or emancipatory. In Chapter 2, we argued that in response to critiques of truth claims, feminist research can reformulate its aims from progress-through-knowledge to overtly political interventions. But still our sense that research can promote social justice, and our belief in the possibility of such 'progress' reveals our own modernist formation. This highlights our ambivalence because whilst we recognize that notions of 'progress' can operate in oppressive ways and require a (self-centring) assertion of value, we would not want to abandon them.

The next sections concern particular aspects of research that serve to construct and affirm the modernist subject (to which 'non-standard' adults and children are expected to aspire). Although the practice as a whole is implicated, we will illustrate how interviewee subjectivity is constructed at three discrete moments: during the interview itself; in the understanding of consent to participate in research; and through the production of an interview transcript.

Eliciting performances of the modernist subject

It requires some distance from the interview to recognize as normative those features that were 'normal' at the time and made for 'successful' research interviews. The implicit expectations are difficult to recognize and only with hindsight can we see qualities that characterize most of the interviews we have conducted. This raises issues of selection and self-selection of/by participants, but we will focus here on normative expectations. The taken-for-granted modes of co-operative communication that function to construct the research subject in a particular way can often only be glimpsed when they are disrupted. When behaviour deviates from general norms of communication, even with subtle variations from the manner, tone and etiquette expected it can disrupt research relations. It might be seen as rude or inappropriate, perhaps even to the extent of breaching the 'research contract' between interviewer and interviewee. This contract of understanding between researcher and interviewee can be seen as having explicit elements, concerning anonymity and confidentiality and publishing intentions, but also implicit terms and conditions.

We can use our experience of discomfort in interviews to reveal our expectations and assumptions and to generate an understanding of how they might differ from participants'. For instance, if an interviewee refuses the narrative task by speaking in a style that is unexpected or does not maintain particular interpersonal boundaries our expectations are disrupted. Being flirted with has felt uncomfortable and disorientating because of its breach of etiquette and undermining of a professional role. Similarly, our feelings of disappointment at an interview can reveal our assumptions about good rapport, which is where we see our own personal investments in being a 'good' researcher and a 'nice' person. Where interviewees go beyond the interview brief or refuse/neglect our agenda we can feel used for their ends. For example, in the course of research conducted by one of us on lesbian parenting, an interview was 'hijacked' and 'used' solely for the narration of a 'coming out' story (Plummer, 1995). At the time this was experienced as frustrating because the relevance to the research agenda could not be drawn out. Only retrospectively did this highlight how obliging all the other interviewees had been, how subtle the negotiation of and compromises over the 'agenda', and what demands were being asked of all participants, in terms of personal confidence and stabilized sexual identity, trust and the establishing of political/ supportive alliances. If interviewees do not perform as a reflexive subject or narrate themselves earnestly through a confessional, self-conscious discourse we might feel disrespected and that they are not taking the interview 'seriously'. The surprises or awkwardnesses can generate important insights when it comes to recognizing difference, and not only in communication styles. It is at these points that the contours of the space for manoeuvre in the position of 'interviewee' are more easily visible.

In our own research, we have both encountered situations where in order to conform to notions broadly accepted as good practice we have unintentionally imposed particular assumptions on interviewees. For example, out of a commitment to include non-white perspectives, when interviewing a couple from Bangladesh, it became clear to one of us that the structure and the content of the interview was predicated on white, Western assumptions about the nature of personhood and agency. The notion of personal decision-making and individualism which underpinned the interview questions made little sense to this couple, who were in effect being asked to narrate themselves as Westernized modernist subjects.

Similarly, one of us interviewed a working-class father, and was disorientated by the random nature of his anecdotes, as his biographical 'narrative' moved backwards and forwards in time with few connecting themes. As a researcher, the compulsion was to try and 'untangle' his account and actively impose a chronological structure on his recollections in order to produce an ordered, cohesive story because the interview agenda assumed individual biographies would be articulated through a modernist discourse of linear development or reflexivity. Life stories are generally expected to have some degree of linearity, not necessarily in the telling, but in the narrative plot, and we expect insight, progress and development. Ironic anti-developmental narratives are possible (e.g. 'I'm getting worse! I don't learn, do I! It's just the way I am'), but the absence of *any* of the narrative conventions would probably be disturbing to hear. It sounds chaotic and confusing if there is no sense of their own reflection on their lives. We might interpret the interview as unsuccessful where an interviewee was not and did not account for his or her actions. Performing what we consider to be reflexive subjectivity is an unwritten rule of the interview. We may only ask for an account of a life (or aspect of it) but what we're really expecting is a self-conscious, reflexive account which describes and comments on (does some analysis of) that account. Not only do we expect the modern subject to illustrate narratives of personal enlightenment and improvement, but these rely on a sense of history or biography which, in turn, rely on a sense of identity. The telling of a narrative also requires a belief that this account is worthy of a researcher's interest (see Birch, 1998).

Reflecting on encounters that felt disturbing, upsetting or disatisfying helps us recognize our active efforts to produce and control the interview process to prompt the construction of selves as modern subjects. In those interviews that 'passed' as successful ones, we must have organised and contained the conversation in order to obtain accounts that have a sense of structure and order (such as a linear chronology) and have probed and coaxed and steered away from certain topics in order to navigate through our research agenda.

Here we can see how the role of researcher is constructed too. We are seeking to perform similar goals and to perceive with a degree of abstraction, reflection and impartiality. In the negotiation of intimacy (over disclosures of distressing personal experiences in particular) are also our own personal boundaries and positionings and our understandings of this peculiar form of passing intimacy (and see Duncombe and Jessop, Chapter 6). We can use our awareness of the ways in which interview interactions can function to constrain as they invite particular modes of being, and how values accord to different behaviour even as we try not to be judgemental of participants ourselves. Whilst concern with researcher reflexivity arose from a critique of scientific objectivity, it too can be seen as modernist in its remedial promise. In addition to the concern to avoid providing an experience that interviewees find normalizing or constraining, eliciting particular performances through interviews means that these modes of being are more likely to predominate and direct our research reflections and are therefore further circulated in these cultural representations.

The consenting subject

The idea of informed consent is central to ethical research practice, but unsurprisingly it too rests on an understanding of the individual as the modernist subject. So even if we strive to conduct interviews that do not elicit and affirm only a narrow range of subjectivities, the explicit and implicit negotiations that precede this, 'speak to' this subject. 'Informed consent' involves the idea that good practice in research means providing 'adequate' information about the study for the researchers' side of the 'consent' procedure to be fulfilled and it constructs research participants as rational beings whose judgement must reflect and guarantee their own interests. This relies on the idea that the information researchers provide is unproblematic (correct, appropriate, accessible, adequate), that the subject has cognitive information processing skills and can make a rational decision in their own interests. As a consequence, responsibility then lies with the individual – a rational, autonomous subject who is in control of their own destiny. There is, therefore, little room to consider how the social context and emotional factors affect such 'processing' and 'decision-making'.

Personal reflections on the research we have conducted with children and young people highlighted two limitations on an entirely rational approach to informed consent for participation in research. The first is concerned with what the would-be participant understood social research to be, since their general expectations of research would inform their decision, in addition to their more specific understandings of the interests, intentions and boundaries of the particular research/ers (Edwards and Alldred, 1999). The fact that future outcomes may not be fully knowable has been raised in relation to medical consent, but this also limits the ideal in social research where we cannot be sure of the personal impact our research conversations might have. The second limitation relates to the abstract ideal of the neutral setting that does not affect decision-making. How 'freely' can we assume children's consent is in an institutional setting such as a school,[2] in which meanings, both moral and educational evaluations ('helping' with research, being mature and articulate) are constantly made across a doubly determined (adult-child, teacher-pupil) power relation?

The argument that children's consent to medical treatment or social research participation should be affirmed or renegotiated throughout the research process rather than consent having been given as a once and one for all at the start (Alderson, 1993; Morrow, 1999; Morrow and Richards, 1996) goes some way to reducing the pressure to make the right decision at the outset, and allows for changes of mind. Trying to open up space in this way (for processing, deciding, thinking and feeling differently) is the most we can do here, since 'informed consent' is still the best practice guideline, but unless we recognize these presumptions we can neither be more ethical to the particular subjects in question or recognize that our culturally particular ways of viewing the individual are presented as if they are inevitable.

In addition to reflecting upon the ways in which our research practices elicit particular performances from participants, and from ourselves, we must consider the way in which our representational practices may serve to depict subjectivity in particular ways. The interpretation of interviews may involve legitimate, unavoidable and unacknowledged processes of projection onto participants, and when we present research accounts we may question our claims about representation in both the literal and political senses of the word. However, next we will highlight one of the taken-for-granted representational processes in research where standard practice may serve to paint participants with greater uniformity, and in this way, reduce the range of subjective forms that research represents.

Producing transcripts

Collecting and processing data are active processes well before what we call 'analysis'. Researchers are 'processing the data' consciously and unconsciously as we make decisions about the form and conventions to use to represent the 'data'. The phrase 'data analysis' implies wrongly that there is a prior stage of data collection that occurs without the interpretive involvement of the researcher. It therefore constructs the object of study as fixed, observable, existing prior to, and independently of the researcher's gaze. Many theorists question positivist assumptions, such as that data analysis is merely the literal re-presentation of data, but few researchers draw on philosophical debates about ethics and representation. James Scheurich (1997: 63) describes it as 'a creative interaction between the conscious/ unconscious researcher and the decontextualised data which is assumed to represent reality, or at least, reality as interpreted by the interviewee'. Unfortunately though, this creativity is 'severely bounded by the restrictions of modernist assumptions about selves, language and communication' (ibid: 63).

Analysis is often assumed to start once the tape of an interview has been typed up and a transcript printed out. The process of transcription – making a written account of the verbal interaction – is one of the least problematized parts of the research process, not generally recognized as an act of representation or embodying interpretation. But transcription tends to affirm a particular theoretical position about the relation between language and meaning and when researchers focus on the mechanics of coding (Strauss and Corbin, 1990), they can fail to attend the complex ambiguities of language, communication and interpretation (Mishler, 1991).

> As transcription has become both more routine and precise . . . emphasis on it as a technical procedure has tended to detach the process from its deeper moorings in this critical reflection on the intractable uncertainties of meaning-language relationships. (Mishler, 1991: 260)

Technical procedures, adopted to ape the systematic rigor of scientific method, mask these uncertainties and 'the unstable ambiguities of linguistically communicated meaning' (Scheurich, 1997: 63). They therefore obscure the active role of the researcher in making meaning of interviewees' utterances.

Transcription is not the straight-forward, passive process it is assumed to be because representing intersubjective interaction on a two-dimensional page entails some compromises. Even rendering the speech alone on the page entails some distinct simplifications and there are strong conventions for it. Grammar and punctuation are required to make verbalizations conform to the rules of written English. But as we punctuate, we produce sentences from what are often streams of phrases and clauses and we fix meaning. Transcribing interviews have demonstrated to us just how ambiguous unpunctuated words can be. For instance, it is surprisingly common for a speaker to begin a negative statement with a 'yes' ('Yeh, no, it's not like that'). The 'yes' is a social emollient, perhaps agreeing with or affirming the previous speaker. Putting a full-stop, rather than a comma, between the 'yes' and 'no' gives the 'yes' more emphasis which makes it seem more of an expression of opinion. Writing it as 'Yeh' suggests a more casual tone, closer to an 'aha' than a decisive 'Yes'. The simplification or loss of tone, pace and volume can mean that emotions are 'sanitized' from the account (Burman, 1992: 47, and see Hollway, 1989). Losing the subtleties of humour can misrepresent emotional tone and meaning. The significance of tone and the difficulty of representing it was highlighted for one of us when interviewing children who spoke sarcastically about wanting their parents to come into school (Edwards and Alldred, 1999). Their words alone contradicted what we understood to be their views and their sarcasm indicated a strength of feeling that '[laugh]' or an exclamation mark seemed to understate. In both these examples, erring on the side of 'meaning', so that we prioritize representing what we believe to be their views over pedantic literality about utterances, shows clearly how we inevitably draw on our own understanding of what the speaker intended, revealing the potential for projection in processes of 'perception'.

It is easy not to type every repetition, or to omit oddly used phrases that sit uneasily in a written sentence and it's hard to resist making sentences neater and arguments clearer when it merely involves transposing the word order slightly. Omitting the question tags that could be reassurance or agreement-seeking, makes an interviewee look more self-assured, the account more confident or rehearsed and the conversation more uni-directional – the delivery of their views – as opposed to being more of a dialogue. Resisting smoothing out hesitancy can leave them looking insecure, and punctuation that implies timing can distinguish clear qualifiers from hesitancy. In addition, it is more comfortable reading an account of an interview which spares us from seeing how messy our own speech is, our requests for affirmation or repetition of 'you know' and 'Right'. We're under greater pressure if we feel our affirming sounds or agreements will be read as reducing the 'impartiality' of our interview or the impact of the account. Furthermore, it is easy to 'amend' word order and 'correct' grammar without being conscious of doing them. The drive to 'sort out' the above is one illustration of how we iron out contradictions, automatically as well as deliberately, either to make the account 'readable', or to capture what we believe they meant, unintentionally, perhaps by convention or deliberately, in order to avoid making speakers look inarticulate. It can be a conscious dilemma about where literal quotations feel unfair because the messiness of the spoken word could be attributed to the participant.

Decisions about what and how to transcribe are often made arbitrarily or unconsciously, so when the task of transcription is passed to someone else, detailed communication about what constitutes a 'non significant' utterance is required. Different projects and styles of analyses will attribute different significance to word repetitions, half-word utterances and 'innit's, and draw the line differently around the ethics of transcribing interruptions from third parties, 'post-interview' talk or discussion of the research contract itself.

Transcripts are artefacts and we should acknowledge that we researchers produce, rather than retrieve them shell-like from the seabed. We are active in producing the particular account and that transcript therefore bears traces not only of ourselves as interviewer, as the culturally situated and particular individuals we are, but also as interpreters. Transcripts do not contain pearls of wisdom allowing insight into the essential truths of other beings. Transcribed interviews function as if their wholeness was more than an arbitrary framing, suggesting a certainty which represents the interview authoritatively. Even if we try to qualify, this embodies a claim of literal representation, and of unmediated access to an authentic, unified subject. These illustrations show how decisions about meaning are being made in the supposed neutral process of transcription, where the demands of communication mean that we err on the side of norms to render an account more fitting of a modernist subject. Our instinct to produce representations of participants that veer towards the norm as subjects whose communication is at least manageably linear and logical is also our own investment in ourselves as modern subjects. It is easy to imagine how an interview that didn't feel successful or a transcript that felt very difficult to work with might not be included in a study and this is the kind of unintentional way in which research ends up representing a narrower range of people, experiences and ways of being.

The Politics of Research

It is because the representations of subjectivities we produce are given the status of research knowledge that they circulate in the public sphere to confirm and bolster the notion of the unitary rational subject. The authority of research means such accounts function in normative ways, where what is written as descriptive ends up functioning prescriptively (Burman, 1994). We can, however, use our recognition of the extent of our interpretive involvement in 'representative' processes to interrupt its implied objective status. We can also admit our own investments in this model of the subject – again at both levels – directly as we are boosted by the interaction, and indirectly as the cultural privileging of the hegemonic Western form to which we subscribe and for the most part succeed in performing. However, bolstering this cultural notion has implications both for Western individuals who struggle to live up to the idea, as well as for the global relations it reaffirms. This is why we argue that researcher ethics should be concerned not only with the individuals who are directly touched by the research, but also with the cultural political relations research promotes or sustains.

In producing ourselves as modernist subjects and eliciting similar performances from interview participants through research practices, we reinforce and bolster this model at a cultural level, thereby sustaining its normative pull. The roots of research lie in the modernist project making the reproduction of the modernist subject in research accounts all but inevitable. Therefore we are not suggesting that this dilemma can be resolved, only that we can and should be more reflexive about the way our practice colludes with the elevated status of the modern subject. Awareness of the way in which we, as researchers, actively reproduce dominant cultural accounts of individual subjectivity works to de-naturalize taken-for-granted assumptions about personhood, opening up greater space to challenge normative, restrictive constructions. While we can not transcend or deny our (or others') investments in the modernist subject, we would want to promote research that, through its own ethical practices or representational function, eschews uncritical acceptance of the culturally dominant mode of subjectivity for a recognition of more diverse ways of being.

Notes

[1] Several chapters in *Feminist Dilemmas* discussed this, for instance, in relation to stigmatized mothers (Standing, 1998) or adults researching childhood (Alldred, 1998).
[2] Accessing children through their home environment is dependant on a similar power relation between parent/guardian and child, as one of us discovered when she attempted to arrange an interview with four children via their mother. Although the mother stated in advance that her children were happy to take part, it emerged during the course of the interview that they had been informed that they would be taking part just five minutes before.

References

Alderson, P. (1995) *Listening to Children*. London: Barnardos.

Alldred, P. (1996) ' "Fit to Parent?" developmental psychology and "non traditional" families', in E. Burman, P. Alldred, C. Bewley, B. Goldberg, C. Heenan, D. Marks, J. Marshall, K. Taylor, R. Ullah and S. Warner, *Challenging Women: Psychology's Exclusions, Feminist Possibilities*. Buckingham: Open University Press.

Alldred, P. (1998) 'Discourse analysis, ethnography and representation: dilemmas in research work with children', in J. Ribbens and R. Edwards (eds), *Feminist Dilemmas in Qualitative Research: Public Knowledge and Private Lives*. London: Sage.

Althusser, L. (1971) 'Freud and Lacan', in *Lenin and Philosophy and Other Essays*. London: New Left Books.

Barrett, M. (1991) *The Politics of Truth*. Cambridge: Polity Press.

Birch, M. (1998) 'Reconstructing research narratives: self and sociological identity in alternative settings', in J. Ribbens and R. Edwards (eds), *Feminist Dilemmas in Qualitative Research: Public Knowledge and Private Lives*. London: Sage.

Blackman, L. (1996) 'The dangerous classes: retelling the psychiatric story', *Feminism & Psychology*, 6(3): 361–79.

Burman, E. (1990) 'Differing with deconstruction: A feminist critique', in I. Parker and J. Shotter (eds), *Deconstructing Social Psychology*. London: Routledge.

Burman, E. (1991) 'Power, gender and developmental psychology', *Feminism & Psychology*, 1(1): 141–53.

Burman, E. (1992) 'Feminism and discourse in developmental psychology: power, subjectivity and interpretation', *Feminism & Psychology*, 2(1): 45–60.

Burman, E. (1994) *Deconstructing Developmental Psychology*. London: Routledge.

Burman, E. (1995) 'Developing differences: gender, childhood and economic development', *Children & Society*, 9(3): 121–42.

Burman, E. (ed.) (1998) *Deconstructing Feminist Psychology*. London: Sage.

Burman, E. and Parker, I. (1993) *Discourse Analytic Research, Repertoires and Readings of Texts in Action*. London: Routledge.

Butler, J. (1990) *Gender Trouble: Feminism and the Subversion of Identity*. London: Routledge.

Butler, J. (1993) *Bodies That Matter*. New York: Routledge.

David, M. (2001) ' "Teenage parenthood is bad for parents and children": a feminist critique of the restructuring of the governance of family, education and social welfare policies and practices', in M. Bloch and T. Popkewitz (eds), *Restructuring the Governing Patterns of the Welfare State*. New York and London: Routledge.

David, M., Edwards, R. and Alldred, P. (2001) 'Children and school-based research: "informed consent" or "educated consent"?', *British Educational Research Journal*, 27(3): 347–65.

Edwards, R. and Alldred, P. (1999) 'Children and young people's views of social research: the case of research on home-school relations', *Childhood: a global journal of child research*, 6(2): 261–81.

Foucault, M. (1988) 'Technologies of the Self', in L.H. Martin, H. Gutman and P.H. Hutton (eds), *Technologies of the Self: A Seminar with Michel Foucault*. London: Tavistock.

Frosh, S. (1987) *The Politics of Psychoanalysis*. London: Macmillan.

Grossberg, L. (1989) 'On the road with three ethnographers', *Journal of Communication Inquiry*, 13(2): 23–36.

Haraway, D. (1990) 'A manifesto for cyborgs: science, technology and socialist feminism in the 1980s', in L. Nicholson (ed.), *Feminism/Postmodernism*. London: Routledge.

Henriques, J., Hollway, W., Urwin, C., Venn, C. and Walkerdine, V. (1998) *Changing the Subject: Psychology, Social Regulation and Subjectivity*. London: Routledge.

Hogan, D. (1998) 'Valuing the child in research: historical and current influences on research methodology with children', in D. Hogan and R. Gilligan (eds), *Researching Children's Experiences: Qualitative Approaches*. The Children's Research Centre, Trinity College, Dublin.

Hollway, W. (1989) *Subjectivity and Method in Psychology*. London: Sage.

Hood, S., Mayall, B. and Oliver, S. (1999) *Critical Issues in Social Research: Power and Prejudice*. Buckingham: Open University Press.

James, A. and Prout, A. (eds) (1990) *Constructing and Reconstructing Childhood, Contemporary Issues in the Sociological Study of Childhood*. London: Falmer Press.

Kitzinger, C. (1987) *The Social Construction of Lesbianism*. London: Sage.

Lather, P. (1991) *Getting Smart: Feminist Research and Pedagogy With/in the Postmodern*. London: Routledge.

Marks, D. (1996) 'Constructing a narrative: moral discourse and young people's experience of exclusion', in E. Burman, G. Aitken, P. Alldred, R. Allwood, T. Billington, B. Goldberg, A.J. Gordo-Lopez, C. Heenan, D. Marks and S. Warner, *Psychology, Discourse, Practice: From Regulation to Resistance*. London: Taylor and Francis.

Mishler, E.G. (1991) 'Representing discourse: the rhetoric of transcription', *Journal of Narrative and Life History*, 1(4): 255–80.

Morrow, V. (1999) 'If you were a teacher it would be harder to talk to you: reflections on qualitative research with children in school', *International Journal of Social Research Methodology*, 1: 297–314.

Morrow, V. and Richards, M. (1996) 'The ethics of social research with children: an overview', *Children and Society*, 10: 90–105.

Nencel, L. and Pens, P. (eds) (1991) *Constructing Knowledge: Authority and Critique in the Social Sciences*. London: Sage.

Parker, I. (1992) *Discourse Dynamics*. London: Routledge.

Patai, D. (1991) 'US academics and Third World women: is ethical research possible?', in S. Berger Gluck and D. Patai (eds), *Women's Words: The Feminist Practice of Oral History*. London: Routledge.

Plummer, K. (1995) *Telling Sexual Stories: Power, Change and Social Worlds*. London: Routledge.

Probyn, E. (1993) *Sexing the Self: Gendered Positions in Cultural Studies*. London: Routledge.

Puwar, N. (2000) 'Making space for south asian women: what has changed since feminist review 17', *Feminist Review*, 66: 131–8.

Ribbens, J. and Edwards, R. (eds) (1998) *Feminist Dilemmas in Qualitative Research: Public Knowledge and Private Lives*. London: Sage.

Rorty, R. (1980) *Philosophy and the Mirror of Nature*. Oxford: Blackwell.

Rose, N. (1985) *The Psychological Complex*. London: Routledge and Kegan Paul.

Rose, N. (1989) *Governing The Soul: The Shaping of the Private Self*. London: Routledge.

Rose, N. (1993) *Inventing Ourselves*. London: Routledge.

Scheurich, J. (1997) *Research Method in the Postmodern*. Falmer Press.

Standing, K. (1998) 'Writing the voices of the less powerful: research on lone mothers', in J. Ribbens and R. Edwards (eds) *Feminist Dilemmas in Qualitative Research: Public Knowledge and Private Lives*. London.

Strauss, A. and Corbin, J. (1990) *Basics of Qualitative Research: Grounded Theory Procedures and Techniques*. London: Sage.

Venn, C. (1985) 'A Subject for Concern: Sexuality and Subjectivity in Foucault's History of Sexuality', *PsychCritique*, 1(2): 139–54.

Walkerdine, V. (1990) *Schoolgirl Fictions*. London: Verso.

Weedon, C. (1987) *Feminist Practice and Poststructuralist Theory*. Oxford: Blackwell.

INDEX